Enterprise Architecture Planning

Books from QED

Database

Managing IMS Databases
Building the Data Warehouse
Migrating to DB2
DB2: The Complete Guide to Implementation and Use
DB2 Design Review Guidelines
DB2: Maximizing Performance of Online Production Systems
Embedded SQL for DB2
SQL for DB2 and SQL/DS Application Developers
How to Use ORACLE SQL*PLUS
ORACLE: Building High Performance Online Systems
ORACLE Design Review Guidelines
Developing Client/Server Applications in an Architected Environment

Systems Engineering

Software Configuration Management
On Time, Within Budget: Software Project Management Practices and Techniques
Information Systems Architecture: Development in the 90's
Quality Assurance for Information Systems
User-Interface Screen Design: Workstations, PC's, Mainframes
Managing Software Projects
The Complete Guide to Software Testing
A Structured Approach to Systems Testing
Rapid Application Prototyping
The Software Factory
Data Architecture: The Information Paradigm
Software Engineering with Formal Metrics
Using CASE Tools for Practical Management

Management

Developing a Blueprint for Data, Applications, and Technology: Enterprise Architecture Planning
Introduction to Data Security and Controls
How to Automate Your Computer Center
Controlling the Future
The UNIX Industry
Mind Your Business

IBM Mainframe Series

From Mainframe to Workstations: Offloading Application Development
VSE/SP and VSE/ESA: A Guide to Performance Tuning
CICS: A Guide to Application Debugging
CICS Application and System Programming
CICS: A Guide To Performance Tuning
MVS COBOL II Power Programmer's Desk Reference
VSE JCL and Subroutines for Application Programmers
VSE COBOL II Power Programmer's Desk Reference
Introduction to Cross System Product
CSP Version 3.3 Application Development
The MVS Primer
MVS/VSAM for the Application Programmer
TSO/E CLISTs: The Complete Tutorial and Desk Reference
CICS: A How-To for COBOL Programmers
QMF: How to Use Query Management Facility with DB2 and SQL/DS
DOS/VSE JCL: Mastering Job Control Language
DOS/VSE: CICS Systems Programming
VSAM: Guide to Optimization and Design
MVS/JCL: Mastering Job Control Language
MVS/TSO: Mastering CLISTs
MVS/TSO: Mastering Native Mode and ISPF
REXX in the TSO Environment, 2nd Edition

Technical

Rdb/VMS: Developing the Data Warehouse
The Wonderful World of the AS/400: Architecture and Applications
C Language for Programmers
Mainframe Development Using Microfocus COBOL/2 Workbench
AS/400: A Practical Guide to Programming and Operations
Bean's Index to OSF/Motif, Xt Intrinsics, and Xlib Documentation for OSF/Motif Application Programmers
VAX/VMS: Mastering DCL Commands and Utilities
The PC Data Handbook
UNIX C Shell Desk Reference
Designing and Implementing Ethernet Networks
The Handbook for Microcomputer Technicians
Open Systems

QED books are available at special quantity discounts for educational uses, premiums, and sales promotions. Special books, book excerpts, and instructive materials can be created to meet specific needs.

This is Only a Partial Listing. For Additional Information or a Free Catalog contact
QED Information Sciences, Inc. • P. O. Box 812070 • Wellesley, MA 02181-0013
Telephone: 800-343-4848 or 617-237-5656 or fax 617-235-0826

Enterprise Architecture Planning

Developing a Blueprint for Data, Applications and Technology

Steven H. Spewak
with Steven C. Hill

QED Publishing Group
Boston • London • Toronto

© 1993 QED Publishing Group
P.O. Box 812070
Wellesley, MA 02181-0013

QED Publishing Group is a division of QED Information Sciences, Inc.

Library of Congress Catalog Number: 92-20028
International Standard Book Number: 0-89435-436-1

Printed in the United States of America
93 94 95 10 9 8 7 6 5 4 3 2 1

Library of Congress Cataloging-In-Publication Data

Spewak, Steven H.
   Enterprise architecture planning: developing a blueprint for data, applications and technology / Steven H. Spewak and Steven C. Hill
      p.   cm.
   Includes bibliographical references and index.
   ISBN 0-89435-436-1
   1. Management information systems. 2. System design. I. Title.
T58.6.S6595 1992
658.4'038'011—dc20   92-20028
                         CIP

Contents

Foreword   xv

Preface   xix

Chapter 1
Introduction   1

What Is Enterprise Architecture Planning?   1
Mission of the Information Systems
    Organization   3
Data Quality   4
Benefits of Enterprise Architecture Planning   6
The Promises of Database   7
Enterprise Architecture Planning Is Different From
    Traditional I.S. Planning   9
The Zachman Framework   11
Components of Enterprise Architecture Planning
    Methodology   13
Conclusion   15
Discussion Questions   17
References   18

Chapter 2
Successful Enterprise Architecture Planning   19

    What Is Successful Enterprise Architecture Planning?   19
    Greatest Obstacles to Overcome   20
    Reasons for Enterprise Architecture Planning Success 32
    Discussion Questions   35

Chapter 3
Planning Initiation   37

    Introduction   37
    Step 1—Determine Scope and Objectives for EAP   38
    Step 2—Create a Vision   48
    Step 3—Adapt a Methodology   50
    Step 4—Arrange for Computer Resources   54
    Step 5—Assemble the Planning Team   63
    Step 6—Prepare an EAP Workplan   72
    Step 7—Obtain Management Approval   76
    Discussion Questions   81
    References   83

Chapter 4
Preliminary Business Model   85

    Introduction   85
    Step 1—Document the Organizational Structure   90
    Step 2—Identify / Define Functions   95
    Step 3—Distribute the Preliminary Business Model   109
    Discussion Questions   111
    References   112

Chapter 5
The Enterprise Survey   113

    Introduction   113
    Step 1—Schedule the Interviews   114
    Step 2—Prepare for the Interviews   119
    Step 3—Perform the Interviews   130
    Step 4—Enter Data into the Toolset   133

Step 5—Distribute the Complete Business Model   137
Discussion Questions   140

Chapter 6
Current Systems and Technology Architecture   **141**

Introduction   141
Step 1—Determine the Scope, Objectives, and IRC
    Workplan   144
Step 2—Prepare for Data Collection   145
Step 3—Data Collection   152
Step 4—Data Entry   154
Step 5—Validate IRC Information and Produce a
    Draft of the IRC   155
Step 6—Draw Schematics   161
Step 7—Distribute the IRC   163
Step 8—Administer and Maintain the IRC   165
Discussion Questions   166
References   167

Chapter 7
Data Architecture   **169**

Introduction   169
Step 1—List Candidate Data Entities for Definition   171
Step 2—Define the Data Entities, Attributes, and
    Relationships   173
Step 3—Relate Data Entities to the Business
    Functions   188
Step 4—Distribute the Data Architecture   194
Discussion Questions   196
References   197

Chapter 8
Applications Architecture   **199**

Introduction   199
Step 1—List Candidate Applications   200
Step 2—Define the Applications   204

Step 3—Relate Applications to Functions 211
Step 4—Analyze Impact to Current Applications 217
Step 5—Distribute the Applications Architecture 219
Discussion Questions 221
References 222

Chapter 9
Technology Architecture 223

Introduction 223
Step 1—Identify Technology Platforms and Principles 225
Step 2—Define the Technology Platforms and the
    Distribution of Data and applications 227
Step 3—Relate the Technology Platforms to
    Applications and Business Functions 235
Step 4—Distribute the Technology Architecture 236
Discussion Questions 238
References 238

Chapter 10
Implementation Plan 239

Introduction 239
Step 1—Sequence the Applications 240
Step 2—Estimate the Effort, Resources, and Produce
    a Schedule 253
Step 3—Estimate Costs and Benefits of the Plan 260
Step 4—Determine Success Factors and Make
    Recommendations 263
Discussion Questions 267
References 267

Chapter 11
Planning Conclusion 269

Introduction 269
Step 1—Prepare the Final Report 271
Step 2—Make Final Presentations to Management 276
Discussion Questions 279

Chapter 12
Transition to Implementation   **281**

 Introduction   281
 Step 1—Plan the Transition   282
 Step 2—Adopt a System Development Approach   284
 Step 3—Arrange for Computer Resources   285
 Step 4—Refine the Architectures   287
 Step 5—Institute Organizational Changes   287
 Step 6—Recruit Personnel   288
 Step 7—Provide Training   289
 Step 8—Establish Programming Standards   289
 Step 9—Establish Procedural Standards   290
 Step 10—Develop Detailed Schedule for the First
  Set of Applications   290
 Step 11—Confirm the Ending of the Transition   290
 References   291

Appendix A
Products for the EAP Toolset   **293**

Appendix B
Consulting Companies   **297**

Appendix C
Duration Estimate for Steps of Each Phase   **301**

Appendix D
Sample Function Definitions   **305**

Appendix E
Sample Business Model Document   **313**

Appendix F
Sample Data Architecture Document   **323**

Appendix G
Sample Applications Architecture Report   **331**

Bibliography   **341**

Index   **357**

List of Figures

Figure

Fig 1.1.   Success factors yield I.S. mission   4
Fig 1.2.   Data quality   5
Fig 1.3.   Business benefits of Enterprise Architecture Planning   6
Fig 1.4.   Benefits to the business of planned systems   7
Fig 1.5.   Promises of the database management system   8
Fig 1.6.   The Zachman Framework   12
Fig 1.7.   Components of Enterprise Architecture Planning   13
Fig 1.8.   Levels of Enterprise Architecture Planning   16
Fig 1.9.   Enterprise Architecture Planning project steps   17

Fig 3.1.   Five dimensions of corporate culture   45
Fig 3.2.a   Nolan's six stages of data processing   46
Fig 3.2b.   Nolan's benchmarks of the six steps   47
Fig 3.3   I.S. planning methodologies   52
Fig 3.4.   Table of contents for an EAP guidebook   55
Fig 3.5.   Ten kinds of EAP reports   57
Fig 3.6.   Selected tool matrix   62
Fig 3.7.   Sample role description for business analyst   66

Fig 3.8.   Sample role assignment   68
Fig 3.9.   Approximate duration percentages   73
Fig 3.10.   Example of EAP project weekly task assignments   75
Fig 3.11.   Planning approach for obtaining a decision from
              management   78
Fig 3.12.   Sample executive announcement letter   82

Fig 4.1.   Strategic business planning areas of interest   86
Fig 4.2.   Formal strategic business plans   87
Fig 4.3.   Strategic business planning process   89
Fig 4.4.   Sample organization unit structure report   94
Fig 4.5.   Porter's value-added chain   96
Fig 4.6.   Utility company value-added functions   97
Fig 4.7.   Functional decomposition of publishing company   99
Fig 4.8.   Hierarchical diagram and an indented
              structure list   102
Fig 4.9.   Effects of function definition change   103
Fig 4.10   Example of matrix relating business functions to
              organization units   107
Fig 4.11   Example of business functions to organization units
              expressed as a cross-reference list   108
Fig 4.12   Example of presentation outline   111

Fig 5.1.   Sample interview confirmation memo   118
Fig 5.2.   Interview schedule chronological (partial list)   120
Fig 5.3.   Interview schedule by team member (partial list)   121
Fig 5.4a.   Sample Function Definition Form (side 1)   123
Fig 5.4b.   Sample Function Definition Form (side 2)   124
Fig 5.5.   Sample Information Source Form   127
Fig 5.6.   18 rules for checking relational EAP database   135
Fig 5.7.   Example of presentation outline for the business
              model   139

Fig 6.1.   Application system description   147
Fig 6.2.   Major input/output descriptions   150

Fig 6.3.   Technology platforms   151

Fig 6.4.   Sample index report   157

Fig 6.5.   Sample input/output files report   158

Fig 6.6.   Sample technology platform matrix   159

Fig 6.7.   Application complexity by number of files used   160

Fig 6.8.   Data file sharing/file usage by number of
            applications   161

Fig 6.9.   Sample IRC document outline   162

Fig 6.10.   Dataflow schematic of an application   164

Fig 7.1.   Other terms for data architecture and data
            entity   170

Fig 7.2a.   Sample entity definition 1   182

Fig 7.2b.   Sample entity definition 2   183

Fig 7.2c.   Sample entity definition 3   184

Fig 7.2d.   Sample entity definition 4   185

Fig 7.3.   E-R diagram for Purchase Goods and Services   186

Fig 7.4.   Database entity-to-function relationships   190–191

Fig 7.5.   Affinity analysis formulas   193

Fig 7.6.   Presentation outline for data architecture   196

Fig 8.1.   Sample application description 1   206

Fig 8.2.   Sample application description 2   206

Fig 8.3.   Sample application description 3   207

Fig 8.4.   Applications supporting Procure Goods and
            Services   209

Fig 8.5.   Concept of a shared data resource   210

Fig 8.6.   Functions supported by Sales Lead Tracking   212

Fig 8.7.   Functions supported by Facility Maintenance
            Planning   213

Fig 8.8.   Functions supported by Production Control System   213

Fig 8.9.   List of functions not supported by applications
            architecture   214

Fig 8.10.   List of organizations supported by Miscellaneous
            Billing   215

Fig 8.11.   Outline for applications architecture presentation   221

Fig 9.1.   Components of the conceptual workstation   230
Fig 9.2.   Example of conceptual enterprise network   232
Fig 9.3.   Example of business system architecture   233

Fig 10.1.   Implementation/migration plan application   244
Fig 10.2.   Database entities-to-applications relationships.   245
Fig 10.3.   Additional sequencing priority criteria for
             applications   247
Fig 10.4.   Structure of the split matrix   251
Fig 10.5.   Applications estimates and implementation plan   257
Fig 10.6   Implementation plan schedule (partial listing)   258
Fig 10.7.   I.S. resources dedicated to architecture
             implementation   259
Fig 10.8.   Administrative database costs   262

Fig 11.1.   Final report outline example 1   272
Fig 11.2.   Final report outline example 2   273

Fig 12.1.   Sample applications prototyping methodology   286

Foreword

by John A. Zachman

I have written the forewords to other books, but I feel especially qualified to write this one as I have spent most of my professional life working in the area of information strategy and architecture. In fact, I have written extensively on this subject as one of the early methodology pioneers.

I acknowledge Dewey Walker, the director of architecture on the old IBM Information Systems Control and Planning staff in the late 1960s, as the "grandfather" of architecture methodologies. It was his internal IBM experience in Information Architecture that later became known as *Business Systems Planning* (BSP). As one of Dewey's early disciples, I had the opportunity to make substantial contributions to BSP, both conceptually and literally. I wrote and/or reviewed significant portions of the BSP documentation as it evolved over the years. I only allude to my experience so that when I claim that this book makes a substantive contribution to the body of I.S. planning knowledge, the reader will not perceive this statement as mere literary formality.

The architecture process begins with an understanding of the enterprise and the data that constitute its information infrastructure. To be most useful, information systems must be derived from this base of knowledge about the enterprise. To do otherwise carries the risk of having limited applicability and ultimately being perceived as more bothersome than valuable. Although this principle has been acknowledged and well understood for many years, we have not been eminently successful in making it a reality. Even if we could document the business strategy (which in many, if not most, cases has not been trivial) and determine how to relate that business strategy into an I.S. strategy by employing relational-type (matrix) techniques, a fundamental problem remained: how to get from those strategy matrices to implementation. Over the years, the strategy and the implementation have remained separated by a cavernous, conceptual "black hole."

During the 1980s, I became convinced that *architecture*, whatever that was, was the thing that bridged the strategy and its implementation. This led me to investigate other disciplines that manufactured complex engineering products to learn how those disciplines crossed the analogous bridge. I published the result of this investigation in the September 1987 issue of the *IBM Systems Journal* in an article entitled "A Framework for Information Systems Architecture."

At the outset, my intention in describing the Framework was merely to improve on the planning methodologies to follow BSP. Little did I expect that the Framework would receive such broad acceptance. Indeed, I read just recently where someone had written that the "Zachman Framework was the de facto architecture standard in the industry!" For me, at least initially, the Framework was simply the logical structure that connected the products of planning with the products of the more technical implementation.

Those of you who have been involved with Business Systems Planning or Information Strategy Planning (ISP) would quickly recognize that those methodologies address the top row of the Framework, particularly producing and relating the top cells in the Data and Process columns (see Figure 1.6). Indeed, most BSP and ISP methods also produce row 2 cells at a high, summarized level of detail. Modern methods that have "architecture" in their names usually address row 2 cells explicitly. This brings me to the methodology in this book referred to as Enterprise Architecture Planning (EAP). The explicit intent of this methodology advocated by Steve Spewak is to produce the top cells of the data and process columns, as well as high-level models in row 2 of the same columns; hence the word "architecture" is quite appropriate in the name.

This book takes a complex subject and makes it more practical for the information-planning professional and understandable for business people who are so vital to the architecture process. It is a methodology book that not only defines the procedure, but also explains its rationale and provides a wealth of practical advice on how to actually make it work. Obviously, Steve Spewak has given this subject much thought, for thought gives lucidity to such complexity. His extensive real-life experience supplies practical advice, such as the use of props in management presentations and a multitude of other valuable suggestions that could separate the successful architecture efforts from those that are not.

Frankly, having been involved in many architecture-planning efforts, I have formed opinions and perceptions about methodologies. As I was reading this book for the first time, I was occasionally skeptical about a particular methodological point. However, *in every instance*, before I had read to the end of the chapter, I was convinced that the innovative and pragmatic approach to accomplish the purpose was sound. This book has given me a wealth of good, fresh ideas about every facet of the architecture process.

There is another very interesting aspect of the book. Even though one may not agree with every facet of the EAP methodology, the book is still useful; Steve has documented his own methodology without excluding other methodological possibilities. I highly recommend providing this book to any enterprise architecture planning team, whether they will be adopting the entire methodology or not. This text should dramatically shorten the time it takes to perform this kind of planning because much of that time is usually spent helping the team understand their goals. Toward this end, the book excels.

If you are an information professional who has a distinct methodological bent, if you are a business executive who is interested intellectually, or even if you are a manager who has more than a little skepticism about participating on an architecture team, you will find this book to be very readable, helpful, and significant in improving your effectiveness in any architecture-planning effort you undertake.

The appendices and bibliography containing lists of tools, consultants, methodologies, examples, and references are worth the price of the book. The lists are carefully and thoughtfully compiled and form a concise guide for where to find the wisdom and expertise available in the industry today.

Many words have been written on the subject of information strategy and planning, but I believe this book will stand the test of time and be recognized as a foremost contributor to our body of knowledge. Thank you, Steve.

John A. Zachman

Preface

THE WINCHESTER HOUSE

In the lower Bay Area of sunny California, on the border between San Jose and Cupertino off I-280, there stands an enormous mansion known as the Winchester House. It was built around the turn of the century by Sarah Winchester, who inherited a large fortune from her husband's rifle company.

As she got on in age, Mrs. Winchester became increasingly eccentric. It seems that she was haunted by the ghosts of the unfortunate people killed by rifles made by her husband. Two full-time spiritual advisors were employed on her staff who told her that she would continue to live as long as she continued to build.

Thus construction on this mansion continued 24 hours a day, seven days a week, month after month, year after year—for 38 years! A new wing here, a tower there; some rooms remodeled more than a dozen times. Workshops, supplies—everything needed for building—were on site. Vast sums of money (for those times) were spent on the house.

Tours are now given through the Winchester House. The grounds are beautiful and the custom-made stained glass, porcelain fixtures, and woodwork are remarkable. However, the highlights of the tour are such odd features as stairways that rise into ceilings, doors and windows blocked by walls, more passageways and halls than rooms, a three-story chimney that falls short of the roof, and many rooms serving the same purpose.

The information systems portfolio of most companies and organizations resembles the Winchester House in many ways. Construction of systems goes on continuously. A new report here, an input screen there; some systems enhanced more than a dozen times. Virtually everything needed for building systems is on site. Vast budgets are allocated to the I.S. organization. The collection of systems has such odd features as reports that are not used, more interfaces and bridges than there are systems, major projects that were not completed, data that is redundant, inconsistent, inaccessible, in incompatible formats, and many systems serving the same purpose.

Another comparison can be made of the Winchester House and the systems portfolio. There was no overall set of blueprints that showed what Mrs. Winchester wanted her house to be. Similarly, most systems organizations have no overall blueprints for the data, systems and technology needed to support the business. The only way to break out of the mode of continuous custom building and replacing of systems that results in such costly odd features is to create enterprise-wide architectures and plans for implementing them.

ENTERPRISE ARCHITECTURE PLANNING (EAP)

As an organization grows and becomes more complex, management makes greater demands of their information systems (IS) function. They require timely access to data whenever and wherever needed, a useful format for data that can be easily interpreted, accurate and consistent data throughout every department, responsiveness to rapidly changing business conditions, and sharing of data across the enterprise. These requirements form the mission of an IS organization—to provide quality data to those who need it. However, data quality does not just happen, nor will it result from focusing on application development productivity. Quality must be planned. Enterprise architecture planning is a modern approach for planning data quality and achieving the IS mission.

Enterprise architecture planning is a process for defining the top two layers of the Zachman Information Systems Architecture Framework. EAP results in a high-level blueprint of data, applications, and technology that is a cost-effective, long-term solution; not a quick fix. Management participation provides a business perspective, credibility, and de-mystifies the systems planning process. EAP can be labeled as business-driven or data-driven because

- a stable business model (independent of organizational boundaries, systems, and procedures) is the foundation for the architectures,
- data is defined before applications, and
- data dependency determines the sequence for implementing application systems.

IMPORTANCE OF ARCHITECTURE

Is the subject of IS architecture important? The Society of Information Management (SIM) and the MIS Research Center at the University of Minnesota have jointly conducted comprehensive studies of practitioners, educators, and consultants to determine the most critical issues facing IS management. The results of the most recent survey, published in December 1991[1] show that the three most important issues (out of 25) were:

1. Developing an information architecture.
2. Making effective use of the data resource.
3. Improving IS strategic planning.

Inn another survey published by the Association for Systems Management[2], 379 respondents were asked cite important IS issues. The five most cited were:

1. Integration of data processing, office automation, and telecommunications.
2. Competitive advantage of technology.
3. Managing data and information resources.
4. Developing a 3 to five year plan.
5. MIS strategic planning.

So the answer to the question is definitely yes—defining strategic enterprise architectures and plans is a very important topic for IS organizations. Why is the interest in architectures and planning increasing? The reasons include the proliferation of products for computer-aided software engineering (CASE), the use of information engineering methods and techniques, the reported benefits of downsizing and business re-engineering, and the advancement of technologies such as client-server networks, relational databases, and object-oriented systems that encourage the sharing of data. IS managers now recognize that a comprehensive enterprise-wide plan is necessary and essential for achieving the full potential of methodologies, tools, and information technology.

OBJECTIVES OF THE BOOK

Two factors common to all successful EAP efforts are solid management commitment and strong project leadership. Therefore, the emphasis of this book is on the interpersonal skills and techniques for organizing and directing an EAP project, obtaining management commitment, presenting the plan to management, and leading the transition from planning to implementation. Specific objectives are to

1. *Define enterprise architecture planning.* A complete methodology for conducting EAP is presented that is flexible and adaptable to different situations.
2. *Provide useful guidelines for managing your EAP project.* Experience shows that every EAP project will be somewhat different, so guidelines, *not rules*, are given for each step of the process.
3. *Separate pragmatism from theory.* Some approaches and techniques described in other books may seem good in theory, but may not be successful in practice. The methodology in this book is based on twelve years of experience conducting EAP projects. Two recurring themes in the book are that there is no single way to do EAP that is guaranteed to be

successful, and theoretical ideas and techniques should not be relied upon.

4. *Suggest ways to handle the political aspects of EAP.* Planning is a political process and, therefore, many of the guidelines are aimed at maximizing acceptance and commitment and avoiding political pitfalls.

5. *Explore the tradeoffs between levels of detail and the time and resources for EAP.* Time and people are the most critical resources for EAP, but the architectures need sufficient detail to be effective blueprints for the developers.

6. *Ease the transition to implementation.* The implementation of the architectures should commence immediately upon completing the plan.

Most of the examples in the book have been taken from actual EAP projects. Actual examples illustrate the variety of reporting formats that can be used, and should carry credibility since they are from successful projects. On the other hand, actual examples may contain errors, and portions may not be as understandable to the casual reader as they would be for a person in the particular organization. A single substantive case study for planning would require much more material, would not appear to be broadly applicable to any business situation, and some people would attempt to emulate the example rather than adapt the methodology to their specific situation.

The audience for this book is Information Resource Managers, Data Administrators, System Planners, and Technology Managers who want to learn about developing a long-range systems plan. This book should also be read by business and systems management whose goal is an integrated shared data environment. Generally, anyone in the midst of developing or who has developed architectures and plans would benefit from the guidelines provided in this book.

This book may also be suitable as a supplementary text to a graduate level course on information systems. The references in the bibliography and the questions and the questions for discussion at the end of each chapter will enable students to gain further insight into the planning issues encountered by systems executives.

ACKNOWLEDGMENTS

This book is the culmination of work that began twelve years ago, During that time, I have worked with outstanding professionals who have shaped the methodology contained in these pages. James Martin, Dixon Doll, Leo Cohen, Ron Ross, and Bernie Plagman were influential in the early years. The late Gary Mortenson gave me the opportunity to hone many of the ideas for the methodology. A particular debt of gratitude goes to Dr. George Schussel and Digital consulting for providing the avenue to convey my experience in a public seminar since 1986.

The clients I have guided through the EAP process over these years are too numerous to individually mention. I appreciate your support and congratulate you for succeeding on the cutting edge of the field.

Finally, I acknowledge my wife Barbara, and sons Jonathan and Matthew, for their support during the long hours and lost weekends required to create this book; and Steve Hill, without whose assistance this book would never have been completed.

REFERENCES

[1]Niederman, Fred, James C. Brancheau, and James C. Wetherbe, "Information Systems Management Issues for the 1990s," *MIS Quarterly*, Volume 14, Number 4, December 1991.

[2]Wood, Wallace A., *Journal of Systems Management*, November 1988.

Introduction to Enterprise Architecture Planning

WHAT IS ENTERPRISE ARCHITECTURE PLANNING?

*Enterprise Architecture Planning is the process of **defining architectures** for the use of information in support of the business and the **plan** for implementing those architectures.*

There are three important words in the above definition. The first is *architectures*—plural because there are three architectures: a data architecture, an applications architecture, and a technology architecture. Architectures, in this context, are like blueprints, drawings, or models. In EAP, architectures define and describe the data, applications, and technology needed to support the business.

The second important word is *defining*. EAP defines the business and defines the architectures. EAP is defining, not designing. EAP does not design systems, design databases, or networks. The design and implementation work is initiated *after* the EAP definition process has been completed.

The third important word is *plan*. Generally speaking, the architectures define *what* is needed, and the supporting plan defines *when* the architectures will be implemented. Architectures by themselves can provide useful definitions, standards, and ideas. But architectures without plans, no matter how thorough or good technically, usually end up sitting on a shelf gathering dust, never reaching implementation. The team conducting EAP must always be mindful that the final product or deliverable is a *long-range* plan to implement the architectures.

In every company and industry, business executives face major challenges to achieve their goals. Unarguably, information provides insights and answers needed to succeed. People at all levels of an organization need information to do their jobs well. When asked, "With respect to information, what is needed to fulfill your objectives or do your job?," presidents, vice-presidents, and on down the line respond with the same five answers:

1. *Access to data in a useful format when and where needed*
   Virtually everyone's job requires data, and access to data is the most frequent request. It is not uncommon to find individuals who spend more than 50 percent of their working time handling data—finding, retrieving, sorting, examining, copying, recording, changing, filing, and sending data. Therefore, being able to obtain data *when* it is needed, *where* it is needed, and in a *usable format* is critical. Being in a useful format means the data is readily interpretable into information and is not buried in a haystack of other, irrelevant data. Purely and simply, access to data is the number one requirement for achieving business goals.

2. *Ability to adapt to changing business needs*
   To thrive in a world economy, modern businesses must be able to adjust and adapt quickly to changes. Executives want information systems that support the business as it changes. In a dynamic business environment, users can no longer afford to wait six months, a year, or longer for I.S. to respond to formal requests. Databases and applications must be flexible and maintainable to quickly accommodate changes involving products, markets, mergers and acquisitions, technology, governmental regulations and deregulations, and competitive shifts.

3. *Accurate and consistent data*
   Executives want and expect the data they receive to be accurate and consistent. The data must have high integrity. It

must not only be correct within acceptable precision, but consistent across the organization. For data to be properly interpreted and combined from all parts of the organization, a common vocabulary, or data standard, is needed. For example, suppose a divisional manager of a large company needed to make a major decision to allocate company resources on the basis of sales levels. The manager could ask the heads of sales and marketing, manufacturing, distribution, and finance, "What are our sales?" and might receive four significantly different answers. Although none of these "sales" figures would be incorrect from the perspective of the person providing them, each would have been determined differently. That is, the word "sales" may have four different meanings across this enterprise. Such differences and inconsistencies must be eliminated. The data provided must be accurate and up to date.

4. *Share data across the organization*
Executives recognize that data must be *shared* across the enterprise to successfully meet business goals. Data must also be shared among departments and organization units, and for this to happen, the data must be centrally administered and coordinated. This statement, however, does not imply a single, centralized database. Rather, it is crucial that the data possess a common organization that eliminates redundancy and ensures the consistency of data wherever it might be.

5. *Contain costs*
Executives want the four above without escalating information systems costs. Double-digit budget increases for I.S. will not be tolerated indefinitely. Data must be provided at a reasonable, affordable cost.

MISSION OF THE INFORMATION SYSTEMS ORGANIZATION

From an I.S. perspective, Figure 1.1 compares the success factors listed above to the I.S. mission:

5 Success Factors Listed by Executives	I.S. Mission
Access to data when and where needed	Timely access to needed data
Ability to adapt to changing business needs	Flexible, maintainable systems
Accurate and consistent data	Data integrity and standards
Share data across the organization	Data/systems integration
Contain costs	Cost effectiveness

Figure 1.1.   Success factors yield I.S. mission.

These five success factors form the mission of the I.S. organizations. Enterprise Architecture Planning is the first step on the road to fulfillment of this mission, and it is the only kind of I.S. planning process that can achieve this mission over the long term.

DATA QUALITY

If one could use a single word to describe these five components, it would be *quality*. In other words, *providing quality data to those who need it* is the mission of I.S. This concept has been the subject of much attention; W. Edwards Deming and others have expounded at length on quality and productivity in business.

If we accept that the mission of I.S. is to provide "quality data," then Deming's 14 Points for Quality[1] can be used to draw a parallel to data quality. Figure 1.2 interprets Demings list into 14 points for achieving data quality.

One important principle to note is that authors such as Deming, Juran, and Conway who write about quality have all stated that *productivity will result from focusing on quality, but quality **does not** come about by pursuing productivity*. This is a vital point because many popular systems development methodologies and tools, such as CASE and AD/Cycle products, have been explicitly touted as improving the productivity of systems development. According to the teachings of Deming, focusing on

Deming's 14 Points for Quality	14 Points of Data Quality
1. Create a constancy of purpose toward improvement (mission and plan).	1. Develop a charter for Data Resource Management (DRM).
2. Adopt the new philosophy (don't accept delays, defects, and mistakes).	2. Manage data as an asset; commit to shared data and data integrity.
3. Cease dependence on mass inspections (require statistical evidence).	3. Develop measures for quality data.
4. Use single sourcing	4. Establish a data-driven migration strategy based on data creation (source data systems).
5. Constantly improve the system of production and service; find problems.	5. Understand your business (functional business model, business plans); correct data errors and eliminate the causes of bugs with better methodologies.
6. Institute modern methods of on-the-job training.	6. Institute DRM training programs.
7. Institute modern methods of supervision.	7. A leader or champion for DRM must be identified; promote teamwork; eliminate short-term performance appraisals.
8. Drive out fear.	8. Focus on long-range goals (architectures clearly establish the future direction, feeding the sense of job security, thus reducing fear).
9. Break down barriers between departments.	9. Develop enterprise business models, architectures, and plans that cross organizational boundaries.
10. Eliminate numerical goals, posters, and slogans for new productivity levels without methods.	10. Develop standards and enforcement mechanisms to ensure data quality.
11. Eliminate work standards that prescribe quotas.	11. Comply with standards through leadership and responsibility for data quality (provide compliance incentives).
12. Pride of workmanship (job descriptions, involvement, tools, methods).	12. Use new methods, techniques, and tools; update position responsibilities.
13. Institute a vigorous program of education and training.	13. Team with the QA function or committee.
14. Create a structure that will push the above 13 points.	14. Management must commit to these data quality principles (establish DRM, reorganize, authorize).

Figure 1.2.   Data quality.

systems productivity alone will not necessarily result in quality data nor enable the mission of I.S. to be fulfilled.

Agreement with and support of the 14 points of data quality is necessary *before* EAP is undertaken; do not believe that it will be easier to gain support on these points *after* EAP has begun. Quality does not simply happen; it must be *planned and designed* into the product of I.S.—that is, data. EAP, then, may be appropriately referred to as *planning for quality data*.

BENEFITS OF ENTERPRISE ARCHITECTURE PLANNING

There are a number of benefits gained by EAP. Figure 1.3 lists some of the benefits the business should experience as a direct

---

- Focus is on strategic use of technology for managing data as an asset.
- Standard vocabulary facilitates communication and reduces inconsistency and data redundancy.
- Documentation increases understanding of the business.
- Models can be used to explain the business and assess the impact of business changes.
- Decision-making policies may be reviewed.
- It considers integration of current systems with new.
- It allows for a comprehensive, objective, and impartial approach.
- The long-range systems plan complements the business plan.
- A cost-effective, long-term solution considers rate of return.
- It involves a feasible migration strategy with short-term achievements.
- It is easier to assess the benefits and impact of new systems and software.
- It allows easier accommodation of dynamic business changes such as mergers, acquisitions, new products, lines of business, and so on.
- Management participation provides a business perspective, credibility, confidence, and demystifies systems development.

Figure 1.3.   Business benefits of Enterprise Architecture Planning.

- More responsive to customer's needs.
- Reduced data entry costs.
- Head count is reduced.
- Increased productivity of personnel permits increased level of business and containment of costs.
- Improving skills raises enthusiasm and loyalty.
- Efficient systems maintenance means improved service.
- Architectures eliminate complex, costly interfaces between incongruent systems.
- Management decisions in all functional areas will be based on more accurate and timely data, leading to various improvements and cost-saving measures.
- End user has direct access to shared data.
- New systems are developed faster and at less cost due to common data, common code, and a shortened requirements phase.
- Easier to evaluate and select vendor software packages.
- Effective use of repository and CASE products.

Figure 1.4.   Benefits to the business of planned systems.

result of EAP, and Figure 1.4 lists potential benefits to the business from having well-planned, integrated systems. When reviewing these lists, circle the two or three benefits most important to your organization. These "hot" issues should be considered when developing presentations made at several stages of the EAP process.

THE PROMISES OF DATABASE

Many of the benefits of EAP may seem familiar to purchasers and users of a Database Management System (DBMS). In fact, some may say, "Wait a minute I've heard this spiel before!" For over 15 years, the vendors of DBMSs have sold their products by a list of benefits similar to those in Figure 1.5, which were alleged to add up to a substantial savings of data processing dollars.

Most businesses and organizations today use a DBMS, and many have more than one. Yet, the benefits in Figure 1.5 remain elusive to most users. Uncontrolled redundancy, inconsistent data definitions, rapid increase of storage, unacceptable response time, and high maintenance costs are just some of the major issues facing organizations using DBMSs. Simply purchasing a new database system will not achieve these benefits, nor will a DBMS in itself lead to quality data. Vendors of DBMSs, and, more recently, CASE tools, have been promising the same advantages. It may be slick marketing on their part, but in reality the claims are not accurate.

The DBMS is merely a tool for accessing and storing data. The promises of database listed in Figure 1.5 cannot be fulfilled by simply using a DBMS. The road to quality data involves planning and change. With EAP, companies have reported achieving these elusive benefits promised by database management systems, CASE, and AD/Cycle.

- Physical and logical independence.
- Improved performance, response time.
- Minimized storage costs.
- Reduced redundancy.
- Data integrity.
- Rapid search and availability.
- Assured privacy and security.
- Adaptable for future requirements.
- Simple, flexible data structure.
- Enforcement of standards.
- Speeded up system development.

$$ SAVINGS

Figure 1.5. Promises of Database Management Systems.

ENTERPRISE ARCHITECTURE PLANNING IS DIFFERENT FROM TRADITIONAL I.S. PLANNING

EAP is different from the traditional method of systems planning used over the history of business computing. Some may label the traditional approach "process driven," whereas EAP can be labeled "data driven." The traditional planning approach is "technology driven," whereas EAP is "business driven." Short term and long term are also labels that have been used. Regardless of labels, EAP is different from traditional I.S. planning in four ways:

1. *Architectures are founded on a **functional business model**.* A functional business model[2] is a knowledge base of what the business is and what information is used to conduct the business. The traditional approach to systems planning does not begin with an overall definition of the business, but it usually starts with a group of systems analysts who walk into an executive's office, sit down, and ask, "What *systems* do you want?" Some other modern systems-planning approaches merely use variations of the traditional approach—replacing the traditional question of "What systems do you want?" with "What are your critical success factors?" This question is usually interpreted as "What information systems do you *need most*?" and leads to setting priorities for building information systems based on the critical success factors of the executives. However, what is critical today may not be so next year. The net effect of both questions is the same. Questions like "What systems do you want?" "What are your critical success factors?" "What information do you need?" lead to information systems that address short-term requirements, not long-term data quality.

   EAP does not ask these questions. Instead, questions for defining an enterprise business model are "What do you do?" and "What information is used to conduct the business?" The business model reflects the nature of the business and offers a *stable* foundation upon which the architectures can be defined. The architectures support the needs of the business, not the requirements of individuals and without regard to the artificial limitations of organizational boundaries. Thus, the label *business driven* is appropriate.

2. *Enterprise Architecture Planning defines data **before** applications.*

   This is the complete reverse of the way planning is done traditionally, where the first step is to determine which applications systems are needed to support the business and what these applications will do. The second step is to determine what data needs to be processed. With EAP, however, the first architecture defines all the data needed to support the business. When that is completed, the second architecture defines the applications needed to manage that data.

3. *EAP uses data dependency to determine the implementation plan.*

   In the traditional approach to systems planning, after the question "What systems are needed to achieve the objectives?," the systems analysts ask, "How important is it?" or "Whose systems should be implemented first?" As an example, the answer may be "The president's executive information system should be implemented first." After all, it is the president who has ultimate control of the budget, holds the most visibility, and commands the highest political power. So, the president's request is accommodated first, often followed in priority by systems for those in descending positions of influence.

   The EAP approach sets priorities differently. In this approach, it is the *data dependency* that will determine the ideal sequence in which applications should be implemented. Data dependency is based on a fundamental principal that says we should develop the applications that *create* data *before* the applications that need to *use* that data. On paper, this principle seems like common sense and is hard to refute, yet data dependency is not an important consideration in the traditional approach to I.S. planning. In EAP, data dependency is the primary criterion used to sequence applications, and hence, it drives the implementation plan—thus the term *data-driven planning*.

4. *Enterprise Architecture Planning considers both a short-term operational and a long-term strategic focus on the use of information and technology to support the business.*

   Traditional I.S. planning focused exclusively on the short term, or "What is critical today?" Many traditional plans only consider automating operational business areas with a high payback or profit contribution in the short run, sacrificing far greater savings in future years. EAP considers the long-term goals of the business, and then it comes up with a feasible plan to achieve those goals at a reasonable and acceptable cost.

THE ZACHMAN FRAMEWORK

In 1987, John Zachman published a paper in the *IBM Systems Journal*, that is considered to be a classic work on the concepts of information systems architecture.[3] The Zachman paper was significant for several reasons. First, it identified a "framework" of six levels of architectures beginning with the conceptual levels of the "ballpark view" and the "owner's view," through the details of the design and construction of a system. Zachman explained his framework for information systems architectures by using an analogy to the process of planning, drafting, and building a new home. Thus he used the terms *owner's view*, *designer's view*, and *builder's view* for increasing levels of detail appropriate for the purpose at hand.

As Zachman points out, consider the analogy that the information systems development process is much like building a home, which requires several levels or iterations of architectures. One must first decide what kind of home to live in, what it will look like, how many rooms it will have, where each will be located, and so on. During this *planning* phase, you would probably meet with architects and come up with rough sketches, drawings, and perhaps two or three sets of blueprints before deciding what you want. But the fact is, the architectures have little real meaning or value until you solidify your plans by contracting with a builder. To construct the house, you would need both the architectures *and* the plans to implement them.

The second significant aspect of Zachman's framework was the clear definition and distinction of three kinds of architectures: data, process (application), and network (technology). The Zachman Framework was a breakthrough in clearly identifying the differing levels of detail or purpose of architectures and the three dimensions of data, applications, and technology. Figure 1.6 is a representation of the Zachman Framework.

	DATA	FUNCTION	NETWORK
OBJECTIVES / SCOPE (BALLPARK VIEW)	List of Things Important to the Business ENTITY = Class of Business Thing	List of Processes the Business Performs Process = Class of Business Process	List of Locations in Which the Business Operates Node = Business Location
MODEL OF THE BUSINESS (OWNER'S VIEW)	e.g., Ent. / Rel. Diagram Ent. = Business Entity Rel. = Business Rule	e.g., Funct. Flow Diagram Process = Business Process I/O = Business Resources (Including Information)	e.g., Logistics Network Node = Business Unit Link = Business Relationship (Org., Product, Info.)
MODEL OF THE INFORMATION SYSTEM (DESIGNER'S VIEW)	e.g., Data Model Ent. = Data Entity Rel. = Data Relationship	e.g., Data Flow Diagram Process = Application Function I/O = User Views (Set of Data Elements)	e.g., Distributed System Arch. Node = I/S Function (Processor, Storage, etc.) Link = Line Char.
TECHNOLOGY MODEL (BUILDER'S VIEW)	e.g., Data Design Ent. = Segment / Row Rel. = Pointer / Key	e.g., Structure Chart Proc. = Computer Function I/O = Screen/Device Formats	e.g., System Arch Node = Hardware/System Software Link = Line Specifications
DETAILED REPRESEN-TATIONS (OUT-OF-CONTEXT VIEW)	e.g., Data Design Description Ent. = Fields Rel. = Addresses	e.g., Program Proc. = Language Stmts I/O = Control Blocks	e.g., Network Architecture Node = Addresses Link = Protocols
FUNCTIONING SYSTEM	e.g., DATA	e.g., FUNCTION	e.g., COMMUNICATIONS

Figure 1.6. The Zachman Framework. (Copyright ©1987, International Business Machines Corporation. Reprinted with permission from *IBM Systems Journal*, Vol. 26, No. 3.)

COMPONENTS OF ENTERPRISE ARCHITECTURE PLANNING METHODOLOGY

Enterprise Architecture Planning, as defined in this book, creates the top two layers of John Zachman's Framework, the ballpark view and the owner's view. The design of systems begins in the third layer, which is beyond the purview of EAP. Restated, EAP focuses on *defining* data, applications, and technology architectures for the overall enterprise as opposed to *designing* these for specific purposes.

The Zachman Framework is very helpful for placing the planning/defining stages into a conceptual framework. It does not, however, explain how to define these top two levels or how to implement these architectures. Figure 1.7 shows the seven components or phases of EAP, which is a "how-to" for defining these architectures and plans. Everyone who follows EAP will go through the seven components represented in this methodology, though different names or terms may be used. These components are in the shape of a layered wedding cake, with each layer representing a different focus of task.

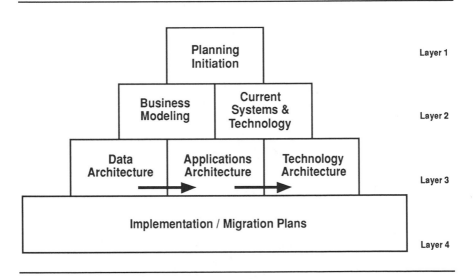

Figure 1.7.   Components of Enterprise Architecture Planning.

Layer 1—Where We Start

Planning Initiation. Starting EAP on the right track, including which methodology to use, who should be involved, and what toolset to use. This leads to producing a workplan for EAP and securing the management commitment to go through the following six phases.

Layer 2—Where We Are Today

Business Modeling. Compiles a knowledge base about the business and the information used in conducting the business.

Current Systems & Technology. Defines what is in place today for application systems and supporting technology platforms. This is a summary-level inventory of application systems, data, and technology platforms to provide a baseline for long-range migration plans.

Layer 3—Where We Want to Be in the Future

Data Architecture. Defines the major kinds of data needed to support the business.

Applications Architecture. Defines the major kinds of applications needed to manage that data and support the business functions.

Technology Architecture. Defines the technology platforms needed to provide an environment for the applications that manage the data and support the business functions.

The arrows on this layer mean that the data architecture is defined first, the applications architecture second, and the technology architecture third. The traditional method of systems planning does the reverse (first determines which hardware you can afford, what applications can run on the selected hardware second, and, lastly, what data needs to be processed).

The question may arise, "Can the three architectures be defined concurrently by three different teams?" This approach has intuitive appeal because (1) overlapping the phases can save time, and (2) data, applications, and technology experts can define their own respective architectures maximizing team productivity and minimizing interpersonal (group) contention. Then, the three architectures can be combined, reconciled, and integrated into a cohesive set of blueprints. However, *in practice, this approach does not work*. The individual architectures turn out to be incompatible or too difficult to combine, because of the following:

1. The teams have different perspectives and levels of understanding of the business.
2. The architectures overlap.
3. There is little or no incentive to be compatible.
4. Without a data architecture, there is no firm foundation for defining the applications and technology.
5. Methodologies, toolsets, and consultants are different; each team wants "to do it their own way."
6. Separate teams point to an inability of the three groups to work cooperatively, which would seem to indicate an unfavorable culture for implementing a shared data environment.

Level 4—How We Get There

Implementation/Migration Plans. Defines the sequence for implementing applications, a schedule for implementation, a cost/benefit analysis, and proposes a clear path for migrating from where we are today to where we want to be.

CONCLUSION

Enterprise Architecture Planning is a planning process for achieving the mission of I.S., which is to provide quality data to those who need it. For EAP to be successful, the 14 points for quality data must be accepted in principle by an enterprise. This recognition should come *before* EAP is initiated and not as an expected result of EAP. Without this acceptance, charter, and support, data-driven planning will inevitably fail.

EAP is different from the traditional method of planning systems. Whereas the traditional method starts by determining current system needs, EAP begins by defining a knowledge base of the enterprise—known as the functional business model. EAP places first priority on defining the data needed to run the business. Once the data architecture has been established, the data dependency determines the plan for implementing applications.

EAP is the "how-to" for creating the top two levels of John Zachman's Framework for Information Systems Architectures. EAP *defines* enterprisewide architectures that serve as blueprints for the subsequent *design* and *implementation* levels of the Zachman Framework.

The seven phases of EAP can be grouped into four layers, each with a particular outlook (see Figure 1.8). The chapters in this book follow the seven-phase methodology for EAP, with the steps, deliverables, procedures, and guidelines described for each phase (see Figure 1.9). Examples based on actual situations are also provided for most of the steps.

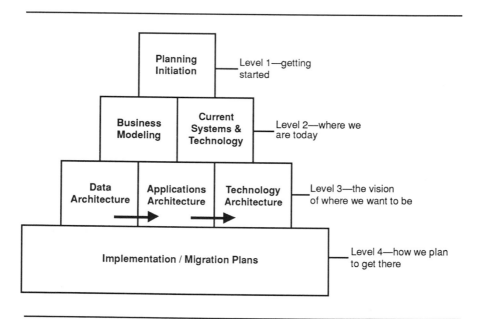

Figure 1.8. Levels of Enterprise Architecture Planning.

STEPS	DELIVERABLES	CHAPTER
1. Planning Initiation	Scope, objectives, vision, methodology, tools, planning team, presentations, workplan	3
2. Business Modeling	Organization structure, preliminary functional business model	4
3. Enterprise Survey	Complete functional business model	5
4. Current Systems & Technology	Information Resource Catalog (IRC), system schematics	6
5. Data Architecture	Entity definitions, E-R diagrams, entity to function matrix, data architecture report	7
6. Applications Architecture	Definition of applications, application matrices, impact analysis, application architecture report	8
7. Technology Architecture	Data/application distribution, technology architecture report	9
8. Implementation Plan	Application sequence, migration plan, costs and benefits, success factors and recommendations	10
9. Planning Conclusion	Final report, presentation	11
10. Transition to Implementation	Improvements to organization, policies, standards, procedures, detailed project plans	12

Figure 1.9. Enterprise Architecture Planning project steps.

DISCUSSION QUESTIONS

1. How long has your organization used database management systems? Have the vendor's promises been completely fulfilled?

2. Most organizations redo their systems plans each year or two. Does your organization have well-defined architectures

and systems plans? Short range (one to two years) or long range (five years)?

3. Are your current planning methods traditional or data driven?

4. Does your I.S. organization have a clearly defined mission? If so, does the mission recognize that I.S's product is data, and does it mention or define quality? Who is responsible for issuing an I.S. mission? If the I.S. mission needs to be updated, how long will that take, including obtaining the required approvals?

5. Has the business side of your organization adopted the quality principles of Deming, Juran, or others? Are there total quality improvement programs, quality circles, team efforts, and quality statistics prominently displayed? Has this culture been passed on to I.S., and if so, what significant changes to I.S. have occurred as a result of focussing on quality?

6. What would be the most important benefits of EAP to your organization? Would different people respond differently to this question?

REFERENCES

[1]Deming, W. Edwards. *Quality, Productivity, and Competitive Position.* M.I.T. Center for Advanced Engineering Study, Cambridge, 1982.

[2]Note: The words "business" and "enterprise" are used interchangeably.

[3]Zachman, John. "A Framework for Information Systems Architecture," *IBM Systems Journal*, Vol. 26, No. 3, 1987.

2

Successful Enterprise Architecture Planning

WHAT IS SUCCESSFUL ENTERPRISE ARCHITECTURE PLANNING?

The vast majority of enterprises that undertake Enterprise Architecture Planning are not successful.

Unfortunately, no one has disputed the above statement. Yet, the precepts of Enterprise Architecture Planning are fundamentally sound, it makes good business sense, and an increasing number of organizations are initiating EAP. EAP is considered to be successful when the following conditions exist.

1. EAP is *completed*. The largest percentage of organizations attempting to define their enterprise architectures and plans never complete the process.
2. The plan is being *implemented*. The completed architectures and plans must be approved upon delivery and then implemented. Plans that are completed but remain on a shelf are not successful.
3. The architectures are *used* to guide new development and are *maintained*. The architectures are overall blueprints for

guiding and directing systems development over both the short and the long term. They serve as standards that must be followed and enforced. For the architectures to remain active and useful, they must be maintained and kept up to date.

GREATEST OBSTACLES TO OVERCOME

When undertaking EAP, be aware of potential obstacles, study the organization, and plan a strategy for overcoming them. The most common obstacles are presented below with a definition, symptoms that indicate its presence, and possible solutions. Particular remedies can be difficult to pinpoint accurately, since each organization is unique, but these suggestions should provide specific strategies for overcoming these obstacles. Beware that many of these problems are interrelated and solving one may provide the answers to others.

Awareness/Recognition/Acceptance by Top Management

Description: This is the most important condition for success. Every successful EAP (completed, implemented, and maintained) has cited this condition as necessary for procuring resources for the project. "Top management" refers to executives both in the area of the business being planned and in I.S. "Awareness" means that executives know about the EAP process, its benefits to the organization, and its products. Management must "recognize" the reasons for developing the architectures and the importance of these architectures to the organization. "Acceptance" means that management understands the rationale for EAP and accepts their role and responsibility to the EAP process for successfully achieving its objectives.

Symptoms: Management questions the purpose, benefits, or need for EAP—identifiable by questions such as "Why should we do EAP?" or "Are other companies using EAP and what have been their results?"

Solutions: Overcoming this obstacle is basically an educational process. The following recommendations are offered for increasing the awareness about EAP and recognizing that architectures and plans are necessary to achieve business goals:

- Make presentations to management on EAP concepts including examples from other companies when possible.
- Arrange for external consultants to present architecture benefits and opportunities, to explain the EAP process, and to discuss success factors.
- Provide management with books and published articles on EAP methods and results of planning in other companies—especially competitors.
- Urge key executives to attend high-level conferences or seminars that discuss the importance of architecture-based I.S. planning.
- Circulate internal reports on the merits of EAP, industry and technology trends, and the role of information technology in the long-term vision of the business. For most organizations, such reports should have a positive tone.

Commitment of Resources to Enterprise Architecture Planning

Description: The development of the architectures and plans typically involves four to eight people from six to eight months and will likely utilize computer and clerical resources as well. Verbal acceptance and support for EAP are needed to gain credibility. *Commitment*, however, means that sufficient personnel, funds, time, and material are allocated to the EAP process. It will be easy to recognize when management commitment is an obstacle. Either resources are made available or they are not.

Symptoms: Statements that begin "We need to do EAP, but we can't afford to do it now because . . . " followed by a list of explanations (i.e., excuses) why EAP is lower in priority or that resources are better allotted other places. These symptoms indicate an intensive "selling" effort is needed to raise the perceived priority of EAP.

A more subtle form of rejection can be recognized by such statements as "Go ahead with your EAP, but you can only use two people for three months." Do not misconstrue such remarks as a conditional or limited approval to proceed. Management's use of words like "you" and "your" indicate that *they* do not accept EAP, will distance themselves politically, and, by limiting resources, may make it impossible to complete EAP or do it well. The final result is that a lack of success appears to be your fault, not theirs. If this situation arises, credibility will suffer from the start. It is unreasonable to expect that two people will produce the same results in three months that truly requires four people six months to complete. Completeness and quality will be severely affected, and the results may be unacceptable or unusable.

Solutions: Prepare a sales pitch to top executives. Without management commitment, EAP cannot succeed. Guidelines for preparing management presentations to obtain management commitment are presented in Chapter 3. With performance evaluations and career paths on the line, it is best to walk away from EAP when management has not demonstrated *full* commitment of resources.

Arrogance of I.S.; Unfavorable Corporate Culture

Description: EAP involves frequent contact with people in the business area being planned. Indeed, business people should participate as members of the planning team. I.S. managers often display an outright arrogance with statements such as "We in I.S. know more about the business than our users do" or "The users don't understand systems, nor do they even understand their own requirements for systems. Therefore, we will tell them what they need." Such arrogant attitudes have understandably caused conflict with users. The architectures and plans will have no credibility with the business in that situation.

Some organizational cultures are better suited for planning than others. EAP is well suited to organizations that have long-range goals and plans, a cooperative team approach to management decisions, total quality management programs, and a desire to invest in new products and procedures leading to significant revenue or savings in the future. Conversely, EAP is not appropriate for an organization that places greatest value on quarter-to-quarter profits, quotas, budget slashing, and short-term projects.

Symptoms: User alienation can be identified by a lack of involvement in the systems development process and a high rate of complaints about support and service levels.

An unfavorable corporate culture is indicated by statements such as "Our company doesn't believe in strategic planning," "Our systems are like a sinking ship, and we must put all of our efforts toward manning the bilge pumps," or "We only have time to shoot alligators, not to drain the swamp."

Solutions: It is difficult to change deep-rooted attitudes in a short amount of time. EAP should not be attempted in an unfavorable climate. Two strategies for preventing this problem when there are minor pockets of adverse culture are the following:

- Avoid selecting team members and leaders who display this arrogance.
- If the first strategy is not possible, perhaps some component of EAP useful in its own right (such as the current systems and technology architecture) can be defined under an acceptable title until a more favorable climate for EAP comes about.

Political Differences Regarding Responsibilities for Enterprise Architecture Planning

Description: Most large data processing shops have several departments that may stake claim to responsibility for one or more components of the enterprise architectures or plans. Typically, these departments have names such as Systems Planning, Data Administration, Technology Planning and Evaluation, Standards and Controls, Systems Architecture, Business Systems Development, Applications Development, and Data Resource Management. Outside I.S. there are additional departments with names such as Corporate Planning, Research and Development, and Strategic Planning.

Symptoms: Multiple departments vying for EAP responsibility. Concurrent independent but overlapping efforts, each being "slices of the EAP wedding cake."

Solutions: The most effective form of responsibility for EAP is to have the ultimate responsibility rest with a single department. This may be a temporary department established expressly to develop the plans and architectures (sometimes referred to as matrix management) or an existing department that is assigned the responsibility. A Steering Committee comprised of I.S. and non-I.S. executives may provide direction and ultimate accountability, but the day-to-day organization for activities should be assigned to a *specific individual* for the duration of EAP. Though having a single person or department responsible for EAP is most effective, all parties with general planning duties should be included as (or invited to be) team members. If a person resents being excluded, he or she may spend time discrediting the work of the planning team.

Shared responsibility for EAP is the least effective form of project management, because the culture of most American companies fosters competition among managers and executives. EAP could easily become a political battleground for competing executives who might take actions or make statements that would damage the credibility or hinder the effectiveness of the EAP team. All attitudes and ambitions toward EAP leadership should be carefully considered, and compromises must be negotiated regarding responsibility, direction, and participation.

Lack of Credibility of Planning Leaders

Description: To be acceptable, the long-range architectures and plans must be credible. Obviously, the credibility of the plans is a direct reflection of the credibility of the EAP leaders and participants. Credibility embodies such personal characteristics as respect, esteem, and integrity. It may take years to establish one's professional credibility and reputation, and considerable attention must be given to maintain it. EAP must be staffed with people who possess high credibility throughout the organization, and measures should be taken to maintain the credibility of the planning team.

Symptoms: Examples of statements that indicate a lack of credibility are: "The EAP team sits in an ivory tower," "*They* really don't understand the way *we* operate," or "Here come the I.S. planners *again*."

Solutions: The EAP team's credibility is on the line at every step. Generally, opinions expressed that reflect a lack of credibility get back to the EAP team through loyal associates. Take steps to overcome a perceived lack of credibility.

* Select respected team members from across the enterprise.
* Use modern EAP methods and tools.

- Place articles about the EAP in an internal newsletter, and present the architectures and plans in a manner that avoids credibility attack. The guidelines contained throughout this book are designed to build and maintain credibility.

Inexperience with Enterprise Architecture Planning; Lack of Training

Description: EAP has been used for a relatively short time in terms of business processing. Few people have completed the process of defining enterprise architectures, putting plans in place, and implementing those plans. Most organizations do not have personnel experienced with EAP. This inexperience often results in a lack of qualified participants or an inability to carry out tasks efficiently or accurately. There are a few books and seminars available for training, but EAP is an exercise in managing interpersonal relationships, and, therefore, one cannot gain valuable experience by reading a technical book on modeling or attending a seminar. Both inexperience and lack of training can lead to deteriorating credibility for the EAP team.

Symptoms: Indications of a lack of experience and training are: difficulty in selecting qualified people for vital roles on the EAP team, slow EAP progress, and statements from team members such as "What will the next step be?" or "What is the purpose of this step?"

Solutions: The lack of training can be overcome by developing an educational program for EAP. This program might include the following:

- Educational seminars taught by experienced practitioners.
- Public seminars and conferences.
- Consultants with EAP experience to make executive overview presentations.
- University classes and programs that include Information Resource Management, Data Resource Management, and Enterprise Modeling classes.

A lack of internal experience can be addressed by hiring employees familiar with EAP or by using external consultants.

Resource Shortages and Large Applications Backlog

Description: Personnel resource shortages and a large applications backlog are the two most common excuses for not committing resources to EAP. EAP may not be dismissed outright, but addressing the backlog of applications takes precedence over EAP. This is a variation of the second obstacle, commitment of resources, discussed above.

Symptoms: This obstacle will surface quickly when the requested number of participants will not be available, or selected individuals are unable to "free up" an adequate amount of their time.

Applications backlog problems are often present in I.S. organizations that have the following:

*   More patchwork program maintenance and enhancements to systems than new system development.
*   Inflexible systems that are time-consuming and costly to change.
*   A proliferation of "interfaces" to transfer files and data among systems.
*   Development priorities based solely on short-term considerations.
*   Frequent reorganizations and business changes that thwart efforts to "catch up" on the backlog.
*   Few standards enforced by a quality assurance group.
*   No formal strategic direction or goal of the organization's systems portfolio.
*   Planning and budgeting focuses on hardware and software technology.

Solutions: Obviously, personnel is a limited resource. It is always a challenge to obtain credible EAP team members and retain them for the duration of the process. Chapter 3, "Planning Initiation," provides suggestions for selecting team members and obtaining management's commitment of time and people to EAP.

A growing backlog will not be reduced by applying more personnel resources or spending more dollars. The current I.S. policies and procedures have contributed to the problem, so a change is needed. The enterprise architectures and plans replace the backlog. Implementing a shared data resource will, over time, substantially shrink the accumulation and fulfill the mission of I.S.

Finding the "Best" Methodology

Description: There is no "best" methodology. Some EAP methods and techniques may seem to work better than others, but such differences are most likely the result of the people involved and the organizational commitment. It is a mistake to dwell only on the technical merits of one methodology over another. Planning involves organizations and people.

Symptoms: There are lengthy debates over methodologies and tools, including exhaustive evaluations of consultants, seminars, and vendors for the purpose of selecting "the best" methodology and products.

Solutions: Any methodology is better than none, and there are good EAP methodologies. By consensus, select a methodology that is understandable, can be accomplished in a reasonable amount of time, and can be completed within the budget—and stick with it. Methodology selection is covered in more detail in Chapter 3, "Planning Initiation."

Educating Information Systems Personnel in New Technologies

Description: The manner in which systems are conceived and developed with a data-driven approach is different from the traditional approach that many systems analysts are accustomed to. Convincing I.S. people that the data-driven approach is better will require a great deal of educating and convincing. I.S. practitioners who have designed and built systems for more than ten years may be the most unwilling to accept the new concepts or adopt new methods.

Symptoms: Low attendance at internal courses and presentations, resistance to new products or techniques such as CASE, object-oriented analysis and programming, and so on.

Solutions: Expect resistance from within I.S., and plan an educational awareness program that will bring I.S. people into the enterprise modeling fold gradually over time.

Satisfaction with Current Applications Methods

Description: There may be I.S. and business people who are set in their ways and will view EAP as a threat. They may, in fact, believe that the current applications methods are not the best, but feel secure with them. "If it ain't broke, don't fix it!" Be prepared to respond to such "don't rock the boat" statements that indicate satisfaction with the current application systems and system development lifecycle (SDLC).

Symptoms: Comments such as "Why do we need EAP when our current applications are operating just fine?" or "There's nothing wrong with the way we've been developing systems for the past 20 years."

Solutions: First, before pointing at problems with current systems, be certain all facts are verifiable. Presenting faults with existing systems rarely generates support for EAP. Understand issues that will affect future systems performance. Second, consider the possible reasons that someone would make the above statements. For example, if the person participated or had responsibility for a current system or procedure, then there may be a fear of appearing inadequate or unsuccessful.

Whether in a one-to-one conversation or in a presentation at a meeting, statements of satisfaction with current systems must be countered directly, tactfully, and with confidence, focusing on the positive impact that EAP will have on *future* systems, and not the causes of current ills. Your actual response, of course, will depend on your perception of the attitudes of the people involved and the impression that you want to give. In response to the question "If EAP is so beneficial, why did we not do EAP several years ago?" point out that EAP is a relatively new process, requires skills heretofore unavailable, and that tools and technology have advanced to the point of supporting EAP.

Few or Inadequate Tools

Description: It is a misconception that better tools must produce better products. EAP is an interpersonal rather than technical process. Tools are no substitute for human experience, intellect, and common sense. They are useful to the extent that they assist with documentation and technical analysis of some data. Budgets are usually too tight to afford expensive tools, and good architectures and plans can usually be developed with products that are presently available to the planning team or are inexpensive to acquire.

Symptoms: Lengthy discussion and evaluation of available products to support EAP. Remarks that "We should wait until the new such-and-such product is released," and "postpone EAP until the decision as to CASE products has been made" indicate the misconception that sophisticated tools are required.

Solutions: Tools are needed to facilitate the plans and architectures. Avoid planning products that claim to "do it for you." Chapter 3, "Planning Initiation," addresses the selection of tools and products to support EAP.

Uncertain Payback and Rate of Return; Expecting Immediate Results

Description: Although EAP is time-consuming, and the implementation of some applications in the long-range plan could take years, the intent of planning is to head the enterprise down a road that will ultimately fulfill the I.S. mission. Planning is an investment in the future, but like any investment, there are no guarantees. There are always alternate routes. EAP will find a good course, show how to proceed, and prepare the organization and I.S. for the journey.

Symptoms: Management wants to know what the short-term payback will be; "What will EAP do for me this year?"

EAP may be seen as the cure-all, end-all planning process, much like the promises of database used to be heralded. "After EAP, everyone will be satisfied."

Solutions: There is bound to be uncertainty regarding the fulfillment of the I.S. mission, but there is less hesitation about using an established methodology such as EAP rather than a traditional or "home-grown" approach. To those who complain of the long payback period, point out these facts:

- The architectures produced by EAP are immediately useful in their own right.

- With sufficient resources, an integrated architecture and plans can be developed in four to eight months.
- New systems developed from the plans can be implemented faster than those without architectures.
- Systems will share data, saving a great deal of money and time building and maintaining interfaces over many years.
- With a phased, data-driven implementation schedule, the systems built in the first and second years will yield significant results.

Fear of Loss of Data Control / Ownership

Description: At the root of many excuses for delaying or postponing EAP is the fear of loss of ownership or control of data. Control provides a sense of security and importance. To some individuals, a shared data resource means that control may be "lost" to a centralized organization.

Symptoms: The symptoms of these obstacles are often subtle and disguised as other obstacles or excuses. Probe beneath the surface of excuses to determine the cause or foundation, which may be emotional (ambition) or political (control). Any statement containing the phrases *"my* (and/or *our) data"* or *"my/our files"* points to an ownership or control issue.

Solutions: Ownership should not be an issue. Who owns the buildings, equipment, furniture, materials, and inventories of the business? Does the purchasing department *own* them? Does the maintenance department *own* the equipment and facilities? Of course not! Those departments are *responsible* for obtaining, maintaining, and providing access to those resources for the people who need them. Data is a shared business resource like any other. Responsibilities will be defined to manage the data resources that will provide a greater degree of control. Redirect statements or questions regarding ownership or control into discussion of responsibility, drawing analogies to the way other familiar resources of the organization are managed.

Substantial Up-Front Cost; Benefits Difficult to Measure

Description: Planning is an investment, and like all investments there are up-front costs. But the expense is not usually substantial relative to the I.S. budget. Considering the total cost of information management for the enterprise (both internal and external to I.S.) over a five-year period, an investment of 1 percent of that figure seems reasonable—indeed downright cheap—to plan a five-year direction for systems aimed at providing stability, reliability, and security into the future. Unfortunately, too often a person's performance objectives and evaluation are entirely based on short-term annual goals and achievements. Except in hindsight, rewards are seldom given for work toward the long-term good of the business.

Symptoms: Questions such as Why is EAP expensive? or What is the payback for EAP? indicate a short-sighted culture willing to ignore or compromise quality.

Information Systems performance evaluations that only consider the accomplishments of a single year.

Solutions: Most people who claim that the benefits of EAP are difficult to measure are using this excuse to mask other deeper-rooted concerns. Deal with those obstacles and this one should disappear.

Establish, up front, a performance evaluation system that rewards steps taken toward achieving long-term business and I.S. goals.

Inaccessible or Uncooperative Users; Delegation

Description: If planning team members do not attend meetings, or they "delegate" project responsibility to staff members below them, STOP! Do not proceed with EAP.

Symptoms: Statements such as "Do *your* planning, but don't involve any of *my* people," or "Submit *your* plan when it is finished, and *we* will evaluate it," indicate a culture in which EAP will not succeed. A statement from an executive, such as "All of *our* best people are fully committed to other activities, but we recently hired two graduates from the university who are not particularly busy, so use them for EAP," similarly indicates a lack of credibility, support, or worse, an attempt to thwart success.

Solutions: EAP should not be attempted without the full cooperation, support, and involvement of the enterprise areas. That means qualified team members directly participate in developing the architectures and plans, and not just reviewing them. Management must view EAP as *their* people producing *their* plans if it is to be credible ("by the people, for the people").

Delusions

Description: The leaders and organizers of EAP may have the following delusions:

- EAP is so simple that external consultants are not needed.
- Business people are incapable of defining architectures.
- The benefits of business models and architectures are obvious.
- Any business participation is better than none (quantity versus quality).
- An I.S. plan can be formulated in far less time than EAP.

Symptoms: Common delusions can be noticed in statements such as "I can do EAP myself," "I don't need consultants or users," or "Though there is currently little support for EAP, when the architectures are presented, management will see and understand the benefits, accept the architectures and approve the remainder of EAP."

Solution: One should be aware of these impressions, and assess them honestly. Understand the risks, rewards, obstacles, and success factors leading to the Planning Initiation Phase of EAP.

REASONS FOR ENTERPRISE ARCHITECTURE PLANNING SUCCESS

With all the obstacles standing in the way, it is no wonder that so many EAP efforts have not been successful. These obstacles are enormous challenges for those attempting to create architectures and long-range plans for integrated systems. Fortunately, companies have succeeded, and their experiences provide insights for those just beginning. By examining successful EAP projects, the following ten factors are common to every organization that has completed, implemented, and maintained enterprise architectures and plans.

Management Commitment and Support

This leads every success factor list—the necessity to obtain adequate funding and gain credibility. To accomplish this, have a common vision in both the I.S. and the business areas. Presentations should explain the concepts, vision, and mission in a manner that virtually assures management commitment and support.

End-User and Management Participation and Cooperation

Management-level business people participate during the entire EAP process. Full cooperation from all business units means that time is scheduled for interviews during the enterprise survey, reviews and feedback are provided, and presentations are attended. Plans are developed by the business and for the business, and are credible and realistic.

Effective Project Leadership and Workplan (Methodology)

Successful EAP projects have leaders who adopt a methodology, develop a clear and concise workplan that is easy to follow, and motivate and guide EAP through to conclusion. The methodology itself is not the success factor, but any methodology is better than none. It is the ability of the project leader to manage EAP that is key to success, and a good leader has a good workplan.

Acceptable Balance of Scope and Objectives vs. Level of Detail vs. Resources and Time Committed

EAP leaders are able to achieve adequate detail in the architectures within the constraints set by available resources and time allotted. The scope of the "enterprise" is not too broad to be accomplished and not too narrow to preclude the sharing of needed data.

Qualified, Trained Team and Use of Consultants

EAP is conducted by well-respected individuals with extensive business experience, credible I.S. personnel, and consultants with practical experience.

Productive Documentation and Analysis Tools

Tools facilitate EAP, enable business information to be analyzed, enhance the presentation of the architectures and plans to the rest of the organization, and enable the developers to build from the blueprints. This success is not based on sophisticated features of the products, but rather on how the tools are used and managed to support EAP.

Compatible Culture

EAP is promoted and performed in a manner consistent with the corporate culture, making it easier for both business and I.S. user, management, and staff to support EAP and cooperate with the team.

Distribution of Intermediate Deliverables

Successful EAP projects maintained a high profile by circulating interim documents for review and comment. Management could monitor the steady progress of the EAP, and business people throughout the enterprise could provide feedback to ensure that the systems defined by the architectures and plans would fulfill their long-term requirements.

Effective Presentations

Successful projects keep team members fully informed about progress and issues, and create a positive image throughout the organization. The presentations keep a business orientation. Expectations of those receiving the presentations are managed so that the purpose and products of EAP and the benefits of EAP were promoted throughout the process.

80/20 Principle

Successful projects followed the 80/20 principle, which—loosely interpreted—states that there is no perfect plan. As planners, we cannot afford to get bogged down by insignificant details. Detail and accuracy may need to be sacrificed somewhat to formulate the architectures and plans in the allotted time. Eighty percent completeness and accuracy in each phase of EAP should be considered "good enough" to produce reasonable, feasible architectures and plans.

DISCUSSION QUESTIONS

1. Which of the EAP obstacles pose the greatest challenge to your effort?
2. Can you describe your strategy to put all ten success factors in place?
3. Have there been successful planning projects in your organization? Why are they considered successful?

Planning Initiation

INTRODUCTION

It was stated earlier that the large majority of EAP projects are never completed. Three contributing reasons for this are (1) the EAP projects may begin on the wrong track by having unreasonable objectives or unrealistic expectations, (2) selecting an approach that will not achieve the desired result in the time allotted, and (3) the participants are unfamiliar and inexperienced with EAP. This chapter, therefore, will explain the EAP initiation steps so that the project can quickly proceed in the right direction from the beginning, be completed on time, and have qualified team members.

There are two major deliverables resulting from the Planning Initiation Phase. The tangible deliverable is the EAP project workplan that specifies the phases and steps necessary to accomplish the goals of EAP, namely, to develop the architectures and implementation plans. The intangible deliverable from the Planning Initiation Phase is the support and commitment of executives and management throughout the enterprise for successfully completing EAP. The term "support" is not simply limited to verbal agreement, but also implies allocation of personnel, budget, and time for EAP.

Seven Steps of Planning Initiation

These are the seven steps of the Planning Initiation Phase:

1. Determine scope and objectives for EAP.
2. Create a vision (initial meetings with management).
3. Adapt a planning methodology.
4. Arrange for computer resources.
5. Assemble the planning team.
6. Prepare EAP workplan.
7. Obtain/confirm commitment and funding.

STEP 1—DETERMINE SCOPE AND OBJECTIVES FOR ENTERPRISE ARCHITECTURE PLANNING

Purpose

In this step, the scope and objectives of the EAP project are formally defined so that management and project participants will understand what will be accomplished.

Deliverables

1. Scope of the enterprise is defined and participating organization units are identified and selected
2. Statement of objectives for what EAP is to accomplish

Tasks and Guidelines

Task 1 Define the scope of enterprise. The "E" in EAP stands for enterprise. So, the first step of the first phase of EAP is to define precisely what *enterprise* means. Since an aim of EAP is to enable an organization to share data, the term *enterprise* should include *all areas that need to share **substantial** amounts of data*. Not simply the periodic rolling up or consolidation of financial figures, but the constant access and use of operational data.

A good and proper scope for enterprise often equates to a business unit, division, or subsidiary because such organization units include all business functions for providing products and services to customers. Also, with responsibility and control of the bottom line, the economic benefits and justification of EAP can more easily be established.

On the other hand, a poor or improper scope for enterprise would be a single department such as Sales & Marketing, Customer Service, Finance, Human Resources, or Administration. These departments depend on and share data with other organization units. If the scope of EAP is too limited organizationally, the architectures will not have businesswide applicability.

Be aware of the risks when the scope of EAP is too narrow or too broad. A scope that is too narrow will result in architectures that are incomplete and lack detail from other areas of the business. If the scope is too broad, there will not be enough time or resources to get sufficient detail into the architectures to make them useful for the design and construction of the systems. Also, the broader the scope, the more politics will be involved. Your definition of enterprise will need to balance these considerations.

Despite the best of intentions, and the intuitive appeal of dividing EAP along departmental lines and subsequently combining or integrating them, experience has shown that this does not happen successfully. Independent architectures for different areas of the business will be inconsistent and virtually nonintegratable into a single architecture. The lesson to be learned is that EAP needs to be properly scoped from the beginning, consistent with the quality data mission given in Chapter 1, or it is best not to do EAP at all.

Task 2   Evaluate favorable versus unfavorable characteristics.   When there are choices of a suitable enterprise for EAP, it is important to evaluate *both* favorable and unfavorable organizational characteristics. There should clearly be more favorable than unfavorable characteristics to consider the environment amenable to EAP. The unfavorable characteristics are still very important, however, since some of them represent potentially insurmountable obstacles for EAP. If a business unit selected as the enterprise has unfavorable characteristics, formulate a strategy to overcome or remove them.

Favorable Characteristics for an Enterprise

- *It has current, strategic, long-range business plans.*
  It is an advantage to coordinate or dovetail EAP with a long-range strategic plan that already exists for the business.

- *Emphasis is on total quality management programs.*
  Since the mission of EAP is to provide quality data, businesses that emphasize total quality management programs are usually receptive to EAP.

- *Existing systems are inadequate and / or too costly to maintain.*
  This represents an opportunity, especially when this situation is the result of a lack of planning and enterprisewide standards. The architectures developed in EAP will provide the needed planning and standards.

- *There is a need to integrate and share data.*
  Since this is a goal of EAP, where the need to integrate and share is widely acknowledged, there is likely to be a favorable climate for undertaking EAP.

- *There are unsuccessful I.S. projects or severe cost overruns.*
  This also represents an opportunity. The reason many I.S. projects are unsuccessful or overly expensive is due to a lack of planning. EAP provides the planning to avoid repeating that outcome for future projects.

- *Budget is approved for major new system development.*
  Funding and personnel are the most difficult resources to obtain for EAP. It can often be shown that a large system uses data in common with other systems. Having a set of integrated architectures to serve as blueprints for the design and construction of major new systems makes plain good sense. In some situations, a portion of the time and resources approved for the development of a major system can be applied to creating enterprise architectures and plans. Many of the benefits of EAP (see Chapter 1) apply to individual applications, and indeed, EAP will enable those benefits to be realized.

- *Major business changes are anticipated.*
  Major business changes underscore the importance of flexibil-

ity in information systems. In organizations characterized by frequent changes such as new product lines, mergers, acquisitions, new competitors or the elimination of competitors, and government regulations and deregulations, management will understand the need for flexible systems. Flexibility must be defined and planned at the enterprise level.

- *There are extensive management changes or reorganization.*
  Again, such changes demand flexible information systems. Where there have been recent executive changes or reorganization, the importance of flexible systems and the role of EAP for creating flexibility will be easier to acknowledge and accept.

- *There is a large I.S. project backlog.*
  A large I.S. project backlog can be used as an excuse not to do long-range planning, but a major reason for the backlog is the lack of adequate enterprisewide planning. Throwing more people and money into I.S. projects will not solve a backlog problem. Management must recognize that reducing the buildup can only come about by changing the fundamental systems development process. As I.S. budgets have increased, backlogs have grown—not shrunk. With EAP, the architectures are the backlog and the plans are aimed at eliminating the backlog by leveraging resources and by having longer-lived systems made from standard components that are flexible, adaptable, and easily maintained.

- *There is an attempt to cope with new technology.*
  If an organization is considering CASE, information engineering, relational database, reverse engineering, networks, rapid application development (RAD), downsizing, object-oriented analysis, and other new technologies, architectures and plans will enable these new technologies to be coordinated, integrated, and employed effectively.

- *The company is able and willing to design architectures.*
  There has to be a "will" and a "capability" for designing architectures. That means the enterprise has a favorable corporate culture that understands and accepts the purpose of architectures, and it has the resources and wherewithal for creating them.

Unfavorable Characteristics for an Enterprise

- *Management is shortsighted (time, budget, other excuses).*
  Where management focuses only on the near term—"What are you doing for me today or this year?"—there is often no interest in establishing long-range plans. This mentality can be identified by an emphasis or preoccupation with the annual budget, quarterly progress reports, and performance reviews.

- *There have been recent unsuccessful planning attempts.*
  If there has been a recent systems planning effort that is not viewed as a success, or there has been a previous attempt to define architectures, management will be reluctant to try it again. In this case, a considerable amount of effort is needed to distinguish how EAP is different from those prior attempts. This will be especially difficult if previous attempts yielded architectures or plans that "sat on the shelf" and were never implemented. In some situations, however, a successful tact is to state that EAP will build upon the prior work, update those architectures, fill in the gaps, and produce an acceptable plan.

- *There is hostility or resentment towards systems people.*
  EAP should be a joint, cooperative effort between I.S. personnel and business personnel. These two groups must work well together. If their relationship is strained for any reason, working together on a team may be difficult and frustrating if not impossible.

- *There is an uncooperative, "hands-off" attitude (delegation).*
  Without complete access to business people throughout the enterprise, defining the business accurately will not be easy. A similar unfavorable condition exists if inexperienced people are assigned or delegated to the EAP project. Do not attempt EAP without the support of upper-level management who can assign the most qualified participants to be members of the EAP team.

- *The company is experiencing less profit, potential downsizing.*
  Downsizing generally results in reducing or eliminating "overhead" functions. Since planning is generally considered

to be an overhead activity and not a necessity, attempting EAP in an atmosphere of cutbacks, reduction in forces, and immediate downsizing is probably futile.

- *There is a lack of or disregard for standards or plans.*
  Again, if the focus is on near-term benefits, then long-term planning and architectural standards will be considered a luxury, and gaining widespread acceptance for EAP will be difficult. If standards and plans are disdained, then the architectures may ultimately end up on a shelf, and the effort that went into creating them will have been wasted. This cultural condition can be identified by (1) no up-to-date I.S. standards, (2) existing standards are unused and unenforced, (3) a lack of a standard systems development methodology where applications development teams may choose any tools and techniques to use, and (4) a lack of or understaffed Quality Assurance function with no accepted measures for ascertaining quality and with little enforcement authority.

After evaluating these favorable and unfavorable organizational characteristics for EAP, there should be clear candidates for businesses and organization units that should undergo EAP. Explain EAP to the management of the candidate businesses and to their respective I.S. functions. Look for signs of enthusiasm and acceptance for EAP in personal expressions of support and cooperation from influential management—that is, those executives with political and/or authoritative power.

Unfortunately, the selection of the organization unit to be the enterprise for EAP is often made politically rather than analytically; you may be told which business unit, division, or subsidiary will undergo EAP rather than choosing the one with the most favorable characteristics. The selection may even be for a single department or support function as a result of traditional DP thinking about having very large systems for Sales and Marketing, Human Resources, Inventory, and Accounting. If this happens, be aware of the obstacles and risks to EAP, and prepare accordingly during this initiation phase. A traditional systems development lifecycle approach is more appropriate for a large integrated system to support a particular department.

Task 3   Understand the enterprise with respect to corporate culture and the evolutionary growth of I.S.   *Corporate culture* comprises the leadership and management styles, decision-making procedures, politics, attitudes, and formal and informal lines of communication of an organization. In an in-depth *ComputerWorld* article, Jane Linder describes corporate cultures along five dimensions (see Figure 3.1).[1] Gaining commitment for EAP is usually easier for those organizations whose cultural characteristics are more toward the left side of Figure 3.1 than the right. The obstacles to EAP success will be particularly difficult to overcome in a *conservative* culture that is headed by a *competitive* executive who manages rather than leads.

Recall from the previous chapter that the top two EAP success factors were management support and the participation of information consumers (users). So, it is most sensible to perform EAP for that part of the organization where those two success factors are most likely to be realized.

As defined by Richard Nolan's six-stage model of I.S. growth[2] (see Figure 3.2), EAP is clearly an advanced stage 5 or stage 6 activity. Though EAP can be used to bring an I.S. organization into stage 5 from a lower stage, doing so will be very difficult as many obstacles will be encountered, especially if attempting to skip or leap over stages. Assess the stage of evolution for your I.S. organization to determine whether EAP is an appropriate process for advancement.

Task 4   List and define EAP objectives and deliverables.   It is important to list formally and define the objectives and deliverables of EAP. Objectives should be written in simple, nontechnical, concise language. Be very precise as to what will be accomplished, and focus on business benefits.

Task 5   Review the list of success factors and obstacles (Chapter 2) and develop a strategy for this initiation phase.   Resolve issues and potential problems during this phase. EAP initiation may drag on for a long time, but do not proceed into the Business Modeling Phase without complete confidence that EAP will be successful. If there are lingering doubts regarding EAP obstacles, these doubts must be completely ad-

Entrepreneurial	Conservative
Risk encouraging	Risk averse
Informal	Formal
Decisive	Deliberate
Results oriented	Process oriented
Aggressive	Defensive

Clear Authority Lines	Ambiguous Authority
Functional or divisional	Matrix
Profit and loss responsibility	Cost and revenue centers
Hierarchical	Consensual

Cooperative	Competitive
Team oriented	"Macho"
Collaborative	Individualistic
Reward oriented	Censure oriented
Merit based	Power based

Led	Managed
Long-term goals	Short-term objectives
Clear, enduring mission	Mixed messages
Big picture oriented	Detail oriented
Creative	Analytical

Ethical	Amoral
Visible ethics and policies	Tacit acceptance of unethical behavior
Ethical leadership and supervision	Hiring for cultural fit
Internal checks and balances	No attention to reconciliation between systems

Figure 3.1. Five dimensions of corporate culture. (*Computer World*, September 23, 1985.)

Growth processes	Stage I Initiation	Stage II Contagion	Stage III Control	Stage IV Integration	Stage V Data administration	Stage VI Maturity
Applications portfolio	Functional cost reduction applications	Proliferation	Upgrade documentation and restructuring of existing applications	Retrofitting existing applications using database technology	Organization Integration of applications	Application
DP organization	Specialization for technological learning	User-oriented programmers	Middle management	Establish computer utility and user account teams	Data administration	Data resource management
DP planning & control	Lax	More lax	Formalized planning and control	Tailored planning and control systems	Shared data and common systems	Data resource strategic planning
User awareness	"Hands off"	Superficially enthusiastic	Arbitrarily held accountable	Accountability learning	Effectively accountable	Acceptance of joint user and data processing accountability

Figure 3.2a Nolan's six stages of data processing growth. (Reprinted by permission of *Harvard Business Review.* "Managing the Crisis in Data Processing" by Richard L. Nolan, March–April 1979. Copyright ©1979 by the President and Fellows of Harvard College; all rights reserved.)

First-level analysis	Stage I Initiation	Stage II Contagion	Stage III Control	Stage IV Integration	Stage V Data administration	Stage VI Maturity
DP expenditure benchmarks	Tracks rate of sales growth	Exceeds rate of sales growth	Is less than rate of sales growth	Exceeds rate of sales growth	Is less than rate of sales growth	Tracks rate of sales growth
Technology benchmarks	100% batch processing	80% batch processing 20% remote job entry processing	70% batch processing 15% database processing 10% inquiry processing 5% time-sharing processing	50% batch and remote job entry processing 40% database and data communications processing 5% personal computing 5% minicomputer and microcomputer processing	20% batch and remote job entry processing 60% database and data communications processing 5% personal computing 15% minicomputer and microcomputer processing	10% batch and remote job entry processing 60% database and data communications processing 5% personal computing 25% minicomputer and microcomputer processing

Second-level analysis	Stage I Initiation	Stage II Contagion	Stage III Control	Stage IV Integration	Stage V Data administration	Stage VI Maturity
Applications portfolio	There is a concentration on labor-intensive automation, scientific support, and clerical replacement.		Applications move out to user locations for data generation and data use.		Balance is established between centralized shared data/ common system applications and decentralized user-controlled applications.	
DP organization	Data processing is centralized and operates as a "closed shop."		Data processing becomes data custodian. Computer utility established and achieves reliability.		There is organizational implementation of the data resource management concept. There are layers of responsibility for data processing at appropriate organizational levels.	
DP planning and control	Internal planning and control is installed to manage the computer. Included are standards for programming, responsibility accounting, and project management.			External planning and control is installed to manage data resources. Included are value-added user chargeback, steering committee, and data administration.		
User awareness	Reactive: Enduser is superficially involved. The computer provides more, better, and faster information than manual techniques.		Driving force: Enduser is directly involved with data entry and data use. End user is accountable for data quality and for value-added end use.		Participatory: Enduser and data processing are jointly accountable for data quality and for effective design of value-added applications.	

Figure 3.2b Nolan's benchmarks of the six stages. (Reprinted by permission of *Harvard Business Review.* "Managing the Crisis in Data Processing" by Richard L. Nolan, March–April 1979. Copyright ©1979 by the President and Fellows of Harvard College; all rights reserved.)

dressed and resolved in the initiation phase. Don't give potential problems the chance to arise later in the EAP process.

Task 6 Put together a schedule for the remaining six steps in the Planning Initiation Phase. Make sure this plan-for-the-plan schedule includes creating the vision, choosing a methodology, arranging for computer resources, assembling the planning team, preparing the workplan, and obtaining executive commitment.

STEP 2—CREATE A VISION

Purpose

Having defined the scope of the word enterprise and identified the business areas to be included, this step investigates the background of the enterprise, systems issues, and opportunities. This knowledge is used to create an I.S. vision of the future for the business. Having management paint a picture of the business vision helps to gain support for defining architectures that will enable the vision to be realized.

Deliverables

1. Vision statement
2. Initial meetings with management (vision confirmed)
3. Expectations, enthusiasm, political support (allies)

Tasks and Guidelines

Task 1 Assemble and read all sources of material about the business (customers, products, objectives, people, and so on). The following are sources for this background information:

- Annual reports
- Budgets and plans (tactical and strategic)
- Discussions with "old-timers"
- Tour of facilities
- Industry books, surveys, and reports

- I.S. executive presentations
- Policies and procedures manuals
- Position papers and memos (potential plans and ideas)
- Product literature and samples

Task 2 Determine influential executives' hot buttons.
Influential executives are those people who will be approving EAP, assigning resources to EAP, and accepting the architectures and plans. Hot buttons are objectives that are important to these executives, both in the near and long term.

Task 3 Visit other companies successful at EAP. Companies in the same or related industry would be ideal, but even companies outside the industry would be beneficial. Examine the methods used to develop them, and if possible, obtain a copy of their architectures. For competitive or proprietary reasons, another company may not divulge the contents of their architectures. However, having architectures from another company or templates provided by a consultant will substantially decrease the total EAP effort as the team can build upon the work of others rather than having to define the architectures from scratch. Examples of the positive benefits and impact of EAP on other businesses can be learned from visits to them.

Task 4 Formulate a* vision *that shows a target data/systems environment fulfilling opportunities and objectives.
A vision will generate enthusiasm and momentum for EAP by establishing a common goal and direction. Determine the most appropriate media to present the vision—it may be verbal, text, illustrations, models, demonstrations, videos, and so on. Compare the vision of information systems to the current situation and highlight the differences. Present the vision to top-level business management, informally when possible, and modify the vision until it is acceptable. Obtain a verbal confirmation that the vision defined is accurate in the eyes of management and clarifies the roles that information and technology will play in achieving it.

Task 5 Make reasonable promises to generate enthusiasm and support. When you are presenting the vision to management, consider the "What's in it for me?" perspective. Be able to show that achieving the vision requires an in-depth understanding of the business, and architectures will enable it to happen.

Sometimes it is advisable to ask each section or department within I.S. to contribute to the vision statement and confirm the vision with all such I.S. areas. This may expand the feeling of ownership and support for the vision, and prevent it from being viewed as a single person's or department's vision. Gaining political support at this point is very important. A major challenge for successfully managing EAP is to maintain the level of enthusiasm and support for EAP generated by this step.

STEP 3—ADAPT A METHODOLOGY

Purpose

The third step in planning initiation is adapting an EAP methodology. The result of this step will be an EAP methodology guidebook tailored to the needs of the business. The EAP methodology provides the outline for the project workplan and team training sessions. Every step of each phase should specify purpose, deliverables, source documents, procedures, guidelines, roles and responsibilities, and a rough effort estimate.

Deliverable

1. EAP methodology guidebook

Tasks and Guidelines

Task 1   Formulate and agree upon the essential principles and requirements of the methodology.   An EAP methodology should possess the following traits:

• It should be different from traditional I.S. planning approaches (see Chapter 1) by (1) defining the business functions first, (2) defining the enterprise architectures for data, applications, and technology in that order, and (3) using data dependency as the primary criterion for sequencing applications.

- It should be "lean and mean." Each task and step should be worthwhile and materially contribute to the architectures and plans. Measure the value of a step against the time and resources required to complete it. The time devoted to EAP is always a critical issue. Some steps may need to be eliminated or modified to reduce the total duration of EAP. Tasks that sound easy and straightforward may be very time-consuming. Tasks in some EAP methodologies may seem important in theory or have enormous intuitive appeal but may add little to the quality of the architectures and plans.
- It should be easy to understand. The methodology should be straightforward, clear, and simple and make sense to everyone. The more difficult to understand, the lower the credibility.
- It should be flexible and adaptable. No two businesses are alike, so the EAP methodology must be adaptable. The objectives, resources, and time requirements of the methodology must be matched to the objectives, resources, and time allotment of the business.
- It should be compatible with the culture and politics of the enterprise.
- It should use automated tools. There is a great deal of information to be gathered about the business, and automated tools are needed to capture and store this information.
- It should deliver a constant stream of deliverables. The EAP team should not be perceived as going off into an ivory tower to emerge months later with the architectures and plans. It is important to continually communicate and be visible throughout EAP using reports and presentations.
- It should result in a long-range implementation plan. Remember that architectures are of limited value unless they are implemented. Be sure that the selected methodology aims at producing a reasonable, feasible plan for constructing the architectures.
- It should recognize planning's interpersonal and imperfect nature. There is no such thing as a perfect plan, no software product that will produce a plan, and no foolproof methodology to follow.
- It should never use words such as "never" and avoid theory.

Task 2 ***Evaluate the current systems planning/development methods and standards of the organization.*** It may be possible to adapt an existing, accepted planning methodology for EAP. But prior to adapting one, be sure that the existing methodology meets the above measures.

Task 3 ***Learn about EAP and other planning approaches from books, articles, conferences, seminars, and consultant's brochures/presentations.*** Figure 3.3 is a list of a few named methodologies used for I.S. planning. Some of these are traditional, such as Critical Success Factors; others are similar to EAP, such as Master Planning. The names in parentheses are the authors who created or published the methodology. I.S. planning methodologies are improving as experience with them increases, but a printed methodology represents a snapshot in time of that particular approach. Thus, it would be misleading to compare methodologies developed by different people at different points in time. Readers interested in I.S. planning methodologies from an academic perspective should read Chapter 6 in the book

---

- Business System Planning (IBM)
- Critical Success Factors (Rockart)
- Strategy Set Transformation (King)
- Business Information Analysis and Integration Techniques (Burnstein)
- Ends/Means Analysis (Wetherbe & Davis)
- Strategic Data Planning (Martin)
- Information Engineering (Martin, Finkelstein, and others)
- Strategic Systems Planning and Tactical Systems Planning (Holland)
- System Architecture (Nolan) and Investment Strategy (Norton)
- Master Planning (Atkinson)
- Strategic Value Analysis (Curtice)
- Information Systems Architecture (Inmon)
- Enterprisewide Information Management, EwIM (Parker)

Figure 3.3. I.S. planning methodologies.

by Dickson and Wetherbe[3] and refer to the article by Karimi.[4] References to the works of other authors on methodologies similar to EAP can be found in section 1 of the Bibliography. Seminars and conferences on the topic are listed in section 10 of the Bibliography.

EAP has its roots in IBM's BSP.[5] Strategic Data Planning,[6] Information Engineering,[7] articles by Lederer,[8] and Goodhue[9] have also contributed techniques and ideas to EAP. Experience has shown, however, that a named methodology is not necessarily better than an unnamed one. Indeed, no one methodology is superior to another in all situations regardless of techniques or related products.

Task 4   Decide whether to develop an approach to EAP internally or obtain a "proprietary" methodology from a consultant. There are three major factors and tradeoffs that will influence the decision of selecting an EAP methodology. First, consider the EAP expertise of your staff. The more internal EAP knowledge and experience, the more detail you will be able to provide in your methodology guidebook. A second factor is the available budget for consulting. The larger the consulting budget, the more external services the business can receive to adapt a particular consultant's methodology. A third factor is the time available for this initiation step and for all of EAP. With more time available, the EAP team will be able to adapt their own methodology and rely less on outside consultants. Consider these factors when making methodology decisions.

Task 5   Tailor the EAP methodology to suit the needs of your enterprise. Every business is different. It is foolhardy to believe that an "off-the-shelf" methodology for planning will suit any business. Therefore, tailor and adapt an EAP methodology to fit your situation rather than religiously follow a "proven" approach.

For some companies, the methodology for EAP might be dictated by management for political reasons or because a particular consultant will be appointed, and the EAP project leader will have no choice in this matter. In this case, one still may be able to adapt a methodology somewhat. Determine the potential obstacles and shortcomings associated with that methodology and resolve these concerns during initiation. Disagreements about the methodology could seriously affect progress later on. *Compromise* on techniques and tools, but not on the principles listed in task one above. Do not proceed with EAP until all methodology issues have been resolved.

The result of this task is the EAP guidebook. Figure 3.4 is a sample table of contents for an EAP guidebook that was tailored to fit one company. For each step in each phase of the guidebook, describe the purpose, deliverables, source documents, procedures, guidelines, participants, and relative effort. Chapters 3 through 11 of this book can be used as the basis for an EAP guidebook.

Task 6 Produce a preliminary table of contents for reports (deliverables). Develop a table of contents for each report to be produced in the EAP phases. A table of contents should have every section of the report identified with a brief description of some of the sections. Sample outlines and sections for reports are presented in subsequent chapters of this book.

STEP 4—ARRANGE FOR COMPUTER RESOURCES

Purpose

The purpose of this step is to put computers and products in place to support EAP, test the products, and ensure that the products are ready for the EAP team. This step also involves developing data entry screens, printed reports, and any programming that is needed to prepare the products for use.

There is no perfect, single product for EAP. A set of products will be used as tools to support the EAP methodology. Henceforth, the word "toolset" will refer to this set of products.

The goal is to have an integrated toolset for EAP that will allow the exchange of data files. Test the selected toolset to ensure acceptable performance and integration. It is important to find any problems that exist between products during the initiation of EAP when they can be eliminated before causing costly and frustrating delays. Stabilize the hardware and software en-

LONG-RANGE DATA/SYSTEM PLANNING GUIDE

I. PLANNING INITIATION STEPS
    A. Determine scope and objectives of EAP
    B. Create a vision (initial meetings with management)
    C. Adapt a planning methodology
    D. Arrange for computer resources
    E. Assemble the planning team
    F. Prepare EAP workplan
    G. Obtain/confirm commitment and funding

II. DEVELOPMENT OF THE BUSINESS MODEL
    A. Document the organization structure
    B. Identify and define the business functions
    C. Document the preliminary business model and distribute for comments

III. EXISTING SYSTEMS ARCHITECTURE AND TECHNOLOGY
    A. Determine the scope, objectives, and IRC workplan
    B. Prepare for data collection
    C. Collect the IRC data
    D. Enter the data
    E. Validate and review the draft of the IRC
    F. Draw schematics
    G. Distribute the IRC
    H. Administer and maintain the IRC

IV. DEFINITION OF THE DATA ARCHITECTURE
    A. List candidate data entities
    B. Define the entities, attributes, and relationships
    C. Relate the entities to the business functions
    D. Distribute the data architecture

V. DEFINITION OF APPLICATIONS ARCHITECTURE
    A. List candidate applications
    B. Define the applications
    C. Relate applications to functions
    D. Analyze impact to current applications
    E. Distribute the applications architecture

VI. DEFINITION OF TECHNOLOGY ARCHITECTURE
    A. Define data and applications distribution architecture
    B. Define technology platforms
    C. Distribute the technology architecture

VII. FORMULATE IMPLEMENTATION STRATEGY AND PLANS
    A. Sequence the applications
    B. Estimate the effort and resources and produce a schedule
    C. Estimate the costs and summarize the benefits of the plan
    D. Determine the success factors and make recommendations
    E. Final report
    F. Final presentation

Figure 3.4. Table of contents for an EAP guidebook.

vironment for the EAP toolset, because changing the computers, operating systems, or software during EAP will be disruptive and consume valuable time.

Deliverables

1. Access to computers
2. Toolset installed and tested
3. Data entry screens, reports, and programs prepared
4. Toolset interfaces developed

Tasks and Guidelines

Task 1   Determine the toolset requirements.   Before selecting the products in the toolset, determine the kinds of reports to be generated by each product. Figure 3.5 lists the ten kinds of reports used in EAP, a brief description of each, and where to turn in this book to see an example.

Task 2   Determine hardware requirements (mainframe, personal computers, and so on).   There are advantages and disadvantages to using either a mainframe or personal computer to support EAP.

Personal computer advantages:

- Ease of setup and use.
- Can be physically located near where it is needed.
- Less cost for both the hardware and the software.
- More control—not at the mercy of downed networks and multi-users.

Mainframe advantages:

- Shared access—important where multiple EAP team members need access.
- Distributed data entry—a single workstation can become a bottleneck during the enterprise survey.

Kinds of Report	Description	EXAMPLE Figure
Matrices/tables	Relates one kind of information to another. For example, a CRUD matrix relating data entity usage by business functions.	10.2
Hierarchical diagrams	A top-down decomposition or division of information, such as an organization chart. Usually drawn with boxes and lines.	4.7
Indented structure lists	Shows the same information as hierarchical diagrams but more succinctly as each level of decomposition is indented from the left.	4.4
Simple lists; cross-reference lists	A single, simple list of items, such as an alphabetical list of data entities. A cross-reference relates one kind of information to another, for example, business functions to organization units.	4.11
Full description (formatted text)	A report containing information about one kind of EAP data. For example, a report for each function that lists a description, purpose, opportunities for improvement, and so on.	7.2
Entity-relationship (E-R) diagrams	A report used to graphically represent the data architecture.	7.3
Gantt charts and schedules	List the stages and tasks of a project on a timeline with the start date, end date, and deliverable dates.	10.6
Dataflow diagrams	A structured analysis diagram.	6.10
Presentation graphics	A drawing or illustration of a concept. For example, a representation of a technology configuration.	9.2
Text (free form)	Documents, typically created with word processing tools.	Appendix F

Figure 3.5. Ten kinds of Enterprise Architecture Planning reports.

A local area network (LAN) can offer both sets of the above advantages.

Task 3 Evaluate the alternatives for the EAP database. When evaluating alternatives for an EAP database, there are three potential choices: (1) extend the current data dictionary if one exists, (2) create your own EAP database capability on a mainframe or personal computer, or (3) license a proprietary package, such as a CASE tool that has its own internal database.

Task 4 Select and acquire appropriate EAP software products. Opt for simplicity over sophistication because the products will be easier to understand and to use. Tools should support the methodology, not the reverse. So, select products based on the requirements of your tailored methodology. Avoid unrealistic expectations from automated tools.

Selection factors include (1) currently available dictionary, repository, and other software products, (2) potential use of products for system development, (3) use of the toolset after EAP, (4) available budget for purchasing software, and (5) the methodology and consultants being considered.

Consider the capabilities required of EAP products. Specifically evaluate the following:

Reporting formats / options.

EAP reports are distributed throughout the enterprise and must therefore be attractive, understandable, and adhere to standards. Some products can only generate reports in a fixed format, which may require subsequent word processing for enhancement. Complicated-looking computer-generated reports can be a turn-off to some readers.

Selectivity and sorting.

Subsets and combinations of EAP information should be able to be selected and then presented in any order requested. Some products are limited to specific, fixed arrangements and views. The ability to summarize, roll up, and infer or trace relationships are valuable toolset features of EAP.

Query.

The ability to examine EAP data from any perspective is useful for understanding the business and the architectures. SQL is an effective query language when a relational database is used for EAP data. Some products have limited query capabilities with fixed presentation formats.

Analyses (integrity, level, affinity, ranking).

The ability to analyze the EAP data can save valuable time. Several kinds of analysis are found in proprietary EAP products. Integrity analysis ensures the consistency of the EAP database. Level analysis checks the consistency of detail among decompositions. Affinity analysis groups data entities according to their usage in the business. Ranking analysis provides support for making decisions by evaluating alternatives based on objective criteria. Products vary on the degree of automation or facilitation brought to these kinds of analyses.

Methodology compatibility / adaptation.

Some products support only one methodology and cannot be changed. So, do not expect such a product to effectively support a different or tailored approach for EAP from the one intended. Be sure the toolset will support your adapted methodology.

Kinds of objects (internal model).

The kinds of data or internal data model (i.e., files, fields, and relationships) to support EAP can vary. The selected toolset should manage every kind of the data and produce the reports required for EAP. Some products are capable of storing more kinds of data than may be necessary for EAP. In this case, avoid expanding your EAP methodology merely to take advantage of toolset capabilities. Some products use names in their internal data model, and on their inputs and outputs, that cannot be changed.

Extensibility.

Some products' internal models are fixed with respect to the information that can be stored. This can be a serious and frustrating limitation when the methodology being followed is not the one intended at the time the product was developed. An extendable internal model has the flexibility to

- define and manage new kinds of files and fields that may arise during EAP,
- relate data in different ways,
- use names for the internal data model and reports that are acceptable to your culture, and
- be adapted to suit a tailored methodology.

Ease of learning, using, and changing data.

Some products have steep learning curves that can delay EAP. Can a clerk enter and use the toolset with minimal training? Data entry may be easy, but making extensive changes may prove difficult or vice versa.

Data entry forms (fixed or variable).

Data entry should be as easy as possible. Can the screens of the product be tailored to match forms for the enterprise survey (see Chapter 5)?

Multiple or single access.

The data entry bottleneck can be avoided with multiple workstations having access to the toolset, but how many copies of the products are needed? Will database consolidation be necessary due to multiple copies of the database?

Performance / efficiency versus size of database.

Products may perform well with small demonstration databases, but will they be efficient with large databases in real situations (in one client situation, a well-known CASE product took three days to produce a matrix report)?

Toolset compatibility and integration—import / export.

Products in the toolset may need to share data or transfer data between them. EAP data may also need to be shared externally with other products not involved with EAP.

In general, opt for flexibility over rigidity in the toolset for EAP. However, flexibility requires greater experience, technical skills, and setup time.

Just as methodologies are continually evolving, products to support EAP are also rapidly improving. Published comparisons of products, such as the article by Holcman,[10] may provide insight about the features and use of products. But do not give such evaluations much weight because

- the products may have added new features and eliminated limitations since the evaluation was written,
- the review may not represent numerous uses of the product in a variety of real-world situations, or
- the author of such reviews may have unstated personal biases or may have a formal or informal affiliation with a vendor.

Create a table showing the products used to produce the ten kinds of reports and the contingency products that will be used if the primary product does not meet expectations. Figure 3.6 is an example of a table of selected products. Each row should have one P and at least one C for Primary and Contingency toolset selections.

Task 5   Prepare procedures to assure proper usage of products.   Clearly defined procedures will save time during training, regardless of the products selected.

Task 6   Develop data entry screens, reports, and routines (macros and programs).   Develop and test interfaces between products to share or transfer data. Acquire the entire set of tool products and prepare any interfaces needed to pass information between them. Do not accept vendor promises on aspects of integration. Assuming the products will properly integrate based on vendor documentation may create major problems and delays during EAP if the products do not perform as promised. Benchmark the toolset with *representative* data. The toolset can facilitate or impede an EAP project; the former can be assured by testing and preparing for EAP.

REPORTS \ PRODUCTS	Product 1	Product 2	Product 3	Product 4	Product 5	Product 6	Product 7	Product 8	Product 9	Product 10
Matrices / tables		P				C				
Indented structure lists	P	C								
Hierarchical diagrams			P				C			
Simple lists; cross-reference lists	P		C							
Full description (formatted text)	P		C							
Entity-relationship (E-R) diagrams			P							C
Gantt charts and schedules						P	C			
Dataflow diagrams			P					C		
Presentation graphics			P						C	
Text (free form)					P				C	

P = Primary product for producing this report
C = Contingency product

Figure 3.6. Selected tool matrix.

Task 7 Estimate the amount of clerical support needed for EAP, especially the enterprise survey, and arrange for clerical resources. EAP collects and generates a great deal of documentation. To store the bulk of this in a computer, a dictionary-based software product is needed. Impressive architecture reports require word processing for text, presentation graphics, spreadsheets (tables), dataflow diagrams, and entity-relationship charts. Therefore, provisions for clerical support must be obtained. There will be substantial amounts of data collected during the enterprise survey that must be entered into the toolset. Arrange to have the personnel for data entry be available for the enterprise survey.

Task 8   Review toolset decisions with other I.S. depart-
ments.   All departments involved with or affected by EAP
should review the toolset selected. Have a contingency plan if a
product does not perform as expected, and document that contingency. This will provide a sense of confidence in the toolset, and if
a problem arises, an answer will have been prepared in advance
so that precious time will not be lost. See Appendix A for a list of
potential EAP toolset products.

STEP 5—ASSEMBLE THE PLANNING TEAM

Purpose

This step is possibly the most important of the Planning Initiation Phase. Whereas there is a great deal of latitude in selecting
methodologies and tools, an ineffective planning team will definitely impede EAP progress and conceivably even prevent success. There are four principles to follow when assembling the
planning team:

1. There must be strong active team leadership and guidance. An
   effective leader can overcome a host of unforeseen problems.
2. Team members should be credible.
3. Team members should understand EAP and be committed to
   its success.
4. Team members must be willing and able to cooperate with
   each other.

Deliverables

1. List of planning team members and confirmation of their
   time commitments
2. Identification of each department involved
3. Roles and responsibilities defined
4. Consultants identified and selected

Tasks and Guidelines

Task 1   Determine the skills required for each of the EAP
phases.   The three most important skills of a planning team

member are broad business experience, credibility, and teamsmanship. Business experience means that a person understands the business well and has solid time invested in a variety of areas. Credibility means that a person is respected by peers and has a good reputation in the company. Teamsmanship means that, in addition to business experience and credibility, a person can cooperate with people from all parts of the company and will work well as a contributing member of a team.

Some EAP phases need additional skills. For example, preparing the data architecture will require people who have data definition experience, and the technology architecture will require people who are up to date on the latest trends in technology hardware, software, and communications. Technical skills, however, are not nearly as important as broad business experience, credibility, and teamsmanship.

Task 2 Estimate the effort needed for each EAP phase. This should be a rough estimate by phase, not down to the step level. Do not try to be too specific at this point. More precise estimates will be determined in the next step for the project workplan.

Task 3 Determine the number of people needed. The number of people needed for EAP will vary considerably from one business to another. EAP can be conducted with as few as 2 people, or may have more than 30 on the team. Do not accept a "typical" number, but let your specific situation, methodology, level of architecture detail, size of business, skill base, and time estimate from the previous task determine the most appropriate number of team members. The time commitment of a person—full time or part time—will effect the number of team members needed.

Task 4 Specify the expected roles and responsibilities of each team member. The roles and responsibilities on an EAP team may include:

Role	Responsibility
Team Leader	Manages the day-to-day activities of all team members, EAP status reports, on-time completion of deliverables, EAP Initiation Phase, coordinates enterprise survey schedule.
Business Analyst	Provides business knowledge and perspective.
Data Analyst	Provides data definition expertise.
Application Analyst	Provides application system expertise.
Technology Analyst	Provides technology expertise.
Toolset Administrator	Oversees the installation, preparation, and use of the toolset products.
Librarian	Data entry, report preparation.
Champion	Presentations and status reports to executive management, obtaining enterprisewide commitment and support for EAP.
Consultant	Technical guidance and methodology direction, quality of deliverables, preparation of reports and presentations.

Strive for a balance of skills and for the participation of nonsystems management. Though there is no typical ratio of systems to nonsystems participants, a 50-50 balance can be effective. Do not get caught in the old I.S. planning trap of having computing people guess what the business people do and need. Have business people participating as EAP team members.

Again, the team leader is the most important role. Be sure to select a leader who is enthusiastic about EAP and is willing to work with the team. In addition to the team leader, select a guide. The guide should have substantial EAP experience and be able to "direct" the team in the methodology. Rarely is the project leader also the guide; the role of the guide is usually played by the consultants who provide the methodology support.

Define the roles and responsibilities of each team member in a brief document, and distribute the information to each participant, their supervisors, and if appropriate, to all management. Figure 3.7 is a sample description of the role for the business analyst on the EAP team. Additional roles should be delegated when appropriate.

BUSINESS ANALYST

A key role in defining Computer Services' long-term direction is that of business analyst, people from our customer's areas who can help define functions and issues in these areas.

Essential requirements for a Business Analyst
1. Knowledge of functions in the business they are representing and the quality issues affecting the functions.
2. Credibility with department and division management.
3　Ability to work on a team.

Computer skills are not a prime qualification for business analysts.

Role of the Business Analyst
1. Confirm the organization chart for their area.
2. Develop a list of the major functions in their area. This list should be arranged in a tree diagram fashion until the major purpose of the function and required information can be defined.
   Much of the function list may already be complete through the quality improvement efforts for the area. This step will involve tapping into these efforts.
3. As a team, compare the list of functions to those developed in other areas. Based upon this, divide functions into those that are unique to one area and those that are performed in more than one area. Assign nonunique functions to a single area for definition.
4. Develop definitions for the functions. The business analyst will work with the employees in his or her area and with I.S. to define their functions. Each analyst will be responsible for the functions unique to their area and for common functions assigned to them.
   We see the definition procedure as selecting employees performing the functions and interviewing them. The definition process will define the function (objectives, indicators of quality, upcoming issues), identify major kinds of information used in the function or produced from it, identify computer applications now used to support the function, and identify opportunities for improvement.
5　As a team, review the function definitions. This is to ensure that the definition of functions that are not unique to an area adequately cover the other areas performing it.

Figure 3.7. Sample role description for business analyst.

6. Participate in the Data Architecture Phase. As a team, refine the list of information types used by functions. Develop definitions for data entities, look for synonyms, and define how the data entities are interrelated.
7. Define broad characteristics of the application architecture. Considering the functions performed, identify the applications to support these functions, and develop a high-level description of each. The description will include a list of business functions supported and the anticipated basic technology (e.g., micro, mini, or mainframe) of the application.
   This phase is a team effort of the business analysts, computer technical support employees, and the consultant.
   The business analysts will also provide the team with feedback from their departments on the application portfolio.
8. Consult on the implementation plan. The development of the plan will be primarily the task of a small core team. Additional business analysts will participate with the cost-benefit analysis and recommendations.

Figure 3.7. *Continued.*

Task 5   Select personnel with appropriate skills and qualifications, and assign them to phases and steps in the methodology.   In addition, select members that are politically astute. Try to minimize political situations that could compromise the effectiveness or objectivity of individuals or of the team. Figure 3.8 is a sample approach for documenting role assignments.

Having defined roles and responsibilities, select the individuals who should participate as team members and determine whether full-time or part-time involvement is expected. Often, a strategy needs to be determined to secure the time commitment of the highly regarded individuals selected. This usually involves presentations described in Step 7 of this chapter. Have a backup or contingency person selected if the primary individual cannot be obtained.

Task 6.   Hold training sessions to explain the methodology and benefits of EAP, and to generate interest and enthusiasm.   After the team has been selected and approved for participation, immediately orient the team in the chosen methodology by holding a two- or three-day training program. This is often the first order of business for the team, occurring in the first

Sample Role Assignment

Role	Planning Initiation	Business Modeling	Current Systems	Data Architecture	Application Architecture	Technical Architecture	Migration Plan
Champion	M	L	L	–	–	–	H
Team Leader	H	H	H	H	H	H	H
Consultant	H	H	M	H	M	M	H
Business Analyst	–	H	L	M	M	L	H
Data Analyst	–	–	–	H	M	L	–
Applications Analyst	–	–	–	M	H	M	–
Technology Analyst	–	–	–	L	M	H	–
Toolset Administrator	H	M	M	M	L	L	M
Librarian	–	H	H	L	L	L	M
Duration (Months)	–	2	2	1.5	1	1	1

Participation/Involvement: H = Heavy   M = Moderate   L = Light   – = None or Little

Figure 3.8. Sample role assignment.

week of meetings. All management throughout the enterprise should attend a two-hour overview of EAP. Having key executives attend these orientations will generate enthusiasm and support at all levels of the organization as the word spreads.

Task 7 "Contract" time commitments from each team member's manager. The EAP team should be comprised of the brightest and best people from the enterprise, and consequently, their availability will likely be limited. It is important to establish the time commitment of each member. Get the commitment confirmed in writing, for example, in a memo. This reduces the possibility that team members will be removed during EAP or will not be available at crucial times in the project.

At the first team meeting, note and resolve dates of known time conflicts for team members, such as vacations, business travel, special meetings, and so forth. Solidify, as much as possible, the availability of all members for scheduled EAP activities. If conflicts would seriously limit a team member's participation or contribution, seek an alternate person as a replacement. It is much easier and less disruptive to replace a team member during initiation than in the middle of important EAP phases when deadlines must be met.

Task 8 Obtain and reserve a workspace such as a conference room for the duration of EAP. The "war room" should have a large table around which all the team members can sit. Don't allow seating arrangements to imply political status. Have as many white boards as possible in the war room; they are erasable and can be seen easily. It is an added benefit to have a white board that is capable of automatic photocopies. It is important to have terminals or personal computers with access to the toolset in the room. Definitions and decisions can be entered directly into the toolset in the war room instead of having to copy them and enter them elsewhere at some later time. There should be ample shelving and filing cabinets for storing and safeguarding the materials gathered during EAP. A drawer or box can be used to keep obsolete material until the end of EAP so that important material is not discarded accidentally.

Task 9 Select and use external consultants. External consultants can provide experience from previous successful EAP engagements, ensure quality, bring credibility, overcome political obstacles, offer an objective point of view, and supply manpower to accomplish some of the steps. The consultant usually leads the team orientation and training sessions and presents the executive overview of EAP. Do not wait until EAP flounders and credibility is lost to obtain the assistance of a consultant.

There are two kinds of consultants: *facilitative* and *operative*. Which to choose depends on who is in control of EAP. A facilitative consultant typically comes from a small consulting firm and provides technical guidance and assistance to the EAP team. The project leaders and EAP team from the business are in control, perform most of the work, and are responsible for the deliverables. An operative consultant, typically a large consulting firm, brings in their own team of consultants, develops most of the EAP, and is responsible for the deliverables of the project.

Consultant selection criteria include the following:

Methodology	Some consultants have their own methodology; some will adapt an EAP approach for you.
Reputation, credibility	Does the consultant have a reputation that lends credibility to EAP?
Experience	How many times have the consultants (the individuals, not the firm) been through the entire EAP process with clients?
Rapport, confidence	You should feel comfortable with the consultant and trust his opinions.
References	The consultant should provide references for previous EAP clients, and you should contact the references and ask about the consultant's role.

Politics, culture	The consultant should adapt to the culture of the enterprise.
Level of support	How many consultants will be needed?
Software products	With some consultants, you must buy or lease the consultant's products. Independent consultants have an unbiased objectivity to assist with the selection and use of products to support EAP.
Control	Will the architectures and plans be developed by the consultant (operative) or by an internal EAP team (facilitative).
Price, total cost (budget)	Consider both the rates and the total cost for consulting for EAP. The total cost of operative consultants for EAP can be several times the facilitative consultants, often into the hundreds of thousands of dollars. One reason is that good architectures and plans are based on business knowledge, and thus, the client is paying for the operative consultant to learn their business.

Unfortunately, the choice of consultant for EAP may be determined politically and not by the EAP team leader. When this happens, the lack of support, trust, credibility, and disputes about methodology can result in architectures and plans of poorer quality, tension and frustration of team members, extended duration of EAP, and a higher total cost for consulting.

See Appendix B for a list of EAP consulting firms.

STEP 6—PREPARE AN EAP WORKPLAN

Purpose

The EAP workplan is the project schedule and plan for all EAP team activities. It is critical that EAP be completed on time. Without a detailed workplan, EAP is likely to fall behind schedule, adversely affect the quality of some deliverables, and it may be cancelled prior to completion. A well-managed EAP project has a good workplan in the hands of an effective team leader.

Deliverables

1. EAP workplan (text, tables, Gantt chart) containing:
    * Introduction (what, why, who, when, where, how much)
    * Task descriptions
    * Expected duration, effort estimates
    * Gantt charts and schedule summary
    * Responsibilities and daily/weekly task assignments
2. An initial status report
3. Team member workbook containing:
    * Workplan
    * Status reports, minutes and notes from meetings
    * Intermediate deliverables and background materials
    * Miscellaneous correspondence

Tasks and Guidelines

Task 1 Complete the previous initiation steps. A workplan cannot be formulated until all previous initiation steps have been completed.

Task 2 Consider dividing EAP into subprojects. It is sometimes necessary—to obtain the commitment of resources—to separate the phases of EAP (as represented in the wedding cake diagram, Figure 1.7) into subprojects. For example, the business modeling and data architecture phases, or the current systems architecture phase that yields the Information Resource Catalog, are sometimes split into separate subprojects, performed and produced by different teams.

However, there is a substantial risk and tradeoff in dividing EAP. Although initial support and commitment to begin EAP might be more easily achieved for one or two phases, experience shows that the subsequent phases of EAP might not be approved. Doing EAP in a piecemeal fashion increases the likelihood that the architectures will be inconsistent, incompatible, and lack enterprisewide credibility. Unless obtaining the commitment for all of EAP is not likely at any foreseeable point, do not split EAP into separate projects—except for the current systems architecture phase, which can usually be split off as a separate project successfully.

Task 3   List all phases and steps in the methodology with team member assignments.   Using the team member availability information gathered in the previous initiation step, assign team members to each step of the methodology.

Task 4   Estimate the duration of each step, and determine the start and completion dates considering the resources assigned.   Overlap tasks where possible. Estimate or assume the expected number of functions, interviews, information sources, entities, applications, and so on. Include a training and orientation step for each phase. Figure 3.9 can be used as a rough

---

Preliminary Business Model 7%   (1)

Enterprise Survey 23%

Current Systems & Technology 15%   (2)

Data Architecture 15%

Applications Architecture 15%

Technology Architecture 10%

Migration Planning 15%

Notes:
1.   Does not include incomplete Planning Initiation Phase tasks.
2.   Often performed concurrently with other phases external to the EAP project team. If so, adjust the relative percentages accordingly.

Figure 3.9.   Approximate duration percentages.

estimate for the duration of each phase of EAP. For example, if EAP is expected to be ten months, then the Data Architecture Phase should be about one and a half months or six weeks. Approximate estimates for the relative duration of the steps for each phase can be found in Appendix C.

Ongoing tasks for EAP project management, coordination, status reviews, and technical direction should be included in the workplan unless contrary to project management standards. Use project management software to document the workplan and monitor the status.

The schedule should reflect the "lean and mean" philosophy—that is, taking the least amount of time possible to obtain the required amount of detail. This means optimizing the tradeoffs of amount of architectural detail versus the time and resources of the EAP team. Start strong and finish strong, which means consider the time for startup, reports, and presentations. Do not take time away from preparing presentations and the final report, as these are the most important deliverables from EAP. The length of EAP projects is typically four to eight months depending on the following factors:

- Scope and level of detail (total effort)
- Executive directives ("complete EAP by the end of the year")
- Staffing and participation
- Use of other applicable architectures

Figure 3.10 contains a sample page from a detailed workplan for EAP. The table displays the allocation of personnel resources to EAP on a weekly basis. Team members are listed in the rows of the table identified by their role. The entry in the table identifies the phase and step of EAP, such as 6.3, 5.5, and so on. The name and description of each step are from the EAP guidebook. The number in parentheses to the right of the step is the number of hours to be worked on that task during that week by that person. The single number to the right of the parentheses is the total number of hours for the week to be contributed by the EAP team member. Steps marked with double asterisks were performed by individuals external to the EAP team. This level of detail in the workplan is needed for EAP projects involving many people.

	11/21–11/25 Week 17	11/28–12/2 Week 18	12/5–12/9 Week 19	12/12–12/16 Week 20
Project Manager	1.5 (21) 35 5.5 (14)	1.5 (14) 35 5.5 (14) 6.1 (7)	1.5 (21) 35 6.1 (7) 6.2 (7)	1.5 (21) 35 6.2 (7) 6.3 (7)
Consultant	5.4 (7) 21 5.5 (7) 6.1 (7)	6.1 (28) 28	6.2 (21) 28 6.3 (7)	6.3 (7) 28 6.4 (7) 6.5 (14)
Lead Consultant	5.3 (7) 21 5.4 (7) 5.5 (7)	5.5 (7) 21 6.1 (14)	6.1 (7) 28 6.2 (21)	6.3 (7) 28 6.4 (3) 6.5 (14) 6.6 (4)
Data Analyst	5.4 (14) 35 5.5 (7) 6.1 (14)	6.1 (35) 35	6.2 (35) 35	6.3 (21) 35 6.5 (14)
Applications Analyst	5.4 (14) 35 5.5 (7) 6.1 (14)	6.1 (35) 35	6.2 (35) 35	6.3 (21) 35 6.5 (14) 6.3 (35) ** 6.4 (21) ** 6.5 (14) **
Technology Analyst	5.4 (14) 21 5.5 (7)	6.1 (35) 35	6.2 (35) 35	6.3 (21) 35 6.5 (14) 6.4 (21) **
Toolset Administrator	1.4 (28) 35 5.4 (7)	1.4 (14) 35 6.1 (21)	1.4 (14) 35 6.2 (21)	1.4 (20) 20
Project Librarian	5.3 (14) 28 5.4 (14)	5.5 (7) 21 6.1 (14)	6.1 (21) 21	6.5 (7) 14 6.6 (7)

Figure 3.10. Example of EAP project weekly task assignments.

Other sections of the EAP workplan would contain Gantt charts and effort summaries for all participants.

Task 5 Establish the project control and status reporting mechanism. Hold team meetings frequently. Status reports should be generated weekly or biweekly. Each status report should include the following sections:

- Accomplishments for the period
- Steps that are continuing or will begin in the next period
- Obstacles and potential obstacles, and the actions being taken or decisions to be made to overcome them

Task 6   Build in contingencies (what ifs).   The team leader should ask "what if" questions relating to situations that could conceivably slow down or block EAP. Develop and document a strategy for each such situation and build contingencies or slack at key points in the schedule.

Task 7   Estimate the costs and budget impact of the project.   Calculate the total cost of the EAP project. Include the estimate of each team member's time, the consultant's fees, the cost of the computing and toolset, and the cost of the clerical support and materials.

Task 8   Distribute the EAP project workbook to team members.   Each team member needs a workbook or filing system to store documents and material produced or collected during EAP. A binder is one convenient means for storing EAP papers. The workbook should include the workplan, status reports, intermediate deliverables, and miscellaneous correspondence.

Task 9   Distribute the workplan to all participants.   Prepare and distribute the EAP workplan to team members to be kept in the project workbook. Also, distribute the EAP workplan to the immediate supervisors of team members and to executives throughout the enterprise.

STEP 7—OBTAIN MANAGEMENT APPROVAL

Purpose

The EAP Workplan is the tangible deliverable from the Planning Initiation Phase, and management approval is the intangible deliverable. Activities aimed at obtaining management approval may occur more than once during EAP. For each kind of approval and commitment, presentations will need to be prepared. Therefore, sequence this step most appropriately for the EAP project.

Deliverables

1. Presentation material
2. Meetings and presentations with management (EAP overseers and participating departments)
3. Status memo confirming understanding of objectives, scope, approach, and the resolution of issues, concerns, and success factors
4. Confirmation memo authorizing the initiation or continuance of EAP
5. EAP awareness throughout the enterprise

Tasks and Guidelines

Task 1   Plan your approach to management.   Be prepared. Know exactly what should be said and how to say it. Plan a strategy for approaching management that anticipates questions and considers the perspective of management. Figure 3.11 is a form for planning an approach for obtaining a decision from management. First, note the position and title of the decision maker (A). Being aware of the performance objectives (B) of the decision maker will enable you to explain what's in it for them. Note the style of leadership and the decision-making process of the executive (C). Does that person have the authority to make the decision? Will it be accepted by others? Write down precisely and succinctly the desired decision (D). How will the decision maker be better off by rendering a favorable decision? Describe the approach to be used (E). Presentations, meetings, and testimonials might have to be prepared, so provide an objective list of reasons to support your position and tradeoffs for the decision. List the potential obstacles or counterarguments to the decision, and be prepared to overcome each of them (F).

OBTAINING MANAGEMENT APPROVAL

For each decision maker, identify the following:

A) Position and title: _____

B) Performance objectives of the decision maker (if known): _____

_____

C) Leadership style _____

Decision process _____

Authority _____

Reputation _____

D) Desired decision, ramifications to decision maker:

_____

_____

_____

E) Specific approach tactics to effect a favorable decision:

_____

_____

_____

_____

F) Potential obstacles. How will you overcome them?

_____

_____

_____

Figure 3.11. Planning approach for obtaining a decision from management.

Task 2   Have an informal meeting with business executives and EAP overseers to review the objectives, scope, potential benefits, and factors critical for success.   Discuss the potential benefits of EAP listed in Chapter 1, the obstacles to EAP, and reasons for success described in Chapter 2.

Task 3   Prepare and deliver executive-level presentations. Prepare summary material appropriate for management. Be aware of what management wants to see and how they prefer to see it. Rehearse the presentations with the EAP team. Work out every aspect and wrinkle of each and every presentation.

Be explicit about the purpose of every meeting with executives. There are three kinds of presentations that may be given. If EAP has been approved, the presentations will be to inform the enterprise about EAP activities and will be a courtesy to management. There may also be presentations to get concurrence, agreement, or support for EAP. Third, the highest form of presentation is for obtaining the resources and/or commitment for EAP.

Be sensitive to the corporate culture and politics. Seek advice from mentors, political allies, and others who have successfully obtained favorable decisions and support from management. Most presentations should be informal. Important decisions are usually made privately—not in a room filled with people at a presentation. So do not force a quick decision in such a setting. Presentations should be short and to the point—20 minutes or less.

Use the nodding-head approach for gaining approval for EAP. A theme that may be useful is "We have the same goals, so we must work together." A typical outline for a presentation intended to obtain commitment of resources to EAP is as follows:

1. State the accepted or generally understood goals, objectives, and plans of the business and, specifically, of the people attending the presentation. Get heads nodding in agreement quickly. Use analogies that establish the I.S. function as a business within the enterprise.
2. Convey the *vision* (see step 2) and critical role of information technology for achieving the vision. Access to data, adapting to changing business conditions, and sharing data are usu-

ally three of the success factors for achieving business goals. Again, heads should be nodding in agreement.

3. Explain EAP as a commonsense, business-oriented planning approach to achieve the vision. Get heads to nod in agreement that blueprints are needed before constructing a long-term solution and that a plan must be formulated before plunging ahead.

4. Having agreed that there are goals to be accomplished, a vision for doing so, that a plan is needed to achieve the vision, and that EAP is a reasonable approach to planning, now state the requirements: commitment, resources, and time are needed to produce the architecture and plans. Since those in the audience have agreed to the previous points, saying no at this point would be contrary to what has already been accepted.

The best kind of presentation is the one with only one logical alternative—an offer that cannot be rejected or disputed. To repeat, draw analogies between conducting the business of the enterprise and the "business" of managing data. Explain the similarities of the products or services of the enterprise and the products or services of the I.S. function. The same sound business practices employed to thrive in a competitive marketplace can be applied to managing the I.S. function.

Determine the best political strategy for delivering presentations aimed at obtaining commitment. If there will be a single presentation to the primary decision maker, then rehearse the presentation until confident that it will succeed. Other presentations may need to be given repeatedly to departments. In this case, do the presentations for the most supportive (easiest) departments first. When you make subsequent presentations, mention that resources have been committed by Departments X, Y, Z and so on. It is unlikely that any department would exclude themselves from a bandwagon gaining momentum.

Task 4 Listen carefully to feedback from management, and discuss their questions.   To be successful when making presentations, exude 100 percent confidence. Be prepared to answer each and every question and respond to every issue. During rehearsals, anticipate hostile questions and antithetical remarks, and be prepared with tactful, acceptable responses.

Task 5 Resolve issues and concerns about funding, scheduling, potential team members, and other resources. Do not begin the modeling phases of EAP unless there is every expectation of complete success. Murphy's Law states that seemingly unimportant, unresolved issues will become major obstacles over time.

Task 6 Obtain approval to proceed with the project. If the EAP workplan has been completed, then this task confirms the acceptance of the workplan. If it has not been completed, this task confirms the duration of EAP phases, completion dates for deliverables, the individuals to be on the team, and the approach for EAP. Upon confirming the above, the workplan can be completed and distributed.

Task 7 Publicize the expressed commitment of management for EAP throughout the business unit with an announcement. Use internal newsletters and bulletins describing EAP and publicizing the commitment and agreement of company executives. Figure 3.12 is an example of an announcement memo from IBMs BSP Guide.

Task 8 Host a general EAP orientation (executive overview) for the entire enterprise. This presentation should be attended by managers and supervisors throughout the enterprise. After EAP commitment has been obtained, this presentation is designed to obtain their cooperation and support for EAP.

DISCUSSION QUESTIONS

1. What are the greatest unfavorable characteristics for you to overcome? Are there more favorable than unfavorable characteristics? If so, what alternative strategies could you employ to turn that situation around?
2. What initiation tasks are on your near-term to-do list?
3. Will you need to develop a formal vision statement?
4. Is long-range planning a part of your corporate culture?
5. Are long-range business plans followed through or are they redeveloped each year as part of the budgeting process?
6. Who is (are) the best person(s) to make EAP presentations?
7. How many nonsystems participants should be team mem-

SAMPLE EXECUTIVE ANNOUNCEMENT LETTER

To: All executives

Subject: Business Systems Planning Study

I am sure all of you are aware of the dynamic nature of our business. Our success in the future will depend greatly on how we plan and react to the business environment. I am pleased to inform you that we are initiating a major effort to analyze our current and future information needs. I have authorized a study group that will conduct an in-depth analysis of how we use information and its relation to our business.

The study project will be directed by Ms. Marilyn Jordan, with other company personnel involved on a full-time basis. Assisting us in an advisory capacity will be personnel from the IBM corporation. We will be using a methodology called Business Systems Planning (BSP), which has been helpful to other companies in evaluating and planning for their information requirements.

Key to the study's success is the precise identification and clear statement of our individual and collective information needs. To this end, the study team will want to discuss our information needs with us in detail in a series of individual interviews. It is essential that each individual who is asked to participate in an interview be completely candid in discussing problems, needs, and plans with the team members. You will be contacted by Ms. Jordan in the near future to set up interview dates and times.

I urge you to give your full cooperation to the study group in this important undertaking. I am confident the study will be of tremendous value to the company and help us accomplish our overall objectives.

Sincerely,

Edward J. Bissel
President

EJB/rth

Figure 3.12. Sample executive announcement letter. (from IBM's *Business System Planning*, GE20-0527-4, Copyright 1984, page 85.)

bers? What is your strategy to obtain the commitment for their time?

8. How much time will the Planning Initiation Phase take?
9. Do you already have an adequate toolset in place? What reporting capabilities are missing? What are the limitations of your toolset?
10. Will it be necessary to split EAP into separate projects in order to obtain commitment?
11. Which type of consulting is most likely to succeed in your corporate culture—operative or facilitative?
12. Can you obtain enterprise architectures from other organizations?

REFERENCES

[1]Linder, Jane. "Harnessing Corporate Culture," *ComputerWorld (In-Depth)* September 23, 1985.

[2]Nolan, Richard L. *Managing the Data Resource Function* (2d ed.), West Publishing Co., St. Paul, MN, 1982.

[3]Dickson, Gary, and James Wetherbe. *The Management of Information Systems*, McGraw-Hill, New York, 1985.

[4]Karimi, Jahangir. "Strategic Planning for Information Systems: Requirements and Information Engineering Methods, *Journal of Management Information Systems*, Vol. 4, No. 4, Spring 1988.

[5]IBM. *Business Systems Planning*, GE20-0527-4 (1984). Available from IBM.

[6]Martin, James. *Strategic Data Planning Methodologies* (1st ed.), Prentice-Hall, Englewood Cliffs, NJ, 1982; and *Strategic Information Planning Methodologies* (2d ed.), Prentice-Hall, Englewood Cliffs, NJ, 1989.

[7]Martin, James. *Information Engineering: Planning & Analysis* (book 2), Prentice-Hall, Englewood Cliffs, NJ, 1990; and *Information Engineering: Design & Construction* (book 3), Prentice-Hall, Englewood Cliffs, NJ, 1990.

[8]Lederer, Albert L., and Kenneth J. Calhoun. "Why Some Systems Don't Support Strategy," *Information Strategy*, Summer 1989; and Lederer, Albert L., and Andrew Putnam. "Bridging the Gap: Connecting Systems Objectives to Business Strategy with BSP," *Journal of Systems Management*, Auerbach, Summer 1987; and

"Connecting Systems Objectives to Business Strategy with BSP," *Information Strategy*, Auerbach, Winter 1986.

[9]Goodhue, Dale L., Judith A. Quillard, and John F. Rockart. "Managing the Data Resource: A Contingency Perspective," *MIS Quarterly*, September 1988.

Goodhue, Dale L., Laurie J. Kirsch, Judith A. Quillard, and Michael D. Wybo, "Strategic Data Planning: Lessons from the Field," *MIS Quarterly*, Vol 16, No. 1, March 1992.

[10]Holcman, Samuel B. "A Review of Three Information Strategy Planning Tools", *Data Base Newsletter*, Vol. 16, No. 4, July–August 1988.

Preliminary Business Model

INTRODUCTION

Business modeling is the process of defining the business. The purpose of the business model is to provide a complete, comprehensive, consistent knowledge base that can be used to define the architectures and implementation plans. In Enterprise Architecture Planning (EAP), business modeling is done in two distinct parts: a preliminary business model, followed by a complete business model. The preliminary business model identifies the functions, provides a brief description of each function, and identifies the organization unit that performs each business function. This chapter defines the steps for defining the preliminary business model, and Chapter 5, "The Enterprise Survey," deals with the steps for compiling the complete business model. In some EAP workplans, business modeling may be split into two phases, with the preliminary functional model consuming about 25 to 30 percent of the combined business modeling effort.

Three Steps to Business Modeling

There are three steps to completing the preliminary business model.

1. Document the organization structure.

2. Identify and define the business functions.

3. Document the preliminary business model and distribute and present it back to the business community for comments.

Strategic Business Planning

Before explaining the steps for developing the preliminary business model, it is important to understand the relationship of EAP to strategic business planning.

Strategic business planning is the process of defining the mission and long-range objectives for conducting the business, and developing the strategies for achieving them.

Strategic business planning is primarily concerned with three interacting aspects, depicted in Figure 4.1.

Figure 4.1. Strategic business planning areas of interest.

The purpose of the first aspect of strategic planning is to define the mission of the business, the specific objectives of the business, and those policies needed to carry out the stated objectives. The second aspect of strategic planning is the organization—or people—and how it is structured as a business to achieve the stated objectives. The third aspect concerns the functions, programs, and procedures initiated to achieve the business objectives.

There are basically four different, distinct kinds of formal strategic plans. Figure 4.2 shows how these plans are related.

Each formal strategic plan serves a specific and useful function. Based on the mission of the company, the current situation, and factors external to the company—strengths, weaknesses, opportunities, and threats—business objectives are formed. Func-

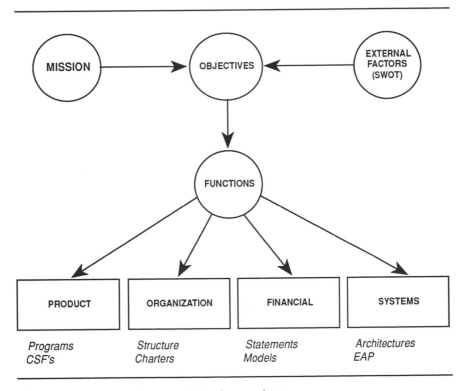

Figure 4.2.   Formal strategic business plans.

tions are established in support of those objectives, and each business area may produce a plan for achieving the stated objectives.

The most common kind of formal strategic plan is a product plan. Product plans are programs and critical success factors that generally focus on the value chain of the organization, and include new product plans (research and development), sales and marketing plans, production plans, distribution plans, and customer service plans—all of which are product/service oriented.

A second kind of strategic plan is the organization plan. This plan is typically produced by the human resources area and consists of items such as organization charts, department charters, responsibility descriptions, and job descriptions.

Finance and accounting areas use a third kind of strategic plan called a long-range financial plan. This plan generally consists of financial statements and various economic and econometric models.

A fourth kind of strategic plan—the one EAP produces—is a long-range information systems plan, which includes architectures for data, applications, and technology and the associated implementation plans. A long-range I.S. plan is an essential part of the enterprise's strategic business plan, since I.S. as a support function is as important as finance and human resources to the enterprise.

Formally defining the business functions of the enterprise in a business model provides a means for directly relating these four kinds of strategic plans together. Often, an enterprise has the first three types of strategic plans, but not an I.S. strategic plan. Also, most enterprises do not have their individual strategic plans *integrated*, though there may be cross-references in those plans. By explicitly relating the components of each strategic plan to the functions in the business model, the plans will be consistent and complete.

The basic strategic business planning process is illustrated in Figure 4.3. Fundamentally, strategic business planning determines what the business is, what the business wants to be, and how the business will get there. The layers of the "wedding cake" described in Chapter 1 show that EAP is essentially the same process.

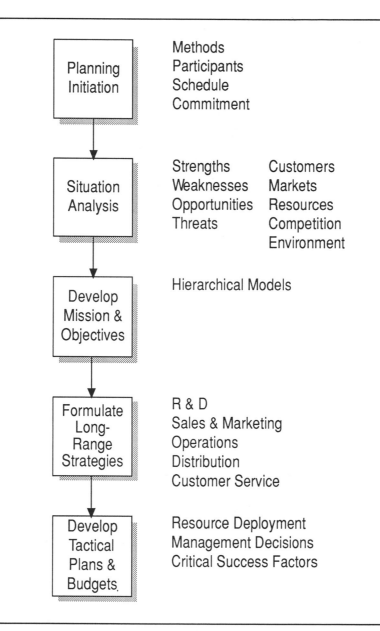

Planning Initiation	Methods Participants Schedule Commitment
Situation Analysis	Strengths Customers Weaknesses Markets Opportunities Resources Threats Competition Environment
Develop Mission & Objectives	Hierarchical Models
Formulate Long-Range Strategies	R & D Sales & Marketing Operations Distribution Customer Service
Develop Tactical Plans & Budgets	Resource Deployment Management Decisions Critical Success Factors

Figure 4.3. Strategic business planning process.

STEP 1—DOCUMENT THE ORGANIZATIONAL STRUCTURE

Purpose

The purpose of this step is to document the structure of the organization and identify the individuals and locations that perform business functions. There are two important uses for this information in EAP: (1) to identify people to interview during the enterprise survey, and (2) to determine the extent of data and application system sharing. This step is short and simple, which makes it ideal as the first to use the data entry and reporting features of the toolset.

Deliverables

1. Up-to-date organization charts
2. List of positions and titles, the locations in which they are performed, and the number of people in the positions
3. Documentation of business goals, objectives, and strategic business plans (optional)
4. Enter the above information into the toolset and generate reports

Tasks and Guidelines

Task 1   Gather recent organization charts, and enter the information into the toolset.   If there are no organization charts, or the ones that exist are not up to date, draw them and make them current. The charts should include as much of the following as possible:

1. Departments (name and location)
2. Title/position
3. People (name and telephone)
4. Reporting lines (direct and indirect)
5. Number of people in position or department

There are numerous sources if the above information is not readily available. Even organizations that claim to have no managerial reporting charts have an inherent structure that can be defined. One source is the budget structure—departments and subdepartments. Nearly every business has a budgeting process based on some kind of hierarchical organizational structure. Another source of information is the company telephone book, which lists departments, organizations, or some other kind of business breakdown, and positions located in each department.

It is important to be thorough with the organization charts, but don't spend too much time on this step. Usually, organization charts can be gathered and updated in one to three days at most.

Do not assume the gathered organizational information can be freely distributed within the enterprise. Get permission to use the organization chart information before putting it into EAP documents. Also, expect changes in the organization structure during the EAP process, and when this happens, update the EAP database accordingly. Always specify an "as of" date on each new version of the organization chart and in the EAP database as well.

Task 2   Identify business locations and relate to the organizational units.   Depending on the importance of location for planning purposes, locations can be entered into the EAP database either as attributes of organization units or as a hierarchical location data structure. In the latter case, organizational units can be related to a business location at corresponding levels of detail.

The following guidelines can be used to determine whether Business Location should be an attribute of Organization Unit or a separate data structure in the EAP database. Business Location should be an attribute if

* most business functions are performed at one site or in one city,
* the structure of the organization at each location is essentially the same, or
* each region or location has an independent organizational structure with only the top level reporting to a central or corporate unit.

Business location should be stored in a separate data structure if

- multiple cities or regions are involved in EAP, or
- the organization structure spans locations—that is, the organization structure does not follow location or geographical lines.

Task 3   Document business goals and objectives (optional).
Business goals and objectives generally have a hierarchical structure. Depending on the standards for planning of an organization, goals may be subdivided into objectives, objectives into goals, or goals and objectives may be treated as two different but related structures in the EAP database. Critical success factors may also be included. If the company has long-range plans that describe goals, objectives, and critical success factors, then gathering this information and entering it into the EAP database will be relatively easy and worth the time. However, a description or full analysis of business goals and objectives is not necessary if they are not readily available. EAP can be successfully accomplished in the absence of strategic business plans, and without defining business goals, objectives, and critical success factors.

An analysis of business goals and objectives is only necessary for those few companies that are characterized by an extremely informal structure or frequent business or product changes—frequent, that is, to the extent that determining the nature of the business is very difficult. In this case, definition of mission and objectives helps to explain the nature of the business and the reasons for the frequent business changes.

Some EAP methodologies mandate that goals, objectives, and critical success factors be determined, documented, and analyzed, or ranked in importance. However, in the absence of a formally documented plan, obtaining accurate business objectives and critical success factors is both difficult and time-consuming, and with EAP, time is one of the most important resources. It is one thing to ask a person in an organization, "What do you do?" and document the functions that person performs. It is an entirely different matter to ask, "*Why* are you doing what you do?" to determine objectives. Answers such as "My boss told me to," "I've been doing this for years," or "Gee, I don't know!" do little for determining objectives. Further, when a person does seem to be aware of objectives and critical success factors, can the accuracy be verified? Goals, objectives, and success factors are extremely political and controversial. Inaccurate or inconsistent documentation of unaccepted, unsupported goals and objectives can destroy the credibility of the business model, which in turn would destroy the credibility of the enterprise architectures and plans. So ask yourself: Is documenting goals and objectives worth the time and risk?

When possible, obtain annual budgets and plans for the organization units within the scope of EAP. This information will contribute to the sequencing of applications (Chapter 10).

Task 4 Produce reports of the organization units, reporting structure, locations, and (optionally) business goals.
Some toolsets may give no warning or could fail if a recursive (cyclic) relationship is entered, such as person A reports to person B, person B reports to person C, and person C reports to person A. Therefore, be sure to review the reports carefully and have business people review them as well. Some toolsets do not permit indirect relationships to be documented. It is important to resolve toolset problems and difficulties before they get out of hand. It is also a good idea to streamline procedures for data entry and report generation, this can save a great deal of time.

Figure 4.4 is an example of an organization chart in an *indented structure list* format. This report shows the position or title and either the name of the person or the number of people in that position. The two columns on the right are not usually distributed outside the EAP team. The first is the internal EAP identification number of the organization unit. Every record in each file or table in the EAP database should have a primary key number assigned for access purposes and to ease data entry. This number is solely for EAP purposes and has no inherent meaning.

Several kinds of internal EAP data have a tree-like hierarchical structure, such as organization unit, business function, and technology platform. When using a relational database for EAP, a column or field known as the hierarchical sort key is used to record the position in the hierarchy and to produce the indented structure list report. This field, shown on the right side of Figure 4.4, is easily manipulated with set-oriented SQL commands.

ORGANIZATION UNITS STRUCTURE REPORT

–PRESIDENT [J.BROEKER]	1	
–EXECUTIVE SECRETARY [C.THACKER]	256	a
–VICE PRESIDENT (SURFACE PLANTS) [J.ESTES]	2	a
–GENERAL ENGINEERING. CHIEF ENGINEER [L.EMMONS]	3	aa
–ENGINEERING SERVICES [T.LATHAM]	4	aaa
–ENGINEERING ANALYSTS [3]	259	aaab
–CONSTRUCTION ENGINEERING [T.MICHAEL]	5	aab
–PROJECT ENGINEERING [4]	6	aac
–CIVIL & MECHANICAL PROJECT ENGINEERING [V.PHAL]	7	aad
–ELECTRICAL & INSTRUMENTATION PRO. ENG. [A.TYLER]	8	aae
–PLANT ENGINEERING [R.BAGBY]	9	aaf
–MILL SUPERINTENDENT [G.ROSS]	12	ab
–MILL GENERAL FOREMAN [M.JONES]	175	aba
–MILL OPERATION SUPERVISORS [3]	176	abaa
–MILL TRAINING/SAFETY [C.COFFEE]	177	abab
–MILL PROCESS IMPROVEMENT [B.HOGMAN]	178	abac
–SMELTER MANAGER [M.JENKINS]	13	ac
–QUALITY FACILITATOR [R.HOOD]	14	aca
–SMELTER PLANT ENGINEER [M.APARICIO]	15	acb
–SMELTER CLERK [A.FAKAYODE]	244	acba
–SMELTER TRAINING [H.MCQUERY]	16	acc
–SMELTER SUPERINTENDENT [M.WEBER]	17	acd
–RSTRS.FCES GENERAL FOREMAN [D.WILLIAMS]	18	acda
–SMELTER SENIOR FOREMAN [M.HARDY]	19	acdaa
–SMELTER RELIEF FOREMAN [Y.KASSADKIN]	242	acdaaa
–SMELTER PROCESS SUPERVISOR [S.GREER]	21	acdaaba

Figure 4.4.   Sample organization unit structure report.

STEP 2—IDENTIFY / DEFINE FUNCTIONS

Purpose

This step defines the structure of the business model. Identifying functions *is* the process of defining the business. This is one of the most important steps in EAP, because defining the business is essential before defining architectures, and the quality of the architectures is derived from the quality of the business model.

Deliverable

1. Functions are identified. Each function
   * has a name.
   * either has a brief description, or
   * is decomposed into subfunctions, and
   * is performed by at least one organization unit (unless it is a future function that is not currently performed).

Definition of Function

A function is any set of actions performed in the course of conducting business.

Any collection of activities done in the business may be called a function, and there is only one rule for defining business functions called *The Fundamental Rule of Functional Decomposition*. This rule states

A function is defined entirely by its subfunctions.

Very simple. A function is defined by its parts—no more, no less. Frequently there is discussion over terms used in business modeling for EAP. Avoid being caught in time-consuming debates over the semantic difference between a function, process, task, or activity. Such discussion is pointless for EAP. Remember, the purpose of a business model is to *understand the business* through definitions. Select one word—like "function"—and use that word to represent "any set of actions performed in the course of conducting business." If there are political reasons to use one word rather than another—for example, if *process* is deemed an acceptable term and *function* is not—then use the politically acceptable term. Attempting to further classify the sets of actions will result in hours of discussion that contribute little to the knowledge and understanding of the business.

Tasks and Guidelines

Task 1 Define the major functional areas using the "value-added" concepts of Michael Porter.[1] How does one begin business modeling? By asking the fundamental question "What *is* our business?" The value-added concept, developed by Michael Porter, provides insight into formulating a good answer to this question—that every major *functional area* of an enterprise makes a significant and identifiable contribution to the overall margin or profitability of the company. Figure 4.5, from

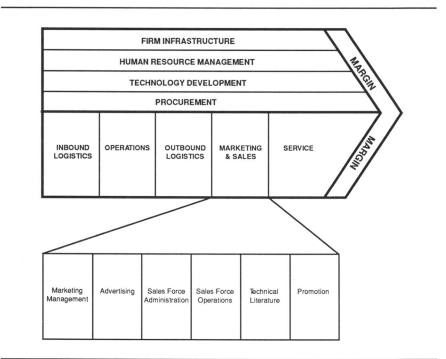

Figure 4.5. Porter's value-added chain. (Reprinted with the permission of *The Free Press*, a Division of Macmillan, Inc. from *Competitive Advantage: Creating and Sustaining Superior Performance* by Michael E. Porter. Copyright 1985 by Michael E. Porter.)

Porter's book *Competitive Advantage*, shows a format for displaying value-added functions. The arrow-shaped figure has two parts. The lower portion, below the heavy center line, identifies the value-added chain functions similar to the product lifecycle or line functions. Each functional area materially contributes to the margin or value of the products or services. Above the center line are the support functions, so named because they provide support to more than one value-added function.

Figure 4.6 identifies the major functional areas of a natural gas utility company. Four of the support functions manage specific resources of this firm, namely money, materials, people, and information.

The EAP team may ask executives in the enterprise for their perspective to identify and define the value-added major functional areas. Initially, the business model may appear similar to the organization chart. This may be in part due to the fact that people tend to define their functions along reporting lines rather than functional lines. The definition of what the business is and its value-added chain are independent of the way the enterprise is structured. A business model, therefore, may be different in some ways from the organization chart.

For example, consider the list of functions for the utility company in Figure 4.6. The organization chart for this company would clearly show that the largest organization unit is called

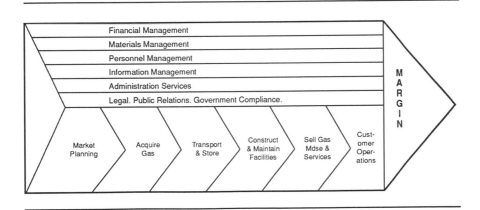

Figure 4.6. Utility company value-added functions.

"Engineering," but there is no function called "Engineering." Why? The answer to the question "What do we do?" is *not* engineering. Indeed, engineers conduct and are responsible for many functions of the utility company. They perform tasks such as storing and transporting the gas and building and maintaining equipment and facilities. The definition of a business function is only based on the actions performed, not the organization, title, or person responsible for or performing the function.

The above is one example of a large organization unit (indeed the largest department) not appearing in a business model. Figure 4.7 is a business model of a company that primarily publishes books of information about manufacturers' products. The functions are displayed in a top-down fashion, like an organization chart, but this too is different from the organization chart of that company. The functions comprising Indexing are, for the most part, performed by a very small group of people that are organizationally many levels down in the Sales and Marketing Department. Yet, Indexing is a separate major functional area because the index code assigned to products and manufacturers contributes a great measure to the value of their product, and because "sales," conceptually, are those activities involving direct customer contact aimed at securing business contracts. Indexing is not conceptually part of the definition of the "Sales" function because it does not involve direct contact with customers, plus it has value-added importance. These two examples, one a large department that does not appear in the business model, the other a small, low-level group being a major functional area, demonstrate that the structure of the functional business model can be quite different from the organization chart.

Task 2   Divide each functional area into its subfunctions by asking the question "What is the function?" or "What does the function name mean?" This is the functional decomposition process. Once the major functions are identified, defining them adds detail to the business model. For the team meetings in the war room, use a large board with colored markers to denote functions, their organization units, major products, and documents. At least one person should carefully take notes during these meetings.

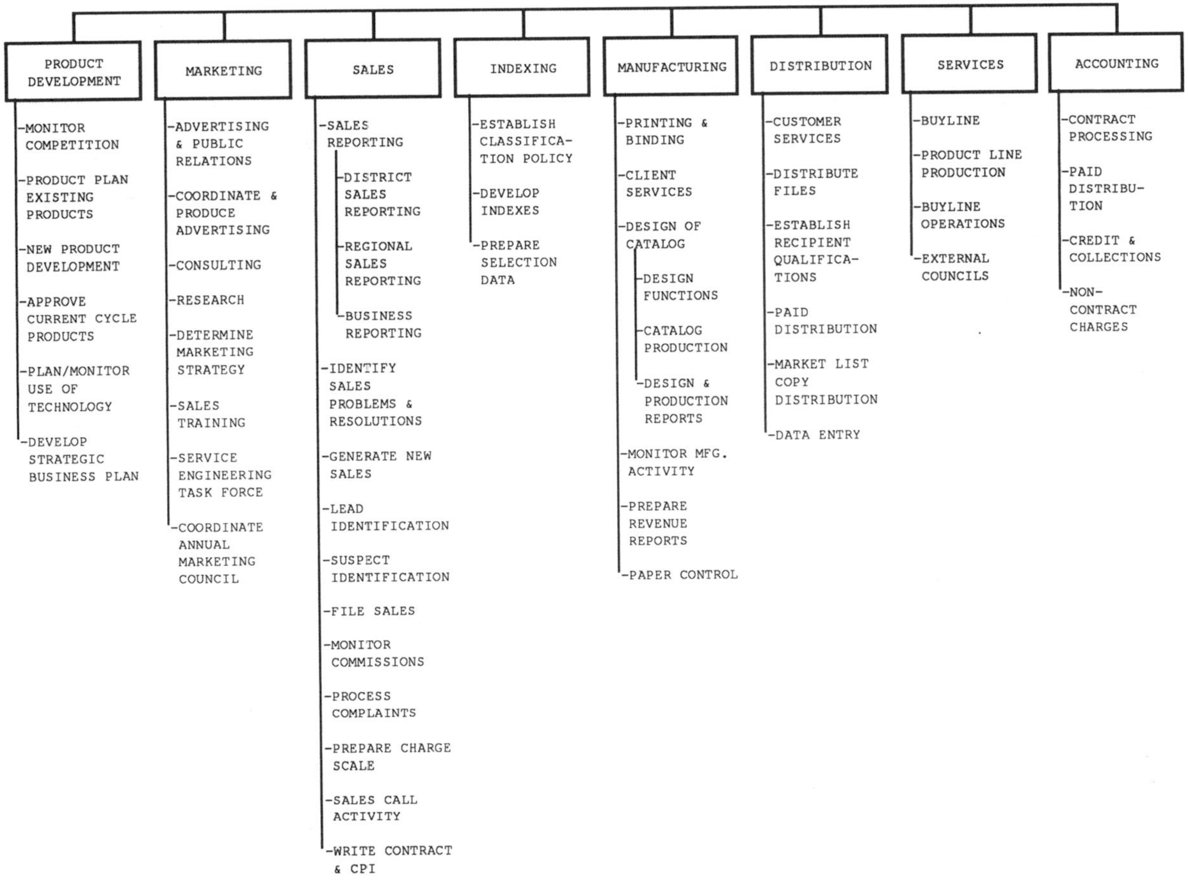

Figure 4.7. Functional decomposition of publishing company.

Identify each function by an appropriate name, one that is descriptive and conveys the meaning of the function. Long function names are usually more descriptive than short ones, especially at greater levels of detail. Avoid one-word names. Function names should have at least two words—one that specifies the action (a form of a verb) and another that identifies the object of that action. Avoid names similar to organization units so that functions are not equated to departments, titles, or people. The fundamental rule of decomposition implies that the name for a function that is decomposed into parts is a heading or descriptive label for the group of subfunctions it represents.

Write a one- or two-sentence description for each function. Every function *without subfunctions* should have a description. Functions that have subfunctions do not need a textual description because those subfunctions collectively *are* the description. Remove the description from a function when subfunctions have been identified.

When dividing a function into parts, do not omit administrative subfunctions. Expect many functions to have parts such as plan, perform, monitor, and control.

Task 3 Continue the functional decomposition until the functions tend to be single-action oriented, executed repeatedly, have an identifiable outcome, or can be associated with a specific organization unit defined in the previous step. The number of levels of detail in a business model depends on the size and complexity of the business and the time and resources for EAP. Do not labor over the levels of detail. The more time and people are devoted to working on the EAP team, the more detail there can be in the business model. Time and people are the two factors that limit the amount of detail in the business model.

The purpose of the business model for EAP is to build an understanding of the enterprise that will enable creating good architectures and plans. Some parts of an enterprise are more complicated than others and will, therefore, require more information to gain that understanding. A few of the EAP methodologies advocate rules such as "all areas should have the same number of levels of detail," or "there should always be three, four, or some given number of levels." In practice, such rules are arbitrary, and adhering to them will consume valuable time that does not contribute to understanding the enterprise.

As a rough rule of thumb, a business model containing approximately 300 functions can be handled by a team of six people in a six-month EAP project. Of course, with more time and/or people, more functions (i.e., detail) can be defined. The enterprise survey, described in the next chapter, collects more information about each detailed function.

Task 4   (Re)Arrange all functions hierarchically to improve the business model.   The order of the functions in a hierarchy is immaterial. There is no left-right or top-down sequencing implied by the arrangement of functions. Move functions in the hierarchy to form groups of similar or related functions by creating a meaningful heading or term as the function name. These collected subfunctions should be grouped based on the *object* of the action—not on *similar* actions. For example, suppose there is a function *design new products*. The word "design" would be the action and the term "new product" would be the object. That function should be grouped with functions such as *build new products*, *sell new products*, and *ship new products*—each of these functions being a subfunction under a heading such as *introduce new products*. All functions that are "planning" would not be grouped together because planning is an action. The object named that follows the word "planning" should be the basis for grouping the functions.

Strictly enforce the fundamental rule of decomposition. The results of a functional decomposition can be presented as either a hierarchical diagram, which reads from the top down, or the equivalent, an indented structure list in which the levels are indented from left to right. Figure 4.8 shows both forms of decomposition using letters to denote function names.

The two diagrams in Figure 4.8 define the same function— function A. Function A has been defined to mean B, C, and D— the order being irrelevant. Similarly, function I is defined as L + M, and function I in turn is part of the definition of function D. If the decision was made to move function I onto the line that contains functions B, C, and D, as in Figure 4.9, what definitions will have changed? The definition of function I will not have changed

RESULTS OF A FUNCTIONAL DECOMPOSITION

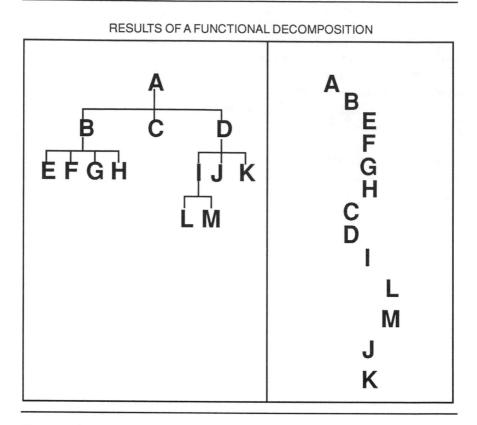

Figure 4.8. Hierarchical diagram and an indented structure list.

because it is still defined as L + M. The definition of function A will not have changed, because function I was implicitly part of the definition of function A, and it is still part of function A, as function A now means B, C, D, and I explicitly. The definition of function D, however, will be different because function I will no longer be part of its definition. Thus, the effect of moving functions in the hierarchical tree is that *it changes the definitions of functions.*

Task 5 Ensure quality of the business model and continue to make it better. The business model contains definitions of functions from the perspective of the EAP team and other contributors. Therefore, the definition of a particular function can be deemed neither correct nor wrong, and the business model is likewise neither right nor wrong. However, a business model can be either good or not good, in the sense that it is either effective or ineffective for planning purposes or any other long-term use.

What makes a business model good or not? There are three criteria for establishing the quality of a business model:

1. It makes sense and is easily understood by people throughout the enterprise.
2. Its scope is complete, meaning that no important functions

---

RESULTS OF A FUNCTIONAL DECOMPOSITION

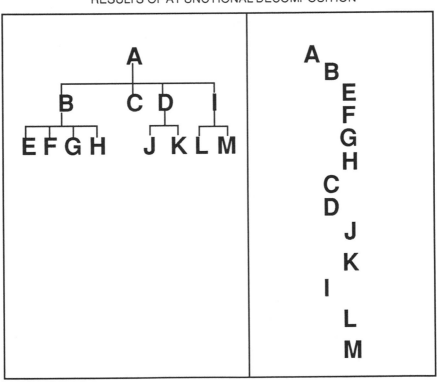

Figure 4.9. Effects of function definition change.

have been omitted from the definition of the business, and it is consistent in the terminology used for names and definitions. For example, each function should be represented only once in the business model, regardless of the number of organizational units that perform the function. There should be no duplicate functions, and function definitions should not overlap.

3. The business model is stable over time; that is, it provides a solid foundation for defining the architectures. A "stable" business model means that the business model *decomposition structure* does *not* show the following:

    *   **WHO** performs the function (organization unit) or the level of responsibility. The definition of a function is independent of who performs it. Functions are not grouped together in the business model because they are performed by the same person or department. An individual may perform functions in several functional areas. The placement of a function in the hierarchy does not imply any level of responsibility. Conceivably, a function performed by the CEO could be next to a function performed by a clerk.

        To prevent the perception of organizational responsibility, avoid using phrases such as *low-level* or *high-level* function. Also avoid phrases like the function *up here* or *down there*, which also imply importance. Instead, use words like "detailed" or "summarized" for functions that, respectively, are or are not decomposed.

    *   **HOW** functions are performed or the ordering (procedures). There is no left-to-right sequencing or chronological aspect to the arrangement of functions.

    *   **WHERE** a function is performed. Functions are not grouped together simply because they are performed at the same location. Thus, there should be no function names such as Region 1 Sales, West Coast Operations, or Philadelphia Manufacturing.

    *   **WHEN** a function is performed. Functions are not grouped together because they are performed at the same time. There should be no function names like Month-End Processing, Weekly Sales Status Reporting.

    *   **IMPORTANCE** or priority. The level in the business

model hierarchy does not indicate importance or priority in any way. High-priority functions are not grouped together.

- **TECHNOLOGY** or resources used. Functions are not grouped together because they use or share common technology. Function names should not reflect technology such as Mainframe Reporting, Network Data Entry, and so on.
- **FLOWS** of inputs, outputs, or personal interactions. Functions are not grouped together because the output of one is the input to the other.

The above list contains those aspects of the business that are most dynamic or most susceptible to change. However, the nature of the business—the "what"—does not change nearly as much as those above. Hence, a good, stable business model captures the essence of the business' nature in the definition (structure) of the functions.

Task 6   Establish the stability *of the business model by continually evaluating the goodness criteria and by asking how the business has evolved over time.*   The business modeling discussion leader should be constantly asking questions to make the definitions better. One method for testing the stability of the business model is to ask how the business has changed over time. If there would have been a business model from last year, five years ago, or ten years ago, would that business model be different from today's? If most of the differences would be with detailed business functions, then the overall structure of the business model would be essentially the same. When this is the case, it is reasonable to assume that the nature of the business will stay the same in the future. In other words, the past stability of the business model implies the future stability of the basic definitions. For the structure of the business model to require change, the nature of the business must change dramatically. Of course, the EAP team should pose questions to top management about the likelihood of such fundamental changes.

Task 7   Relate the detailed functions to the organization units that perform them, and produce a matrix report.   In the previous step, the organization structure of the enterprise was identified and documented. This task relates the organization units to the lowest level subfunctions—the functions that are not subdivided into parts. Since a function is defined entirely by its parts, it would not be meaningful to relate organizations to summarized functions.

The word "performs" is important. Relate functions to the organizations that perform the functions, not the organization responsible for them. It is relatively easy to establish that a department or position performs a function. Responsibility, however, requires a subjective interpretation and may be a political and controversial subject. It is reasonable to assume that a higher-level organization unit is responsible for the functions performed by those organization units and positions reporting to them.

A tip for managing this task is to use the toolset to generate a large, empty matrix. The matrix should have organization units listed on one axis and detailed functions listed on the other. Fill in the boxes of the matrix in a meeting of the EAP team. Figure 4.10 is an example of a matrix relating business functions to organization units.

The matrix of organization units to business functions is rarely distributed outside the EAP team. The reason is that the matrix can be used for organizational planning and other political purposes. It shows, by glancing across a row, all of the functions performed by a person that can raise questions such as "Why does a high-level person perform so few functions?" or "Why are so many functions performed by this department?" Similarly, glancing down the columns could raise political issues such as "Why are so many people performing the same function?"

Every function at the greatest level of detail should be performed by at least one organization unit. An automated function is performed by the person who "owns" or is responsible for that function. Each position in the organization unit structure should perform at least one function. These conditions can be used to check the completeness of the business function-to-organization unit relationships.

The toolset should be able to produce an indented structure and a cross-reference list. This is a more appropriate format for displaying and distributing the relationship of organization units to the business functions. Figure 4.11 is a portion of a com-

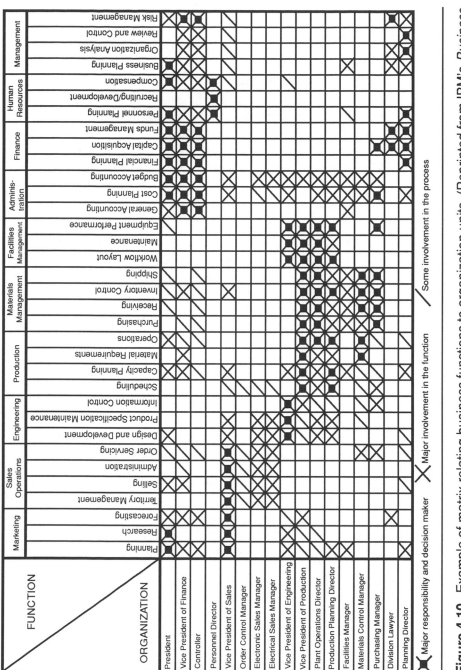
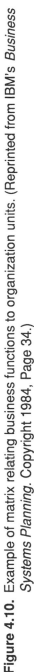

Figure 4.10. Example of matrix relating business functions to organization units. (Reprinted from IBM's *Business Systems Planning*. Copyright 1984, Page 34.)

bined indented structure and cross-reference list that includes the brief description of the detailed functions. The numbers in brackets are internal to EAP and can be omitted on reports distributed outside of the EAP team.

The relationship of functions to organization units is important. In Chapter 5, "The Enterprise Survey," the EAP project team goes into the business to gather the details about the business functions. The best people to provide information about a function are those people who actually do that function. A matrix report relates functions to the organization units, thereby pro-

---

WAREHOUSING [240]

    RECEIVE MATERIAL [255]

        Physical receiving of material into the warehouse.

           RECEIVING AND HEAVY STORAGE FOREMAN [230]

           MATERIAL RECEIVERS [231]

    RECEIVING PROBLEM SOLVING [256]

        Resolving issues outstanding from the receipt of particular items.

           MATERIAL RECEIVERS [231]

           GENERAL FOREMAN, ALL AREAS [33]

    SUPPLIES STORAGE [244]

        The storage of supplies.

           WAREHOUSE SUPERVISOR [129]

           GENERAL FOREMAN [32]

    ISSUING SUPPLIES [245]

        The issuing and delivering of stock supplies to the using department.

           GENERAL FOREMAN, ALL AREAS [33]

           WAREHOUSE SUPERVISOR [129]

           YARD CREW [234]

           CLERK [255]

Figure 4.11. Example of business functions to organization units expressed as a cross-reference list.

viding the EAP team with a map of where to go to gather the detail about the business.

STEP 3—DISTRIBUTE THE PRELIMINARY BUSINESS MODEL

Purpose

In this step, the business model reports are distributed to verify that the definitions and relationships are correct, so that the next phase, Enterprise Survey, will proceed smoothly.

Deliverables

1. Preliminary business model report
2. Preliminary business model presentation
3. Comments on the business model

Tasks and Guidelines

Task 1.   Collect all notes and charts from the previous step. Number the business functions. Everything in the EAP database should be numbered, including business functions, organization units, data entities, applications, and so on. Sequential numbering is best, because numbers as identifiers are not subject to revisions and do not imply a sequencing or priority. Once a function is numbered, its name may change, but its number will stay the same. Numbers are much easier than names for entering and maintaining relationships. Do not make this number also a hierarchical key. In an EAP database, a hierarchical key should be established as a field of the function record separately from its sequentially numbered primary key. As functions are rearranged in the hierarchy, new functions will be created and others eliminated. Do not reuse function numbers. New function names should be assigned the next available sequential number.

Task 2   Enter the functions names, numbers, subfunction relationships, brief descriptions, and the organization units performing the functions into the toolset.   Functions need not be directly related to business locations if it is reasonable to assume, within the 80/20 principle, that the locations of an organization unit are where the business functions are performed. When relating functions directly to business locations, the toolset or team members should verify that no inconsistencies are introduced. If organization units, business locations, and business functions are three separate "entities" in a relational EAP database, then to avoid inconsistencies there should be an internal EAP database table whose primary key is the concatenation of the three identifiers for organization unit, location, and function.

Task 3   Generate business model reports (indented lists, diagrams, matrices, formatted text, summaries).   Generate decomposition reports with different levels of detail. Summary reports may show only two or three levels of detail. The toolset should be able to limit the amount of detail in reports. Some toolsets can automatically "roll up" and summarize relationships at various levels of detail. The value of a flexible, adaptable toolset for EAP will be demonstrated in this step.

Task 4   Present, fully explain, and provide copies of the preliminary business model reports to management.   It may be necessary to explain repeatedly the differences between a business model and an organization chart. Some will grasp the fundamental concept easily; others will not. The EAP leader must have great patience and tolerance for these situations. Figure 4.12 is a suggested presentation outline for this task of the EAP process.

Task 5   During the presentation, solicit comments and suggestions about the preliminary business model for discussion.   The EAP team should review the comments from the business community. Update the business model to make it better, not just to satisfy particular people. Expect numerous changes to the business model as EAP progresses.

Task 6   Explain the Enterprise Survey Phase and obtain permission to contact people for interviews.   Ask managers to recommend people to be interviewed. Explain the questions to

---

OUTLINE FOR
PRELIMINARY BUSINESS MODEL PRESENTATION

I.   Introduction
    A. Purpose of presentation
    B. Agenda
II. Overview of Business Modeling
    A. Phases of EAP and team members
    B. Purpose of business model
    C. Interpreting the business model
    D. Characteristics of a good business model
III. Business Functions
    A. Overview of Major Functional Areas
    B. Detail of Functional Area Definitions
IV. Next Steps
    A. Review of business model and comments
    B. Enterprise survey steps
    C. Interview questions
    D. Interview recommendation

Figure 4.12. Example of presentation outline.

be asked, and show a draft of a Function Definition Form to be used in the enterprise survey.

DISCUSSION QUESTIONS

1. Will the function to organization matrix be distributed?
2. Is management familiar with the "value-added" concept?
3. How many functions and how much detail do you expect in your business model?
4. Has any other form of business modeling been used by your organization?
5. Do you expect to compile business plans (mission, goals, objectives, critical success factors) in your EAP database?

6. Who is the best person(s) to make business model presentations?
7. Which executives or managers have perspectives that could shape the overall structures of the business model?
8. What EAP project policies, procedures, or actions can be adopted to ensure the quality of your business model?

REFERENCE

[1]Porter, Michael. *Competitive Advantage*, Free Press, New York, 1985; and Porter, Michael, and Victor E. Millar. "How Information Gives You Competitive Advantage," *Harvard Business Review*, July–August 1985.

The Enterprise Survey

INTRODUCTION

The purpose of the Enterprise Survey Phase is to gather details about the business to complete the business model, including the following:

- What information is used to perform a function
- When that function is performed
- Where the function is performed
- How often the function is performed
- What opportunities exist to improve the function

The enterprise survey is part of the business modeling of EAP identified in the EAP "wedding cake" of Figure 1.7. For most EAP projects, however, the enterprise survey is managed as a separate phase of the project. The method for gathering, organizing, and verifying the information needed to complete the business model is presented in five steps.

Five Steps for Performing Enterprise Survey

The five steps of the Enterprise Survey Phase are

1. Schedule the interviews.
2. Prepare for the interviews.

3. Perform the interviews.
4. Enter data into the toolset.
5. Distribute the business model.

For some EAP projects, the word "interview" may be considered too formal. If that is the case, substitute the word "meeting" or "session." In the discussion about the EAP project workplan in Chapter 3, a rough time estimate for all of business modeling was 30 percent of the EAP process, with most of that time consumed by the enterprise survey. Therefore, streamlining the process for conducting the enterprise survey will significantly reduce the overall amount of time for EAP. A well-managed EAP project is efficient, making the best use of precious time.

During Planning Initiation, the questions may arise, "Do we need to spend so much time on the enterprise survey?" or "Do we need to have detail in the business model in order to conduct EAP?" To answer these questions, consider the stated purpose of the business model: to provide a complete, comprehensive, consistent knowledge base that can be used to define the architectures and the plans to implement them. Hypothetically speaking, if an individual or group of individuals had this "complete, comprehensive, consistent knowledge" of the business, then the answer to the above questions would be "No, an enterprise survey is not needed." But in the real world, it is unlikely that such vast knowledge would be so highly concentrated and involved on the EAP team to the extent needed. Even if a single person with this knowledge did exist, that person may not be available for EAP as much as necessary. EAP is a team effort, and *all* members of the team need this business knowledge. Therefore, a business model would still be required in some documented form to be of use for the team to define the architectures; so the answer to the questions above should be "Yes, we do need a detailed business model."

STEP 1—SCHEDULE THE INTERVIEWS

Purpose

In this step, all interviews will be scheduled and the time allocated to this phase in the EAP workplan will be verified. Measures may need to be taken to keep the EAP project on track.

Deliverables

1. Schedule of interviews showing the following:
    Interviewee name and phone number of the person to be interviewed
    Date, time for which the interview is scheduled
    Location in which the interview will be held
    Interviewers who will perform the interview
    Functions being defined during the interview
2. Adjustments to the EAP workplan

Tasks and Guidelines

Task 1   Select the people to interview. Use the function-to-organization unit relationship matrices or the cross-reference lists created during the Preliminary Business Model Phase. All functions at the lowest level of detail in the decomposition should be covered by at least one interview. The person or persons who perform the function should be interviewed, and this means that EAP interviews will be conducted at all levels of the organization, from clerks to executives. It is far more credible to ask "What do you do?" than to ask "What do you think someone else is doing?"

For many of the functions, there may be several people and organization units who perform that function. It is neither practical nor necessary to interview each person performing each function. Select and interview the *best representative(s)* of a function, one who understands and has performed the function for some time. If defining a function seems to require interviewing three or four people, re-examine the function to see if it is possibly two or more distinct functions that can be split apart and interviewed separately. Consider the location of interviews and avoid extensive or expensive travel. By selecting the best representative, travel can be minimized. Suppose, for example, that a business conducts operations in six cities (or regions, territories). Within the 80/20 "good enough" principle, one or two cities may be sufficient to define and understand the business functions of all cities. Though there may be local differences in the functions, for the most part they are the same.

Task 2 Assign interviewers to functional areas. It is best to assign team members to interview familiar functional areas. For example, if there is a representative from the marketing department on the planning team, then that person should be assigned to interview marketing functions. Interviewers experienced and familiar with a functional area may have a rapport with the person to be interviewed, and may also have established credibility in the eyes of the interviewee.

Best results are obtained when two team members are assigned to an interview—a systems person and a business (user) person. However, time and resource limitations may dictate that only one team member conduct an interview. Good results can still be achieved with single interviewers, especially when interviewers are paired for a few initial interviews prior to conducting them separately.

Suggestions may be put forth to conduct *group* interviews as an alternative to the one-on-one or two-on-one interviews recommended for EAP. Joint Applications Design (JAD) style interviews will significantly *reduce* candor, accuracy, thoroughness, and credibility of the business model. Remember, the purpose of interviews is to *define* the business, not *design* systems. Group meetings or interviews have a tendency to focus on design or "how-to" issues that are not appropriate for EAP.

Watch for signs of personal disagreements or conflict that might exist between interviewer and interviewee, and avoid pairing them. Ask team members to identify such situations.

Interviews should generally last one to three hours, depending on the scope and complexity of the business functions being interviewed. Morning is usually the best time for an interview, since people are more alert at the beginning of their day, and there will be less chance that they have been sidetracked and may lag behind their daily schedule.

Task 3 Verify that the workplan has allocated sufficient time for this phase. Once the interviews have been scheduled, compare the scheduled amount of time with that allocated in the workplan for this phase. Anticipate schedule changes and follow-ups, and make sure there is sufficient time to conduct all interviews. As a rule of thumb, 20 percent of the interviews may need follow-up sessions; if so, schedule it at the end of the initial session. If the time allocated for this phase is *not* sufficient, there are at least five courses of action:

1. Extend the completion date for EAP to accommodate the time needed to complete the interviewing process, probably the least available action. In this case, all subsequent phases will need to have their schedules extended as well. Evaluate the tradeoffs of this decision. Extending EAP to accommodate more interviews may improve the thoroughness, detail, and credibility via greater participation. On the other hand, it will take more time, be more costly, and could damage some credibility by demonstrating an inability to plan for EAP accurately .

2. Reduce the number of functions to define by summarizing portions of the business model. In this case, the interview is conducted at one level higher than in the preliminary business model. The set of lower-level functions are combined into their parent functions, and the detailed functions are removed from the business model. This reduces the amount of work but sacrifices detail or precision. Again, the 80/20 principle should guide the decision.

3. Group or omit the documentation of information sources, particularly reports. *Information sources* are defined in the next step (step 2).

4. Reduce the scope of EAP. There may be functional areas that have minimal or no impact on the architectures, for example, Maintain the Corporate Airplane, Provide Legal Services, or Support the Community are likely candidates. If such functions are identified, eliminating them from the enterprise survey will reduce the number of interviews and save time.

5. Add people to the Enterprise Survey Phase of EAP, especially for interviewing and entering the interview data into the toolset. Supplementary interviewers may be from I.S. or business organizations, and additional data entry personnel could come from a secretarial pool or temporary agency.

Task 4   Write a template interview confirmation memo.
Write a template for an interview confirmation memo such as the example in Figure 5.1. Fields or variables can be used to repre-

---

To: J. A. Broeker, Vice President of Production

From: John P. Jones, Vice President of Information Systems

Subject: Enterprise Architecture Planning Study (EAP)

The information systems planning study that Mr. Wilson announced in the EAP executive orientation has begun. As you will recall, the objectives of the EAP team are the following:

- Document an overall understanding of the business and how information systems currently support the business

- Define data, application, and technology architectures that will support the business

- Make recommendations for I.S. improvements

- Formulate a long-range systems implementation plan

- Create a tactical plan for the first and most important subsystems

To assist the EAP team in this effort, the team members will be interviewing people throughout our organization. You have been selected to contribute to this important project. This will confirm that [team member(s) and telephone number(s)] will meet with you:

Date: _____

Time: _____

Place: _____

The discussions will focus on (1) the business functions you perform, (2) the information you use or generate when performing these functions, and (3) opportunities for improving your functions. The interview should take one to three hours.

Prior to the meeting, please review the attached list of business functions and preliminary descriptions. We would appreciate your having sample copies of all reports, forms, memos, screens, or other kinds of information that you use or generate. We will keep the samples for subsequent analysis.

If you have any scheduling problems, please contact the team member(s) given above or the EAP Project Manager, Jim Johnson, at extension 1234. Please call me if you have any questions. Thank you for your cooperation.

Sincerely,

John P. Jones

Attachment

Figure 5.1. Sample interview confirmation memo.

sent the information for specific memos. A handy toolset for EAP can record the interview schedule and use the schedule to generate the confirmation memo automatically. This memo will help the interviewee be prepared for the session, so the interview will go more smoothly and require less time.

Task 5   Contact each person to be interviewed and arrange a mutually convenient time.   Interviewers should contact the people they are assigned to interview and make mutually convenient arrangements for the date, time, and place for the interview. Enter the interview scheduling arrangements into the toolset and generate schedule reports chronologically as in Figure 5.2, and by team member as in Figure 5.3.

Task 6   Send a memo confirming the interview appointment and explaining the interview process to each interviewee and their manager.   The memos should be addressed from an executive such as the head of the business unit or I.S. expressing the importance of EAP to the business and asking/thanking them for their support and cooperation. In some companies, it is protocol to send a copy of the memo to the supervisor of the person being interviewed. Be sure to follow any such formalities. Figure 5.1 is an example of a template for a confirmation memo. Notice that the memo lists the data, time, place, agenda for the interview session, and requests that the interviewee have samples of forms, memos, reports, code lists, or anything used and generated by the function that the interviewer might keep for further analysis.

STEP 2—PREPARE FOR THE INTERVIEWS

Purpose

To prepare for the interviews, forms are created to help guide the interviewing process, and the EAP team members learn to conduct interviews.

Deliverables

1. Interview forms
   - Function Definition
   - Information Source Definition (optional)
2. Interview training

DATE	TIME	NAME	EXT	DEPT/TITLE	LOC	MEMBER	FUNCT.
May 28	10:00	E. Johnson	6069	Indexing	PP-09	M. Hardy	107
May 29	9:00	B. O'Hara	8231	Reg Sls Sec	PP-09	G. Wilson	121
June 1	9:30	M. Thacker	1221	Reg Sls Mgr	PP-09	M. Hardy	120
June 1	10:00	J. Estes	6504	Spec Systems	NY-20	M. Jones	051
June 4	9:30	R. Bagby	3933	Buyline Mgr	NY-20	G. Wilson	050
June 5	10:00	B. Coffee	9815	VP-Marketing	NY-19	G.A. Ross	009
June 13	9:00	M. Emmons	4240	VP-GM	SD	G. Wilson	021
June 14	10:00	J. Broeker	7112	Cost Accting	Chi	G.A. Ross	099
June 15	9:30	K. Johnson	8110	Distribution	NY-18	M. Jones	076
June 17	9:30	B. Hogman	5890	Manufacturing	NY-18	M. Hardy	033

Figure 5.2. Interview schedule chronological (partial list).

MEMBER	DATE	TIME	NAME	EXT	DEPT/TITLE	LOC	FUNCT.
M. Hardy	MAY 28	10:00	E. Johnson	6069	Indexing	PP-09	107
M. Hardy	June 1	9:30	M. Thacker	1221	Reg Sls Mgr	PP-09	120
M. Hardy	June 17	9:30	B. Hogman	5890	Manufacturing	NY-18	033
M. Jones	June 1	10:00	J. Estes	6504	Spec Systems	NY-20	051
M. Jones	June 15	9:30	K. Johnson	8110	Distribution	NY-18	076
G. Wilson	May 29	9:00	B. O'Hara	8231	Reg Sls Sec	PP-09	121
G. Wilson	June 4	9:30	R. Bagby	3933	Buyline Mgr	NY-20	050
G. Wilson	June 13	9:00	M. Emmons	4240	VP-GM	SD	021
G.A. Ross	June 5	10:00	J. Broeker	7112	VP-Production	Chi	099
G.A. Ross	June 14	10:00	B. Coffee	9815	VP-Marketing	NY-19	009

Figure 5.3. Interview schedule by team member (partial list).

Definition

Information Source: Anything used or produced by a person or computer performing a business function that conveys information (i.e., report, document, form, memo, message, screen, index card, letter).

Tasks and Guidelines

Task 1 Decide what information to obtain through the interviews and, therefore, what questions to ask. These questions will determine the items on the forms that will be designed in the next task. Be sure to include questions to assess the (dis)satisfaction and performance of current systems. This information will be valuable for identifying opportunities for business function improvement. A good business model is stable over time, and the stability is derived from function definitions and decomposition independently of who, where, when, and how. But those aspects of functions are important for a complete understanding of the business. The enterprise survey questions about a function should therefore include who performs it, how often it is performed, the place where it is performed, sequencing and timing, and resources used.

Task 2 Design the Function Definition and Information Source Forms. These forms should guide the interview process and be suitable for entry into the toolset. Consider the data entry features and constraints of the selected toolset. Some EAP toolsets only have fixed format data entry screens that might constrain the layout of these forms.

A shortage of time and/or resources for the enterprise survey may mean that individual information source usages will not be documented, though samples of the sources will be collected. In this case, leave plenty of room on the Function Definition Form to describe the information used and the source of the information.

Figures 5.4a and 5.4b show the front and back sides, respectively, of a sample Function Definition Form. The fields in this example are described below:

DATE: _____

FUNCTION NO.: _____

FUNCTION NAME: _____

SUBFUNCTION OF: _____

PERFORMED BY: _____

RESPONSIBILITY: _____

LOCATION: _____

DESCRIPTION: _____
(What)   _____
           _____
           _____
           _____
           _____
           _____

PURPOSE: _____
(Why)   _____
         _____
         _____
         _____

STATUS: Active _____   Inactive _____   Proposed _____

FREQUENCY: _____   times per _____

              Exception on Condition: _____

DURATION: _____

DECISIONS: _____
(How)   _____
           _____
           _____
           _____

INTERVIEWEE: _____

AUTHOR: _____

Figure 5.4a. Sample Function Definition Form (side 1).

FUNCTION
IMPROVEMENT
OPPORTUNITIES: _____

_____

_____

_____

_____

_____

_____

_____

_____

POSSIBLE ORGANIZATIONAL/
PROCEDURAL/FUNCTION
CHANGES: _____

_____

_____

_____

_____

_____

_____

_____

_____

INFORMATION USED: _____

_____

_____

_____

_____

_____

_____

Figure 5.4b. Sample Function Definition Form (side 2).

Date:	Every form should have the date that it was filled out, which should be the same as the interview date.
Function number:	The key from the preliminary business model.
Function name:	The (long) name that may be updated to better describe the function.
Parent functions:	The function numbers in the decomposition hierarchy.
Performed by:	List of organization unit numbers that perform the function.
Location:	Business locations where the function is performed.
Definition:	A one-paragraph description of the function; avoid lengthy definitions. The definition may also describe the purpose of the function, how decisions are made, and success factors.
Status:	Most functions will be *active*, that is, currently performed. Future or *proposed* functions may also be documented.
Frequency:	How often a function occurs expressed in a unit and measure such as *five* times per *week*.
Frequency condition:	Conditions that affect when a function is performed.
Duration:	The average or approximate amount of time to perform the function in unit and measure, such as *15 minutes.*

Duration condition:

Factors that affect the duration.

Interviewee:

The name(s) of the person(s) who provided this information. Generally, their names *will not* appear on business model reports in connection with the function so that the interviewees can be candid and accurate.

Interviewers:

The names or initials of EAP team members who completed this form. This will be handy in the event that a data entry person cannot read the handwriting on the form.

Function improvement opportunities:

A paragraph to document ideas that would make the function better with respect to quality (effectiveness) or productivity (efficiency). Although the focus of EAP is information systems, interviewees should not limit their ideas to those that are I.S. related.

Information used:

If information sources are documented separately, this space can list the information source numbers. Otherwise, identify all major sources of information and describe the information used. Additional pages may be used and attached for this section. Understand the kinds of information used by the functions and the context of terms mentioned by the interviewee, but do not *attempt to define standard entities or terms*.

Figure 5.5 shows a sample Information Source Form. The fields in this example are described below:

DATE: _____

FOR FUNCTION: _____

SOURCE NAME: _____   SOURCE NO. : _____

DESCRIPTION: _____

_____

_____

_____

_____

_____

_____

_____

RECEIVED FROM: Yes _____   No _____

FORWARDED TO: _____

SAMPLE ACQUIRED: Active _____   Inactive _____   Proposed _____

MEDIUM: Excellent _____   Good _____   Fair _____   Poor _____

STATUS: Acceptable _____   Unacceptable _____

ACCURACY: _____

CURRENCY: Acceptable _____

VOLUME: Changes Required: _____

FORMAT: _____

_____

AUTHOR: _____

Figure 5.5.   Sample Information Source Form.

Source number:	The key unique to the information source.
Source name:	The name generally appears at the top of the source. Commonly used names should also be noted.
For function number:	The description and usage of the information source is given in the context of a particular business function.
Description:	A paragraph explaining the information in the source and how the information is used by the above business function.
Medium:	The physical characteristics of the source.
Received from:	The business function, information system, or organization unit that provided the information source.
Forwarded to:	The business function, system, or organization unit that is given the source by or at the conclusion of the business function.
Quality:	The opinions of the interviewee regarding the usefulness or quality of the information source as to its accuracy, currency (up-to-date), and format. Problems or suggestions for improvement may also be described.

The interview date, interviewee, and interviewer should be recorded on every form. If strategic business plans are documented in the EAP toolset, interviewees may be asked to relate business functions to objectives, opportunities, and critical success factors.

Task 3* *Develop an interview format and have a training workshop to "practice" interviewing within the planning team. An experienced interviewer should lead the first few practice interviews during the training workshop. Interview the business members on the planning team to define their functions as part of the workshop. This will give the rest of the planning team experience in interviewing, an idea of what to expect, and comprehension of the questions that need to be asked. After interviewing the business members on the planning team, arrange the initial interviews with tolerant and cooperative people willing to be early in the interview process.

It does take time for team members to become accustomed to conducting this kind of enterprise survey interview. Few team members emerge from the workshop as expert interviewers. Even those with systems analysis experience will find these definition interviews to be markedly different from those aimed at designing systems. With this in mind, select initial interviews that are expected to be the easiest. Send an experienced interviewer to accompany new interviewers for their initial sessions until they become confident with proceeding on their own.

The enterprise survey workshop lasts about one day and includes the following topics:

- Status of the business model
- Interview schedule
- Interview forms
- Interview agenda
- Practice interviews and discussion

Task 4* *Establish interviewee profiles and specific questions. Each interviewer should prepare for individual interviews ahead of time. If possible, learn something about the person who is being interviewed. Anticipate responses to the interview questions. Prior to the interview, fill in the forms for function and information source items known or expected.

Task 5* *Gather materials to be used for the interview into a folder. Such materials include organization charts, the preliminary business model, copies of relevant correspondence, interview schedule, blank definition forms, samples of expected information sources, and partially completed definition forms.

STEP 3—PERFORM THE INTERVIEWS

Purpose

The focus of this step is not on interviewing techniques, but on managing the EAP effort and the enterprise survey so that the interviews proceed smoothly.

Deliverables

1. Completed Function and Information Source Definition Forms
2. Samples of information sources cataloged and filed

Tasks and Guidelines

Task 1   Perform each interview at the scheduled time.
Establish a reputation for punctuality that will help the team meet the schedule and maintain a positive team image. Postponing or missing interviews will hurt the team. To repeat, team members on their initial interviews should be accompanied by an experienced interviewer until confident in proceeding on their own.

Task 2   Fill in the Function Definition Form during *the interview.*   Do not wait until after the interview to fill in the Function Definition Form. Taking notes during the interview and attempting to translate those notes into answers on the form after the interview is *not* a good practice. In many cases, a team member will have multiple interviews in a single day, and trying to reconstruct an interview from memory, even with notes, will cause errors. It does not take many mistakes before the credibility of the entire business model will be called into question. Don't allow this to happen. The best approach is to fill in the information as the interview proceeds, and allow the interviewee to review the information on the form and verify that it is correct.

Pause every few minutes during the interview, summarize, fill in part of the form, and then continue. This will ensure not only that the information and definitions are concise, but it will help keep the interview on track and on time by avoiding lengthy, extended, and possibly circular answers.

During the interview, identify problems and/or opportunities for a function, but do not try to solve them. Don't even offer suggestions, which may be misconstrued as promises.

Several functions and information sources may be defined concurrently. Find ample space on a desk or table to spread out the interview forms and materials. When two people conduct an interview, one interviewer (usually the business team member) can direct the discussion while the other interviewer fills in the form. Another approach is to have one interviewer fill in the Function Definition Forms and the other interviewer fill in the Information Source Forms.

Task 3   Identify the information sources for each function and fill in the Information Source Forms during the interview.   This form should also be filled in and verified during the interview. Carry plenty of extra forms to document business functions that are not in the preliminary business model. The team members may determine that the function name and description from the preliminary business model was not appropriate. Several changes to the business model structure or decomposition may be required, such as

- Changing a function name or the name of its parent(s)
- Splitting a function into separate functions and placing them in appropriate positions in the decomposition
- Moving a function in the decomposition to improve the overall definition
- Combining functions that are essentially the same
- Decomposing a complicated function into subfunctions (increasing detail)
- Eliminating a group of detailed functions by merging them into their parent(s) to be treated as a single function (summarizing)

Make sure that the completed forms are legible and accurate to avoid misinterpretation and data entry errors. When a new function is discovered, it too must be completely defined.

Task 4 Ask the interviewees to describe the information that they use from the information source. Identify what information is used (candidate data entity) and how it is used. For example, a person may receive a very large report from which only a single number from the last page is used for the function. That number on the last page is what is to be described on the back of the Function Definition Form or the Information Source Form.

Task 5 Obtain a sample copy of each information source. The information source sample should have a number, name, function number, and may have notes on it from the interview. For information sources that are standard printed business forms, try to get several examples of filled-in forms, not blank ones.

Task 6 At the end of an interview, summarize what has been written, schedule a follow-up session if necessary, confirm copies of sources that the interviewee will provide, and extend proper courtesies. After the interview, complete any missing information on the forms.

Task 7 Meet regularly as a team to discuss the status and results of the interviews. More frequent meetings will be required during the early stages of the interviewing, and, as interview teams gain experience, fewer meetings and less time will be required. Team meetings should discuss issues that arise during the interview process, such as regulating the amount of time for interviews, handling complicated situations and questions, or ensuring a consistent level of quality for the definitions. Distribute business model changes to all team members.

Task 8 Number every business function and information source. All new functions and information sources must have a unique identifier. The next available number may be assigned by a team member, a data entry operator, or may be automatically generated by the toolset, which would be the preferred method.

Task 9   File the forms and make a copy of each one before giving them to data entry people.   Take the copies of the forms and sample information sources and assemble them into a binder or folder. Keep them in the planning area (war room). It is important to have a backup copy of all completed function and source forms. Losing a form without a copy can be embarrassing and time-consuming to replace.

Task 10   Pass the forms to the clerical support group for entry into the toolset.   One team member should have the responsibility of making sure that all forms are complete as they are handed in. This person should review and verify the forms *before* they are passed to the data entry group.

STEP 4—ENTER DATA INTO THE TOOLSET

Purpose

In this step, all the information gathered in the interviews will be entered into the toolset and verified. Entering the interview information into the toolset may seem straightforward and obvious, but this step hurts or kills more EAP projects than any other step in the entire EAP process, outside of planning initiation. The reason is that many of the products used for toolsets, while they can produce impressive reports and diagrams, do not have a data entry capability that will handle large quantities of data that must be input quickly into their databases. This situation is often referred to as the "data entry bottleneck." The tasks and guidelines of this step will help prevent this from occurring.

Deliverables

1. All interview forms entered into the toolset
2. Verified EAP database (inconsistencies resolved)

Tasks and Guidelines

Task 1   Arrange to have data entry personnel.   Data entry personnel will key the information on the forms into the toolset. Forms should be reviewed, verified, and forwarded to data entry from team members as they are filled in—not accumulated until all interviews have been completed. The flow of forms from interviewing through data entry should be maintained at a reasonably constant pace so that the backlog of forms to be keyed does not become overwhelming. The professionals on the planning team should be spending their time gathering and analyzing business information and improving the business model. Team members should *not* be spending their time typing. The data entry personnel can either be assigned from inside the company, such as a secretarial pool, or contracted through an outside agency. No knowledge of the EAP process is required, but some amount of learning for the toolset will be needed, depending on the products.

One person on the EAP team should oversee the data entry effort and make sure that it proceeds on track. This person should be the focal point for receiving the forms and should be responsible for reporting any toolset problems to the planning team and project leader.

Task 2   Design data entry procedures and screens.   If the EAP toolset has modifiable or extendable data entry procedures and screens, design them to facilitate the data entry. Using multiple personal computers or terminals will improve the throughput. However, data entry on unconnected workstations may require database consolidation procedures, such as combining individual files into a single master database for EAP. Procedures may need to be established for batch loading files each day into the master EAP database, unless the master EAP database is being shared by workstations on a local area network. Consider the significant time it may take to develop these consolidation procedures to ensure the integrity of the EAP database.

Depending on the toolset, programs may need to be developed in the language of the toolset to facilitate data entry and reporting. This is often the case when a general DBMS is used for EAP

COMPLETENESS AND CONSISTENCY RULES

1. Functions must have hierarchical sort keys.
2. Higher-level functions must have at least two children.
3. Every lowest-level function must have a description.
4. No higher-level function should have a description.
5. All lowest-level functions must be mapped to an organization unit.
6. Responsibility mappings must exist
   a. for all functions referenced.
   b. for all organizations referenced.
7. All lowest-level functions should have had an interview.
8. Interviews should not have been interviewed for
   a. nonexistent functions.
   b. higher-level functions.
9. There should not be source usage for functions that do not exist.
10. Source usage should only be linked to lowest-level functions.
11. Higher-level functions should not be mapped to organization units.
12. All functions should have parent function numbers.
13. Descriptions should exist for
    a. all organization units.
    b. all information sources.
14. All lowest-level functions should have source usage.
15. There should be no orphan records based on the hierarchical sort key.
16. The initials for team members must be valid
    a. for functions.
    b. for organization units.
    c. for information sources.
17. Initials must be present for
    a. functions.
    b. organization units.
    c. information sources.
18. Information sources must have at least one source usage.

Figure 5.6.   18 rules for checking relational EAP database.

instead of a software package specifically for EAP. As mentioned in Chapter 3, the tradeoff for flexibility in the toolset is a greater time and experience requirement for effective use.

Task 3   Take steps to avoid a data entry bottleneck. Streamline data entry procedures and make them as easy to follow as possible. Have default values on data entry screens and have repeated values generated automatically. Use automatic sequential numbering for new functions and information sources. Use numbers instead of names to refer to database records and to establish relationships, and have the toolset retrieve the names and place them on the data entry screens. Consider the use of overtime and/or temporary help for entering the data.

Task 4   Check that the interview forms are understandable, complete, and consistent before giving them to the data entry personnel.   Resolve any difficulties immediately with the EAP team member who wrote the interview form.

Task 5   Enter the data on the forms into the toolset.

Task 6   Produce reports to verify that the data was entered correctly and that the EAP database is complete and consistent.   Use the query and reporting facilities of the toolset to verify the data entry and the consistency of the EAP data, that is, objects and relationships. Figure 5.6 is an example of completeness and consistency rules that can easily be translated into SQL statements for a relational database. The toolset should have facilities for easily changing data after entry such as SQL, forms, matrices, decomposition pruning and grafting and so on.

Team members should correct the data for which they are responsible and resolve inconsistencies with other team members. Team members' initials should be associated with all data in the EAP database. This task can consume a substantial amount of time, especially when using a general DBMS for the toolset. So allocate sufficient time in the workplan to "clean up" the database.

Task 7   Send the interviewees a copy of the data they provided.   A *very important* task indeed, this is both a courtesy and a protection of the team's credibility. If there have been any misunderstandings of the information gathered during the interview, this task will ensure that these errors are promptly corrected. When the business model is distributed, there should be no attacks on its credibility.

STEP 5—DISTRIBUTE THE COMPLETE BUSINESS MODEL

Purpose

In this step, the complete business model will be distributed to the management of the enterprise.

Deliverables

1. Complete set of business model reports
   - Diagrams and/or indented structure lists
   - Organization unit description
   - Function definition summary
   - Full function description
   - Information source description
   - Information source usage summary
   - Goals, objectives, and critical success factors
   - Relationship reports and tables (matrices)
   - Current application/function support tables (If the Information Resource Catalog discussed in Chapter 6 has been completed at this point)
2. Introduction to the business model
   - What it is
   - Why it is important
   - How it was determined
   - How to interpret the reports
3. Presentation materials
4. Feedback, comments, and suggestions on the business model

Tasks and Guidelines

Task 1   Analyze the enterprise survey information.   Summarize the most significant business opportunities and relevant findings. Focus on such problems or opportunities as data redundancy, duplicate functions, manual manipulation of data, and inefficient data flows. Be as quantitative as possible given the supporting data.

Task 2   Generate a complete set of reports on the business model from the toolset.   Use the toolset to generate the kinds of reports listed above. The planning team should review all reports before they go into a document or are made available for distribution. Large, voluminous reports are not generally distributed in printed form. Such reports may be made available for browsing in files on a network or mainframe, or distributed on floppy disks. Appendix D contains several examples of function definitions.

Task 3   Write an introduction to the business model. This introduction should use business terminology and stress the importance of the business model to the organization. Summarize the findings using tables and graphs to illustrate those that are most significant. See Appendix E for a sample business model report introduction.

Task 4   Develop a 15- to 20-minute presentation about the business model.   Figure 5.7 is a typical outline for the business model presentation. Include the findings and observations from the interviews and specific opportunities for substantially improving the business via information management.

Task 5   Deliver the business model presentation to the managers and supervisors of the enterprise.   Have a *well-respected* business unit manager (preferably a member of the planning team) make the presentation. When it comes to defining the business, it is the *business* person on the EAP team that will have the most credibility. A copy of the complete business model should be given to each manager and/or supervisor in the enterprise. The presentation may need to be delivered to each area of the business.

Task 6   Solicit comments and suggestions.   Use a cover letter from the head of the enterprise that acknowledges the EAP

OUTLINE FOR
THE BUSINESS MODEL PRESENTATION

I. Introduction
    A. Purpose of presentation
    B. Agenda
II. Overview of Business Modeling
    A. Phases of EAP and team members
    B. Purpose of business model
    C. Interpreting the business model
    D. Characteristics of a good business model
III. Business Functions
    A. Overview of major functional areas
    B. Detail of functional area definitions
IV. Significant Findings and Opportunities
V. Next Steps
    A. Review the business model and provide comments
    B. Information resource catalog
    C. Data architecture

Figure 5.7. Example of presentation outline for the business model.

team effort, reaffirms the importance of EAP and the business model, and requests comments and suggestions within one week. People throughout the enterprise should be asked to provide comments. If necessary for expediency, have all responses directed to the head of the enterprise. Of course, the enterprise executive will not be reading these responses, but having the comments and suggestions addressed to the highest executive will motivate a timely response.

Task 7 The planning team should review all feedback and change the business model as appropriate. Respond via memo to valuable feedback when it is politically expedient to do so. Distribute the changes to the business model.

DISCUSSION QUESTIONS

1. How many interviews would you expect to have?
2. Will there be sufficient time for the enterprise survey in your workplan? What alternatives would be considered for making the most of the time available?
3. Will your interviews be conducted by two-person teams?
4. What assumptions and actions can be taken to minimize geographical travel?
5. Will current issues or challenges of your enterprise influence the questions or items on the interview form? What particular items do you foresee?
6. What steps will you take to avoid the data entry bottleneck?
7. Do you have a contingency alternative if your primary toolset does not facilitate data entry, reporting, or making changes easily?

Current Systems and Technology Architecture

INTRODUCTION

The purpose of this phase of EAP is to document and define all of the systems and technology platforms in use within the enterprise. The major deliverable of this phase is called an Information Resource Catalog (IRC), but it is also called a Systems Encyclopedia or Systems Inventory. The IRC is at a high summary level and does not go into exhaustive detail for every system. It is *not* a data dictionary that documents files, data elements, and records, and it is *not* an equipment inventory of all items used for computing.

Benefits of an Information Resource Catalog (IRC)

There are many benefits from having an IRC. Perhaps the most important of these is that the IRC replaces intuitively perceived issues with substantiated, documented information about the current state of technology within the enterprise. The report of these findings can often provide justification for EAP. There are at least eight reasons why every enterprise should have an IRC:

1. The IRC provides a reference to all information resources. It contains a definition and description of all application systems

(including *major uses* of personal computers, locally defined applications, and important spreadsheets), data (inputs, outputs, major files/databases), and technology platforms (hardware, software, communications).

2. The IRC shows the distribution of information resources throughout the enterprise; where the applications and technology physically exist. One company that had grown through mergers and acquisitions discovered upon compiling their IRC, that there was a data center that corporate I.S. was not aware existed.

3. The IRC can be used as an information locator for management throughout the enterprise. For example, if the sales manager wants to compare revenues for the past five winter seasons in the Midwest, the IRC could locate the system or files that would provide that information. Potentially, the IRC could go further and initiate the retrieval of the requested information.

4. The IRC can be used to orient new personnel to the I.S. department. Illustrations that show the "big picture" of how systems fit together will be enlightening for nearly everyone in I.S.

5. The IRC is used by the EAP team as a baseline for long-range planning. It defines what is currently in place, whereas the architectures define a vision for the future. The IRC will highlight critical opportunities for improvement that should be considered by the EAP team. The kinds of opportunities that can be determined by an IRC include the following:

   - More applications than expected found to be supporting the enterprise; expanding the definition of a system and the scope of the I.S. organization.
   - The approximate total cost of information management, both internal to I.S. and external throughout the enterprise.
   - The over- or underutilization of technology platforms.
   - The degree to which data is integrated and shared by applications.
   - Measure of the extent of data redundancy, data accuracy, and data consistency throughout the enterprise.

- Measure of the extent of application redundancy—applications performing essentially the same function.
- The use of and reliance on obsolete technology, and the insignificant and inefficient use of new technologies.

6. Budgeting and cost control decisions can be directly linked with the IRC. For instance, those organizations that have a charge-back system can link budgeting decisions to the IRC and show expenditure patterns.
7. The IRC is a quick success at reasonable cost. A good IRC can be developed for most enterprises by one or two people in approximately 12 weeks. When an IRC is complete and accurate, it can establish the credibility for leading an EAP project, especially when the IRC is the first deliverable of EAP.
8. The IRC represents an internal use of documentation tools; that is, I.S. personnel can use CASE and database products for their own use and not only as tools for generating systems for users.

The IRC is often a project separate from EAP that can be conducted concurrently with other EAP phases, or it can begin prior to Planning Initiation. Regardless of when the IRC is initiated, it is far better to complete the IRC *before* beginning the architectural phases of EAP so that this current information is available to the team for the impact assessment. As primarily an internal I.S. activity, this phase may be assigned to people other than EAP team members. Assigning the IRC to non-EAP team members will enable the IRC to be compiled concurrently with EAP.

Steps for Building the IRC

There are eight steps for building an IRC:

1. Determine the scope, objectives, and IRC workplan
2. Prepare for data collection
3. Collect the IRC data
4. Enter the data
5. Validate and review the draft of the IRC
6. Draw schematics

7. Distribute the IRC

8. Administer and maintain the IRC

STEP 1—DETERMINE THE SCOPE, OBJECTIVES, AND IRC WORKPLAN

Purpose

The purpose of this step is to determine the scope and objectives of the IRC and to develop a workplan and schedule for the IRC when it is managed as a project separate from EAP.

Deliverables

1. Scope and objectives of the IRC

2. IRC workplan

3. Preliminary presentation

Tasks and Guidelines

Task 1   Determine the objectives.   Clearly define the objectives for the IRC. Some of the common uses and benefits of an IRC have been explained above. The important issues and opportunities to be examined should be listed.

Task 2   Determine the scope.   Establish the criteria for identifying which applications to include in the IRC and what information about those systems will be collected. Applications may include the following:

- mainframe systems
- application software packages
- departmental systems
- personal computer-based application software
- systems developed and/or maintained by the I.S. department
- major *uses* of spreadsheets and databases on personal computers

Task 3   Select the toolset for the IRC.   The IRC is typically made available throughout the I.S. community and possibly beyond. The IRC database and reporting facilities may be part of the EAP toolset, or it may be a separate set of products. Of the ten kinds of reports produced by EAP (see Chapter 3, Figure 3.5), the only kind of report not produced in this phase is the entity-relationship diagram.

The IRC toolset should be prepared to produce all of the reports in the subsequent steps. This means that the products should be installed and available, internal data models implemented, data entry and reporting procedures prepared, and screens and reports programmed. The products used for data entry and initially compiling the IRC may be different from those used to distribute and maintain it. For example, the IRC may be initially compiled on a personal computer, and when completed, uploaded to a mainframe.

Task 4   Prepare an IRC workplan.   Regardless of whether the IRC is a phase of EAP, a subproject, or a separate project, it must still be properly planned and managed. The steps and tasks of this effort to document the current state of technology and applications for the enterprise should be assigned to participants, a leader should be appointed and assigned responsibility for the IRC, and time and resources committed.

Task 5   Deliver a presentation to prepare for the IRC.   A presentation should be made to all levels of I.S. management. The presentation should explain the purpose and benefits of the IRC, the procedures for collecting the data, and the need for cooperation and support to complete the process on time.

STEP 2—PREPARE FOR DATA COLLECTION

Purpose

The purpose of this step is to determine the kinds of data to be compiled in the IRC and to design forms for collecting that data.

Deliverables

1. Data collection form(s) for applications and major files
2. Instructions for completing the form(s)
3. Technology platforms identified

Tasks and Guidelines

Task 1 Determine the data to be compiled about applications. There is a great deal of information that may be compiled in an IRC. Decide which data will be most useful and worthwhile to collect. The example in Figure 6.1 illustrates the data collected about applications for one company. Data items usually compiled for applications that are shown in this figure include the following:

- A short name (acronyms or abbreviations) and the long name (official name) assigned to systems.
- The project manager or person responsible for maintaining that application, along with the phone number.
- The owner or business department responsible for the requirements and functions of the application.
- A plain language definition of this application and what it does. The definition is intended to be read by people throughout the organization. However, it does not describe "how" the application works.
- The status of the system, such as operational, planned, or obsolete. The status notes include changes scheduled for the coming year.
- Long-range issues are changes that may occur in the future, but are not definite.
- Organization units identified in the business model may be linked to the application.
- The business functions supported may also be listed.
- Maintenance or other direct budget costs to the application, if known, may be given.
- The number of people in I.S. are assigned to maintain this application.

Page 2 of this example documents the more technical aspects.

- Whether the application is primarily batch, online, or both.
- The frequency of running the system, such as daily, weekly, or monthly.
- The time within the frequency when the application runs.

APPLICATIONS SYSTEM DESCRIPTION

Short System Name: DAILY EDIT   System Group: FEDS

Long System Name: EDIT PREMIUMS   No. 132

Project Manager: Jeff Broeker   Ext. 5387   ADD Division Head: Thacker

User Department: Stat Services

User Contact (s): Shelley Greer

Description:

> This system is the data entry for all manually written policies. Premium transactions are keyed into the computer at the branches. Data is batch-transmitted to the central data center where records are verified, formatted, edited, and distributed. Edit rejects are returned to the source. Minor errors cause records to be suspended and turnaround documents transmitted to the source for correction. Reconciliation reports are created for transmission, and output of valid data sent to month-end and various billing systems. The basic purpose of this system is to capture premium data at the transaction level (not policy level) to be used by most of our reporting systems.

Status: OPERATIONAL

> System developed in 1978. Interfaces for computer-assisted coding, XXX, PRISM, Direct Bill added in the interim. XXX is a company that creates a tape, mails it to us, and is included in Friday's processing. PRISM is the Canadian version of the system.

Long-range Issues:

> Front end systems are being designed to replace Edit Premiums-processing at some point in the future. Until then, the system is maintained in ongoing mode, and commercial line systems will be feeding the (EDIT) XYZ system.

Top-level Organization: ACTUARIAL

Major Business Functions Supported: PREMIUM ENTRY (POLICY WRITING)

----------------------------------- BUDGET CONTRACTS -----------------------------------

1986	1987
Amount: 1,057,565.39	Amount: 1,423,585.00
Numbers: A0440/51 A0440/5G A0440/6C	Numbers: A0440/51
Comments: And also A0440/83	Comments: Combined 1986 crtcts & /53 covers 3 sys

Number of People Supporting This System: 6

Figure 6.1.   Application system description.

Batch or On-line: BATCH DAILY

When Run: 8 PM–9 PM

Equipment Used: System 36 entry at branch, Mainframe, DASD, Tapes for
                       backups, 3800 printer, COM

Networks Used: RJE IN/OUT

Preceding Systems: RJE SPLIT

Succeeding Systems: Month-End Premiums, Billing, Comm'l Direct Bill, Assigned
Risk Direct Bill

Additional Notes:

   There is no editing of the policy number. The billing systems reconcile the
   EDIT PREMIUM transactions against client accounts and policy billing. Fifteen
   percent of Personal lines are written manually. Most commercial lines are
   manual presently.

   The above information was originally written on MM/DD/YY and last updated
   on MM/DD/YY, and was written by Timothy Michael.

Supplemental Material Submitted? (Yes or No): Y

Figure 6.1. *Continued*

- The equipment, hardware, or physical technology platforms
  used.
- The network(s) or communication platforms used.
- The software platforms used.
- Preceding systems are those systems that must execute be-
  fore this application.
- Succeeding systems are those systems that can only be ex-
  ecuted after this applications has been run.
- Additional notes are for miscellaneous material relevant to
  this application.
- Who provided this information, when they provided it, and
  the most recent update.
- Finally, a note whether supplemental material or documen-
  tation was collected.

Other items not shown in Figure 6.1 that can also be documented about applications include opportunities for improvement, the year implemented and latest revision, the existence
and currency of documentation, and business location(s).

Task 2 Determine data to collect about the **major** *inputs, outputs, files, and databases of an application.* The word "major" means there is a great degree of summarization. Large systems can have hundreds of physical files, inputs and outputs—far too many to document each and every one in an IRC. Therefore, summarize or categorize the kinds of data that come in, that go out, and the data that is stored internally to the application. An application may produce 100 reports, but there may be only two kinds of significant outputs, each having 50 different varieties. Figure 6.2 includes two examples, the first an input to the edit premiums application, the second an internal file or database. Some of the data collected includes the following:

- Whether this is an input, output, file, or database.
- A short or common name and a long name for the major I/O of this application.
- Where the input comes from, or where an output goes to (files and databases are internal or are shared by other applications).
- The physical location from where the input comes or to where the output goes.
- The physical medium or technology platform of the input, output, file, or database.
- A brief definition in plain language that describes what this is and the purpose for which it is used.
- Who originally provided this information, when they provided it, and the most recent update.

Task 3 Identify technology platforms. Define a hierarchical decomposition of the kinds of technology platforms. Figure 6.3 is an example of the technology platforms used by one enterprise. The numbers in parentheses are for internal EAP reference and have no other meaning. This report may be produced by the toolset, and, being in this format, it can be used for relating an application to the technology platforms. Having an extensible and flexible toolset can facilitate the IRC phase of EAP.

Task 4 Create forms for data collection. After determining the data to be compiled in the IRC, design forms that will aid in gathering the data. Examples of forms can be found in the books by Burke and Horton[1] and Marilyn Parker.[2]

MAJOR INPUT/OUTPUT DESCRIPTIONS

<--- INPUT --->

For Application: EDIT PREMIUMS

Short I/O Name: CAC

Long I/O Name: COMPUTER-ASSISTED CODING

Input From/Output To: RJE SPLIT

Location (of above): DOMESTIC BRANCHES

I/O Medium: DASD, SEQ. RJE SPLIT

Description: Computer-assisted coding of Commercial Auto, GL (General Liability), and Fire batched input. CAC operates on the System 36 and edits premium transactions locally. The mainframe EDIT system re-edits these transactions with 99 percent usually passing. Program changes (new codes for example) take six weeks to make and get them out to the System 36 files. In the meantime, branches will use the Edit System for entry instead of CAC.

The above information originally written MM/DD/YY and last changed on MM/DD/YY

--> FILE/DATABASE <--

Short I/O Name: SUSPENSE

Long I/O Name: EDIT PREMIUM SUSPENSE FILE

Input From/Output To: INTERNAL

Location (of above):

I/O Medium: DASD/SEQUENTIAL

Description: Recycling sequential file maintaining transactions awaiting matching corrections from branches. Bimonthly, the branches get a full listing of transactions awaiting correction.

The above information originally written MM/DD/YY and last changed on MM/DD/YY

Figure 6.2. Major input/output descriptions.

TECHNOLOGY PLATFORMS

Hardware (1)

Mainframe (4)
- ☐ Amdahl (IBM equivalent) (10)

Minicomputers (5)
- ☐ DEC 11 series (11)
- ☐ Foxboro (12)
- ☐ DEC/VAX (13)
- ☐ System 36 (82)

Microcomputers (PCs) (6)
- ☐ IBM/PC, XT, AT, & Compatible (7)
- ☐ EPSON equity series (8)
- ☐ IBM PS2 (9)
- ☐ Compaq, Zenith, & others (80)
- ☐ Hewlett Packard (84)

Input Devices (14)
- ☐ Terminals (15)
- ☐ Diskette Reader (16)
- ☐ Sensors (17)
- ☐ Mouse (18)
- ☐ Digitizing Table (19)

Output & Graphics Display (20)
- ☐ Line Printer (21)
- ☐ Dot Matrix Printer (22)
- ☐ Laser Printer (23)

Plotters
- ☐ Hewlett Packard (27)
- ☐ Versatec (28)
- ☐ Calcomp (29)
- ☐ Graphics Display (26)

Storage Media (30)
- ☐ Magnetic Tape (31)
- ☐ Fixed Disk (32)
- ☐ Removeable Disk (33)
- ☐ Floppy Disk (34)
- ☐ Winchester Disk (35)
- ☐ Compact Disk (91)

Software (2)

Operating Systems (36)
- ☐ VM/CMS (37)
- ☐ CICS (38)
- ☐ MVS/TSO (39)
- ☐ MS/DOS (40)
- ☐ RSX (DEC) (41)
- ☐ UNIX (42)
- ☐ VMS 5.0 (96)

DBMS—Database Mngmnt Sys (46)
- ☐ ADABAS DBMS (47)
- ☐ TOTAL DBMS (48)
- ☐ dBase II/III (49)
- ☐ R:Base (50)

Language (51)
- ☐ COBOL (52)
- ☐ Assembler (53)
- ☐ FORTRAN (54)
- ☐ Natural-report Mode (55)
- ☐ Natural-structured Mode (56)
- ☐ REXX (57)
- ☐ VM Exec (58)
- ☐ BASIC (59)
- ☐ 'C' Language (60)
- ☐ FORTH (61)
- ☐ DCL—Digital Cmd Lang. (92)

Spreadsheet (62)
- ☐ Lotus 1-2-3 (63)
- ☐ E.S.S. (64)
- ☐ QUATTRO (65)
- ☐ Surfer (81)

Other Software (85)
- ☐ Autocad (87)
- ☐ Micro Miner (88)
- ☐ PC-XPLOR (89)
- ☐ Other Software (90)
- ☐ IGDS—Interactive Graphics (95)

Figure 6.3. Technology platforms.

Communications (3)

Networks
☐ LAN—Local Area Network (67)
☐ Line-to Mainframe (68)
☐ LAN with Gateway to mf (69)
☐ DATAPAC (83)
☐ DECNET (93)
☐ XNS—VAX (94)
Signal Devices (70)
☐ Modem (71)

☐ Concentrators (72)
☐ IRMA (73)
Virtual Devices (74)
☐ VM Reader (75)
☐ VM Punch (76)
☐ VM Disk Linking (77)
☐ VM Sharepack (78)
Security (43)
☐ ACF2 (44)
☐ Natural2 (45)
☐ CICS Security (79)

Figure 6.3.   *Continued*

Task 5   Prepare detailed instructions for using these forms, with samples of completed forms.   Be sure to state all expectations in the instructions. Provide the criteria to determine what is an application and what is not. Include examples of completed forms to provide sample answers for reference. Samples should be provided for large (mainframe), medium (departmental), and small (personal) applications. Instructions should include this information:

• The kinds of responses desired.
• A date by which the form should be returned.
• A contact person in case there are questions about any item on the form.
• How the forms will be collected—either by sending them to the IRC leader, or if time permits, to be picked up in person and reviewed.

STEP 3—DATA COLLECTION

Purpose

In this step, the forms for collecting the information for the IRC will be distributed and collected. The applications will be related to the functions supported as defined in the business model. The applications will also be related to the technology platforms defined in the previous step.

Deliverables

1. Completed forms for applications and major inputs and outputs
2. System documentation assessment (optional)
3. Applications are related to business functions
4. Applications are related to technology platforms

Tasks and Guidelines

Task 1   Distribute the blank forms.   Distribute the blank forms, instructions, and samples prepared in step 2 to anyone who may be responsible for an application. Typically, I.S. project managers and systems analysts are the best sources for information. If the IRC will include major uses of personal computers and applications outside I.S., distribute the forms to all people and locations that potentially have applications.

Task 2   Locate and/or obtain access to system documentation and file descriptions.   This may be a good opportunity to inventory and assess the quality of application documentation. If current documentation is lacking, then this can be cited in the IRC report.

Task 3   Relate current applications to business functions supported.   If the business model has been defined, relate the applications in the IRC to business functions defined at the lowest level of detail. It is best if the EAP team establishes this relationship rather than the person responsible for an application.

If information sources have been documented during the enterprise survey, be sure that the relationship of current applications to the business functions is consistent with the information source usage for the functions.

Task 4   Relate the applications to technology platforms. The technology platforms defined in the previous step should be related to the applications defined in the IRC. The relationship should be established at the lowest level of detail or specific technology platform. The person responsible for the application or completing the IRC forms should determine the technology platforms used. A form, such as the one shown in Figure 6.3, is a convenient and easy way to indicate each technology platform used by an application.

Task 5   Collect the completed forms.   There are two ways to collect the forms for the IRC. The best approach is to meet with each person contributing to the IRC and review the information on the forms together. This is the suggested approach because

- It ensures the forms are complete.
- It ensures the information and detail is appropriate and consistent.
- It ensures the information is legible and understandable.
- It may review the business functions supported.

The other approach is to have the completed forms sent back to the person or team responsible for the IRC. The primary advantage of this approach is that it consumes much less of the IRC project people's time. However, it increases the time for validation (step 5), and there may be a greater number of tardy forms returned after the date due. Forms and instructions may also be distributed using electronic mail.

If travel and busy schedules make it difficult to have meetings, the telephone or transmitting forms via fax can substitute for an in-person meeting. Also, if the majority of contributors to the IRC have access to personal computers, networks, or other online facilities, the IRC forms can be distributed and collected electronically using the toolset, substantially reducing the time for data entry (step 4).

STEP 4—DATA ENTRY

Purpose

The purpose of this step is to enter the information on the forms that have been collected into the toolset. The tasks and guidelines for managing this step are much the same as the data entry for the enterprise survey (step 4 of Chapter 5). If the same toolset and personnel are used for the IRC information, take advantage of the kinds of streamlined processes established for the enterprise survey.

Deliverable

1. Forms entered into the toolset
2. Application to business function relationships entered

Tasks and Guidelines

Task 1   Make a copy of each form before giving them to data entry people and store the copy in a safe location. Assemble the copies of the forms into a binder or folder. Keep them in the planning area (war room). It is important to have a backup copy of all completed forms in case any originals are misplaced.

Task 2   Pass the forms to the clerical support group for entry into the toolset.   Regardless of whether the IRC is a phase of EAP or a separate project, one person should have the responsibility of verifying that all forms are legible, understandable, complete, and consistent *before* they are passed to the data entry personnel.

Task 3   Enter the data on the forms into the toolset.   Prepare screens, menus, and procedures for streamlining the data entry and for generating reports from the toolset.

STEP 5—VALIDATE IRC INFORMATION AND PRODUCE A DRAFT OF THE IRC

Purpose

The integrity of the information about the current applications and technology platforms should be verified before widely disseminating it. Each contributor to the IRC should have the opportunity to check his information. The findings and opportunities should be summarized and presented in an IRC report.

Deliverables

1. Verified IRC database (inconsistencies resolved)
2. Complete set of draft IRC reports
   - Full description reports
   - Summary, index, and cross-reference reports
   - Relationship reports and tables (matrices)
         Current applications to business functions
         Current applications to technology platforms
3. IRC is introduced.
   - What it is
   - Why it is important
   - How it was determined
   - How to interpret the reports
4. Observations and findings prepared

Tasks and Guidelines

Task 1   Produce reports to verify that the data was en-
tered correctly and that the IRC database is complete and
consistent.   There are several kinds of reports that should be
generated:

- Full description reports (see Figures 6.1, 6.2)
- Index report (Figure 6.4)
- Input/output files report (Figure 6.5)
- Technology platform matrix (Figure 6.6)

Task 2   Send to each person who completed a form a copy
of the data they provided.   This is an important task because
it will prevent misunderstandings of the information gathered
and will ensure that errors are promptly corrected.

Task 3   Prepare observations and findings, summarize
significant opportunities.   Analyze the data collected for the
IRC to determine significant opportunities for improvement.
Some of the kinds of opportunities were listed in the first section
of this chapter.

MM/DD/YY   APPLICATION INDEX BY SYSTEM GROUP

Group	No.	Short Name	Full Name

Security

	48	SECPRG	Hazardous Vehicle Registration
	111	CCINFO	Hazardous Materials Info Retrieval
	132	SMMATRQN	Create Material Requisitions
	149	SMLTCNL	Process Control
	151	SMTRBOOK	Books

Supplies Management

	1	EMSALES	Employee Sales
	5	VENDINFO	Vendor Information
	11	WHRECEIV	Receiving
	12	WHISSUES	Warehouse Issues
	17	PURNONST	Purchasing Non-stock
	18	QUOTEMGT	Price Quotation Management
	20	PURSTOCK	Purchasing Stock
	27	SUPPCOST	Supplies Costing (Stock and Non-stock)
	30	INVCNTRL	Inventory Control
	74	TRANSCNT	Collect and Record Transaction Counts
	75	VNANOTES	Monitor Vendor Related Problems
	76	CREDISSU	Credit Issue Monitoring
	77	INDICE	Monthly Progress Application
	78	BUYACT	Buyer Activity Status
	79	ARITMISS	Monitor Issues on ARP and ARW
	120	STKREV	Supplies & Obsolete Stock Review
	121	ISSUE	Monitor Warehouse Issue Systems
	170	SYNCDBAS	Keep Supplies Management Databases Synchronized

Traffic and Transportation

	2	FREIGHT	Freight Reconciliation
	107	TRACESHP	Tracing Incoming Shipments
	108	INVOIC	Invoice Preparation
	109	TTPRDSHP	Product Shipment Application
	110	TTCUSTOM	Monthly Customs Summary

Figure 6.4.   Sample index report (partial listing).

MM/DD/YY

RACLNJVS (193)
Name: EDITED JOURNAL VOUCHERS
DSName:XXX.P.RA.CLN.TRANS
Media: S   Type: DISK
Description: These are month-end journal vouchers (J.V.s) that
have passed the edits. They are recycled as input
along with other J.V.s, and the file is recreated until it
contains all the month-end J.V.s and they are all
error-free.

RACSTVAR (194)
Name: COST VARIANCE LIMITS
DSName:XXX.P.RA.BUDG.ACT.LIMITS
Media: S   Type: DISK
Description: This is a table of cost centers and acceptable
variances between budgeted dollars and actual costs.
This table is used to print the selected cost variance
report.

CAPSUTBL (195)
Name: ANNUAL PLAN PREFIX TABLE
DSName:XXX.P.RA.ANNUAL.PLAN.PREF
Media: S   Type: DISK
Description: This is a list of cost centers that will be reported on
the cost statements that print the actual costs
compared to the budgeted annual plan run for the
surface.

DCSVCREC (196)
Name: SERVICE PURCHASE ORDER RECEIPTS
DSName:XXX.P.RA.DLY.RCPT.RECS
Media: S   Type: DISK
Description: These are the service receipts automatically
generated by the non-stock system whenever a
purchase order is created to cover services, not
actual supplies.

MDCMPERR (197)
Name: MDCOST DATA COMPRESSION ERRORS
DSName: XX.P.MIDCOST.F140.LOAD.ERRORS
Media: S   Type: DISK
Description: This file is usually empty but may contain errors from
the ADABASE compression utility when it is
compressing the sequential file of cost data prior to
being loaded into MDCOST.

Figure 6.5. Sample input/output files report (partial listing).

Figure 6.6. Sample technology platform matrix (partial listing).

Application	Application Software	Purchased Software
86 "Forms"	OGL,MacDraw,CricketDraw,ADRS	
85 "Inventor"	ADRS	
90 A/P	COBOL,MARKIV,VIDEO370	
172 Accident Reporting	LOTUS	
112 Accounting Reporting	ADRS	
182 Administrative Sys	ADRS,LOTUS	CALMA
89 AM		INTERGRAPH
127 AM/FM	COBOL	
139 Applicance Control	ADRS	
36 Accounts Rec.	COBOL, VIDEO370	
79 Aviation Budgeting	LOTUS	
171 BDRS	ADRS	
133 BUD	LOTUS	
142 Budget Reporting	LOTUS	
115 Budget Reports	ADRS,APL	
173 Business Charting		FLOWCHARTING II
15 C.S.		
54 C.S. Reporting	DC-COBOL,CICS,GA,IDMS,ADSO	
43 C.S. Reporting Sys	ADRS	
174 CAA1	COBOL	
47 Capital Budget	LOTUS	
109 Capital Budgeting	ADRS,LOTUS	
135 Capital Budgets	ADRS	
175 Capital Budgets Rep		

The matrix records, for each application, check-marks (X) under the grouped hardware columns (Host, Mini, Micro), Type of Process, Storage, Output, Input, Network, Operating System, and Security.

159

Use graphics to summarize the findings and observations. For example, Figure 6.7 shows that the majority of current applications use only 0–4 files, which indicates that most applications are not complicated with respect to the usage of data. Figure 6.8 shows that 85 percent of the data files are used by only one application. Is data being shared in this organization? Definitely not. In a shared data environment, there would be a gradual decline of the bars on this graph.

If budget information about information systems and technology has been collected, a report can be generated showing the distribution of expenditures. For organizations that require a formal assessment or audit of their I.S. function, the book by Dickson and Wetherbe[3] has a section on that subject.

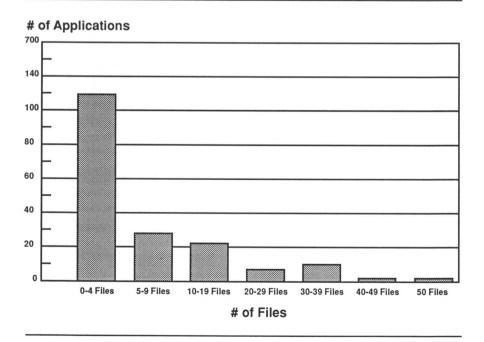

Figure 6.7. Application complexity by number of files used.

# of files

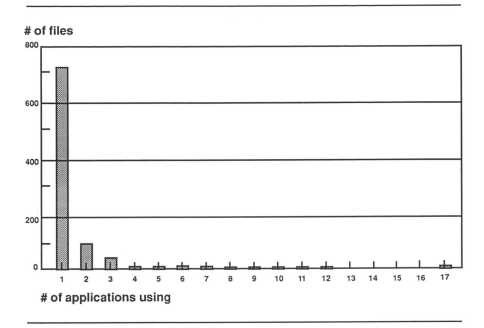

# of applications using

Figure 6.8.   Data file sharing/file usage by number of applications.

Task 4   Prepare a document for the IRC.   Prepare a document in which the IRC is described and explained. Highlight significant findings, problems, or opportunities. Use tables and graphs, such as in Figures 6.8 and 6.9, to support the findings. A suggested outline for the IRC document is in Figure 6.9.

STEP 6—DRAW SCHEMATICS

Purpose

Schematics are application-level diagrams that graphically depict the "flow" of each system's inputs, outputs, and files. Schematics provide an overview of the IRC showing how the applications of the enterprise interconnect. This is the role of dataflow diagram reports, one of the ten kinds of reports identified when selecting a toolset for EAP (step 4 of Chapter 3). If the

---

OUTLINE FOR
INFORMATION RESOURCE CATALOG DOCUMENT

I. Introduction to the IRC
    A. Purpose
    B. Scope
    C. Methodology
    D. Contributors
    E. Summary of findings
    F. Maintenance of the IRC
    G. Description of Available Reports

II. Findings and Observations
    A. Data redundancy and integrity
    B. Technology utilization, redundancy, obsolescence
    C. Data integration and sharing
    D. Documentation

III. Business Function Support
    A. Extent of support
    B. Functions unsupported
    C. Application redundancy

IV. Conclusion
    A. Opportunities
    B. Recommendations
    C. Next steps in EAP

Figure 6.9. Sample IRC document outline.

time and resources for compiling the IRC are limited, this step may be postponed.

Deliverable

1. Application schematics

Tasks and Guidelines

Task 1   Draw schematics for applications that show the inputs, outputs, files or databases, and the source of inputs and destination of outputs.   The schematics can facilitate understanding the current applications portfolio and will complement the other IRC reports. Artistic creativity is an important skill for drawing schematics. Place as many applications as possible in each diagram. The diagrams should not look cluttered or have lines that cross.

For the Edit Premium application in Figure 6.2, there were nine inputs, outputs, and files, which are shown on the schematic in Figure 6-10. Dots at the end of inputs or outputs signify other applications.

Dataflow diagrams are usually used to show intricate detail of process and data flows. Schematic is a better term to use because these diagrams are at a high level of summarization, showing how applications are related, and avoids confusion with typical dataflow diagrams.

Task 2   Verify the interapplication consistency of the IRC.
Verify the sources and destinations of inputs and outputs between applications. If Application X has an output to Application Y, then Application Y should have a matching input from Application X.

STEP 7—DISTRIBUTE THE IRC

Purpose

After the IRC data has been verified, the draft document edited, and the schematics drawn and reviewed, the IRC should be distributed or made available throughout the enterprise.

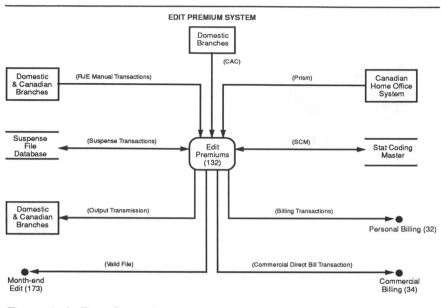

Figure 6.10. Data-flow schematic of an application.

Figure 6.10. Dataflow schematic of an application.

Deliverable

1. IRC document
2. IRC presentation
3. Comments and suggestions on the IRC

Tasks and Guidelines

Task 1   Distribute the complete IRC (or make it accessible) throughout I.S. and to the enterprise.   The IRC can be distributed in alternative mediums including paper (reports, notebooks), mainframe or network files for browsing, floppy disk files (with utilities), or as database files to those who have access to or can use the toolset. Providing the IRC in a database form, either on a mainframe or personal computer, will allow sophisticated query and reporting facilities to be used for accessing the IRC.

Task 2   Prepare and deliver presentations summarizing the findings and opportunities presented in the report. IRC presentations are commonly delivered within the I.S. organization and may also be made outside of I.S. to executive committees or management meetings. Ask for comments about the IRC information and suggestions for improving it. The presentation should focus on the uses and benefits of the IRC to the enterprise, findings and opportunities, and maintenance procedures to keep the IRC up to date.

STEP 8—ADMINISTER AND MAINTAIN THE IRC

Purpose

To be widely used as a reference, the IRC information must be kept reasonably current. In this step, procedures are developed to keep the IRC up to date. Generally, it is the responsibility of each contributor to update the information about their applications.

Deliverable

1. Responsibilities assigned for maintaining the IRC
2. Procedures for maintaining the IRC

Tasks and Guidelines

Task 1   Assign responsibilities for maintaining the IRC. Two responsibilities should be assigned. First, each contributor to the IRC should be required to update the information about their applications periodically. Second, the responsibility for administering the IRC should be assigned to a position in the I.S. organization. Specifically, the administration responsibilities are to

- provide IRC information to those who request it,
- ensure that updates are performed on a timely basis,
- create procedures and mechanisms to access and update the IRC,
- correct errors or inconsistencies in IRC data,

- update technology data and business model relationships, and
- maintain the list of contributors.

Task 2   Develop policies and procedures for maintaining the IRC.   Two approaches can be used to update the IRC. One is to have contributors send their updates periodically (i.e., quarterly, semiannually, or annually) to the IRC administrator who will effect the changes and disseminate them. The second approach is to provide direct access to the IRC database so that contributors can make changes themselves. Those without direct access can resort to the first approach.

In environments where the IRC is widely accessible, the IRC administrator should create automated mechanisms for ensuring the IRC information is updated. If, for example, the policy is to update the IRC semiannually, then every six months the IRC administrator can

- check that each contributor accessed their information and either updated it or stated that no change was needed,
- issue a series of memos via print or electronic mail to contributors who have not updated their information, and/or
- widely disseminate a summary of changes, and send details of changes to the business functions and organization units affected.

DISCUSSION QUESTIONS

1. Will user-developed systems be included in your IRC?
2. How many systems do you expect to have?
3. What are the "burning" issues that the IRC will address?
4. What will be the best way to obtain the IRC data?
5. How will the IRC be distributed, and who will (should) be given access to it?
6. How will you keep your IRC up to date?
7. How much time and effort are required to produce the IRC?
8. Who must "approve" the resources for creating your IRC? When do you expect to obtain the commitment?
9. Will the IRC be a phase of EAP or a separate project?

10. What toolset will be used for your IRC (data collection and distribution/access)?

REFERENCES

[1]Burk, Cornelius F., and Forest Horton. *INFOMAP: A Complete Guide to Discovering Corporate Information Resources*, Prentice-Hall, Englewood Hills, NJ, 1988.

[2]Parker, Marilyn M., Trainer, H.E., and Benson, Robert J., *Information Strategy and Economics*, Prentice-Hall, Englewood Cliffs, NJ, 1988.

[3]Dickson, Gary, and James Wetherbe. *The Management of Information Systems*, McGraw-Hill, New York, 1985, pages 177–185.

7

Data Architecture

INTRODUCTION

The *data architecture* identifies and defines the major kinds of data that support the business functions defined in the business model. The data architecture is one of the three enterprisewide architectures identified in the Zachman Framework for information system architectures (Figure 1.6). It is the first of the three architectures to be defined because quality data is the basic product of the I.S. function. Data is the first column of the Zachman Framework, and the enterprise data architecture corresponds to the top two rows of that column. The data architecture definitions become the standards to be subsequently used for the systems design phases commonly referred to as logical database design (row 3), physical database design (row 4) and database creation (row 5).

The data architecture consists of *data entities*, each of which have *attributes* and *relationships* with other data entities. Definitions for these terms follow, but a reader unfamiliar with these terms will gain a better understanding by reading further.

ENTITY: Any person, place, concept, thing, or event that has meaning (information) in the context of the business, and about which data may be stored.

ATTRIBUTE: A named characteristic of an entity that further describes what that entity is.

RELATIONSHIP or RELATIONSHIP ATTRIBUTE: An attribute whose value is that of another entity (identifier), which serves to further define the business context of the entity (referred to as foreign key in logical relational database design).

There are other terms that have been used for data architecture and data entity. Some of these are given in Figure 7.1. Readers may be familiar with the three-schema architecture proposed by a national standards committee.[1] The data architecture corresponds to the conceptual schema of that framework.

Four Steps to Data Architecture Phase

The books and articles listed in section 3 of the bibliography describe different methods, techniques, and diagramming symbols for conceptual data modeling. Some of these approaches, such as those by Nijssen,[2] Ross,[3] and Thompson,[4] are very thorough and result in precisely defined, detailed conceptual models. Though detailed conceptual models will serve well as blueprints for the subsequent design of databases, the price of such detail is time and effort—more than is usually available for one phase of EAP. A data architecture only requires *sufficient detail for planning purposes.* After the implementation plans have been accepted,

EAP TERM	OTHER TERMS
Entity	data entity, object, data object, conceptual data entity, entity type
Data Architecture	conceptual data model, conceptual schema, conceptual database design, enterprise data model, global data model, object definition, logical data model, information model

Figure 7.1. Other terms for data architecture and data entity.

there will be time to add detail and semantic constructs to the conceptual data architecture.

This chapter presents a simplified, streamlined approach to conceptual data modeling. First presented in 1982,[5] this approach is neither rigorous nor unique. But it is sufficient for planning purposes, and business participants with no prior systems training can contribute quickly.

There are four steps for the Data Architecture Phase:

1. List candidate data entities.
2. Define the entities, attributes, and relationships.
3. Relate the entities to the business functions.
4. Distribute the data architecture.

The time required for this phase is about 15 percent of the EAP project. Thus, for an EAP project of an expected duration of 39 weeks (nine months), the Data Architecture Phase should be about six weeks. Within this phase, the relative percentage of effort for each step is

$$
\begin{array}{ll}
\text{Step 1} = & 10 \text{ percent} \\
\text{Step 2} = & 60 \text{ percent} \\
\text{Step 3} = & 20 \text{ percent} \\
\text{Step 4} = & \underline{10 \text{ percent}} \\
& 100 \text{ percent}
\end{array}
$$

STEP 1—LIST CANDIDATE DATA ENTITIES FOR DEFINITION

Purpose

The purpose of this step is to identify all potential entities of data needed to support the business. This step does not take much time, usually only a few days.

Deliverable

1. List of the names of candidate entities. The list may include a preliminary definition, synonym designation, an indication

of the functions that use the data, and the team member who proposed the entity name.

Tasks and Guidelines

Task 1   Divide the business model among team members.
To formulate the list of entities, the following documentation should be completed and available for the EAP team: function definitions from the business model, information source forms, information source samples (reports, forms, memos), interview notes, existing systems and files descriptions, previous data architectures or database designs of the organization, and conceptual data models that can be obtained from other companies.

Divide this material among EAP team members along functional lines. That is, one team member may have the Manufacture Products function, another Manage Human Resources, and so on.

Task 2   Each team member develops a list of entities (people, places, things, concepts, events) for definition.
Scan through the following to search for candidate entities:

- Function definitions
- Information source forms
- Samples of information sources
- Interview notes
- Existing systems and file descriptions
- Other data architectures or database designs

Recall that the name of a business function has two parts—a verb form that is an action and a noun that is the object of that action. These objects, or nouns, may be candidate entities. However, not all nouns are entities! List only likely candidates, those that the enterprise will probably store as data. Apply the following guidelines when creating a list of entities:

- Use the singular form of a noun, for example, *employee* rather than *employees*, *product* instead of *products*, *customer* instead of *customers*.

- Include relevant descriptive adjectives with the noun, for example, *domestic* customer, *back-ordered* parts, and *part-time* employee. These adjectives are often initial indications of entity subtypes.
- Note possible synonyms and preliminary definitions.
- Note the person or group who proposed each entity name and where the name came from, that is, its source.

Task 3 Combine the individual lists into one. Team members, the project librarian, or clerical assistants can enter the individual lists into a product of the toolset. The toolset can create the combined list and sort it by entity name. For this task, the toolset should allow duplicate names.

Review the entire list at a group meeting and remove *obvious* duplicates. The team members who proposed two similar entities on the list may be asked for their opinion as to whether the entities are indeed identical.

As a very rough estimate, the number of candidates to expect may be 50 percent of the number of business functions. For example, if the business model identifies 300 business functions, expect approximately 150 candidate business entities. Do not be concerned if the number is much higher than expected. The larger the business model and supporting documentation, the more terms (nouns) will have been used.

STEP 2—DEFINE THE DATA ENTITIES, ATTRIBUTES, AND RELATIONSHIPS

Purpose

The purpose of this step is to create a standard definition and description for each entity in the data architecture and to provide a graphical illustration of their interrelationships. The material below is not intended to provide complete instructions on the semantic subtleties of defining entities or conceptual data modeling. There are entire textbooks devoted to this subject. Rather, the focus is on managing this step to have good results in the time allotted. For this step, it is recommended to have an experienced data modeler as part of the team. If a member of the team does not have this expertise, arrange for external training and assistance for this step.

Deliverables

1. Entities defined and documented
2. Entity-Relationship (E-R) diagrams drawn

The components of an entity, attribute, and relationship are defined below with further explanation to follow in the examples. Components not marked with an asterisk are essential components that should be part of every definition. This step does not attempt to identify and define *every* attribute of a data entity— only those that further the understanding of the data entity and its meaning in the context of the business.

ENTITY	Person, place, thing, concept, or event.
Entity name:	An entity name represents the term being defined. For example, Employee, Sales Territory, Product Type, Promotion, or Shipment.
Alternate names:	Other standard, acceptable names for the entity, but not the preferred name. For example, if the preferred name for an entity is Employee, then alternate names might be Staff, Personnel, or Worker.
Identifier:	Every entity must have an identifier. An identifier is an attribute whose value can uniquely distinguish each individual occurrence or instance of the entity. For the entity Employee, the identifier might be Social Security Number, and a serial number is an identifier unique to each automobile. An identifier may be a combination of attributes. For example, Volume and

	Number together can identify one issue of a journal.
Definition:	A short, textual description of the data entity.
Is-a-kind-of entity: *	One entity might be "a kind of" another entity. For example, a Full-time Employee is a kind of Employee. In addition to having the same attributes of Employee, a Full-time Employee would have additional attributes.
	An "is-a-kind-of" entity is useful for differentiating between different kinds of similar entities. For example, a business function may involve a Part-time Employee, Contract Employee, or Temporary Employee with different data associated with each one. In database parlance, the is-a-kind-of entity (Employee) is called a "supertype" and the entity (Full-time Employee) is called a "subtype."

ATTRIBUTE	A characteristic that serves to define and describe the entity further.
Attribute name:	A name assigned to a characteristic. For example, attributes for the entity Employee might include Employee Name, Employee Home Address, Salary History, and Performance Reviews.
Definition:	A short, textual description of the attribute.
Value set: *	The range of values, domain, or kinds of values for the data represented by this attribute. An attribute is not the same as a data element in a logical database

	design and may, therefore, not have a simple value set.
Business rules: *	Rules or conditions that govern the value of the attribute.

RELATIONSHIP	An association between two entities that serves to further the definition and understanding of both entities.

Relationship name:	All relationships have names. A relationship name has a form of a verb phrase that describes the relationship between two entities. For example, an Employee "works in" an Organization Unit. The verb phrase "works in" is the relationship name.
Related entity name:	The second entity in the relationship. In the above example, Employee "works in" an Organization Unit. Organization Unit is the name of the related entity.
Cardinality:	Describes the number of entities involved in the relationship, expressed in terms of *zero, one, or many*. For example, in the relationship Employee "works in" Organization Unit, the cardinality might be expressed as one Employee works in one Organization Unit, with the reverse as one Organization Unit employs *many* Employees.
Definition & rules: *	A further explanation of the relationship and any business rules that might effect it. For example, a business rule might state that "At least one Employee *must* work for an Organization Unit."

Tasks and Guidelines

Task 1   Prepare for the entity definition.   Read books and articles about entity definition, conceptual and logical data modeling, and object-oriented design, such as Flavin,[6] Flemming and von Halle,[7] Coad and Yourdon,[8] and Shlaer and Mellor.[9] Again, this chapter focuses on managing this process rather than the technical intricacies of data modeling.

The EAP team should have at hand the business model and information resource catalog on which to base the definitions for entities. All definitions should be proposed in meetings of the *entire* EAP team. Entity definitions will be agreed upon by a *consensus* vote. Therefore, one of the first tasks is for the EAP team to decide what "consensus" will be. Unanimous agreement of entity definitions will be too difficult and time-consuming to obtain. Lengthy debates on the wording of definitions will prevent completing this phase on time. A "consensus" is a much more reasonable goal to achieve. For example, if the EAP team consists of eight people, decide how many of the eight votes will constitute a consensus. It might be five, or six for this example. Decide on a specific number of team members that will determine an agreement or approval. When a consensus has been reached, then the discussion will move on to another definition.

The essential skills for this step are creativity, wisdom, ingenuity, and a command of the language. Have a dictionary and thesaurus handy in the meeting room in addition to any company and industry standard references.

Task 2   Define the entities on the candidate list.   If you have another data architecture that is accepted in some parts of the business, then begin by modifying the definitions of complicated fundamental entities (such as Customer, Product, Supplier, Material, Equipment, Employee, Account) to be agreeable from the perspective of all business functions. If there are no prior definitions, data models, or standards, then define the easiest entities first—those that are the most obvious, have the fewest relationships, or are least controversial.

As you select entities, fill in the components of a data entity described at the beginning of this step. Often it will be easier to define several related entities concurrently. For example, if the team selects the entity Employee, it may be easier to define that entity concurrently with Organization Unit, Position, Skills, and Benefits, because a clear understanding of Employee may depend on understanding those other entities, and the definition of Position and Organization Unit may influence the definition of Employee.

As the definitions are proposed, write them on a whiteboard rather than flip-charts. There will be many changes during this process, and a whiteboard is easily erased. Be sure that the whiteboard has enough room for each entity being defined. When a consensus agreement is reached by the team, enter the definitions, attributes, and relationships into the toolset. Distribute the complete set of definitions to team members prior to each meeting.

A meeting should have one person designated as the discussion leader who is responsible for moderating the discussion and calling for a consensus when agreement seems at hand. The discussion leader should allow everyone to express his or her views and attempt to negotiate compromises when needed. When the discussion does not progress toward a consensus definition for the entity or set of entities, move on to the next one. In many cases, consensus will not be reached because a definition depends on another entity that has not been defined. The discussion leader needs to be aware of these situations and able to move on.

The discussion leader is usually someone with data modeling experience. However, as team members become familiar and competent with the data definition process, the role of the discussion leader may rotate or be assigned to other team members.

A data modeling expert should point out the ramifications of definition and relationship decisions during the meeting. Allow many-to-many relationships in the data architecture; these are not permitted in logical database designs but are acceptable in a data architecture because this is *not* a process to design databases, but to *define* data entities.

Every entity must have at least one attribute that is not the identifier. Without an attribute there is no data; and with no data, there is no entity. Attributes in a data architecture are not the same as attributes or data elements in a logical database design. In a data architecture, attributes often represent sets of data. For example, with the entity Employee, an attribute might be Physical Characteristics, meaning a person's height, weight, eye color, hair color, and so on. If there is a business need for data about the physical characteristics of an employee, then only the understanding that an employee has physical characteristics is important for planning purposes during this phase without going into detail about which characteristics there may be. During the design of a database, these physical characteristics would become a number of data elements and possibly a record or segment unto itself during physical database design.

Reports and forms identified as information sources during the enterprise survey are not usually entities in a data architecture. They often appear on the candidate entity list from the previous step because business functions use reports and forms, and people are accustomed to seeing their data in that fashion. Reports and forms often contain data from one or more fundamental entities.

One way to understand the difference between forms, reports, and entities is to realize that the physical media of data may change in the future. Paper may be all but eliminated as pocket-sized computers, voice and imaging systems, and other technological advances change the physical form of data and improve how business is conducted. For example, there may be many business functions that use a multipart Work Order Form, but it is the fundamental concept of "Work" that should be defined first, and then the stages of Work (events) can be defined. For example, "Work is Requested, Scheduled, and Performed." In a paperless environment, the physical multipart Work Order Form disappears, but data about Work exists.

Expect the initial consensus definition of an entity to be changed as this step proceeds. Indeed, an entity definition may change several times during this phase and beyond. Be certain that the EAP toolset can easily handle changes such as adding, removing, and updating entities, attributes, and relationships. One change may cause many others to be needed. Removing an entity means changing all other entities related to it. Avoid being slowed down by clerical duties, or having to halt or postpone meetings due to an inefficient toolset.

Work on the most difficult entity definitions in the morning. People are most alert in the morning and more capable of conceptual thinking. Also, the team members will have had some time to consider difficult definitions from the previous meeting and may be able to provide new insight leading to consensus.

The easiest way to identify most entities is to have an entity-name-number, such as Employee Number, Equipment Type Number, Customer Number, and so on. However, for many entities there may be no such enterprisewide identification or numbering scheme in current use. For those entities, a new identifier should be designated. New standard identifiers (keys) should be highlighted in the data architecture material. One way to distinguish a new identifier is to place an asterisk (*) before or after its name. Often, significant business changes are needed to accommodate new standard, enterprisewide identifiers.

An optional attribute, which is a characteristic that a particular instance of an entity may not have, should also be highlighted. Again, an asterisk could serve this purpose. A business rule may further explain the reason an attribute is optional.

Data modeling methods differ in their treatment of relationships. One method has an object distinct from an entity, called a relationship. A relationship associates *two or more* entities, and it may have attributes of its own. The entity-relationship method espoused by Chen[10] employs a relationship object that is drawn as a diamond-shaped box. The second method has an entity as the only object, and a relationship is a name given to an association of exactly two entities. The entity-relationship method known as IDEF1X[11] draws a relationship as a line that connects two entities. These two methods for handling relationships are often referred to as the n-ary and binary methods respectively.[12] For a data architecture that is one component of an EAP, the second binary method of having only one object called an entity is recommended, because

1. it is simple and easy for business people to grasp and apply,
2. the conceptual model will be easier to use for a logical database design, especially when a relational DBMS will ultimately be used, and

3. there are more software products available that use the binary method to document and illustrate the data architecture.

Each entity will have at least one relationship unless it is truly independent of any other kind of data or is-a-kind-of another entity, in which case the subtype entity is said to inherit or participate in the relationships of its supertype.

There is no single report format accepted as a standard for displaying the components of an entity definition. Figure 7.2 shows partial definitions of entities from a data architecture. They are presented to illustrate common situations and as an example of one report format. Further suggestions regarding reports are in step 4. The EAP team should decide on a format for the reports that best suits the team and the people throughout the enterprise who will be reading the reports.

An asterisk beside an identifier name, such as Product Type Number in Figure 7.2a, indicates that an enterprisewide identifier for that entity does not currently exist. The symbol "(o)" on an attribute or relationship means that it is optional, or that a particular instance of the entity may not have that attribute or relationship. Internal EAP entity numbers appear in parentheses after the entity name in relationships.

The Physical Specifications and the Packaging Specs attributes of the Product Type entity in Figure 7.2a show that attributes are not data elements; indeed Packaging Specs can be a thick document of instructions, but that document is considered to be an attribute of Product Type because (a) it serves to further clarify the understanding of the concept of a Product Type, (b) defining Packaging Specs in more detail as an entity would not significantly add to this understanding, and (c) Packaging Specs is not related by itself to another entity (within 80/20 significance).

Product Type has a relationship that one Product Type *consists of* other Product Types; in other words, products can be combined to form other products.

A data architecture will usually have several type-item combinations. In Figures 7.2a and 7.2b, Product Types are the classes or categories of products, such as Widget; whereas the

Product Item represents data about a particular widget with a Product Item (serial) Number, for instance, of 7239531. Equipment, Goods and Services, and Materials are terms that typically have type-item pairs of entities.

An example of the is-a-kind-of, or supertype-subtype, pairs of

---

Entity Name: PRODUCT TYPE   Entity Number:009

Alternate Name: SERVICE, PRODUCT FAMILY

Identifier: PRODUCT TYPE NUMBER *

Description: A kind of goods or services that can be developed, produced, sold, leased, purchased, provided, or used by the company.

Attributes ---

Name: PRODUCT TYPE NUMBER

Description: A unique identifier assigned to each Product Type.

Name: PRODUCT TYPE NAME

Description: The official name assigned to a Product Type.

Name: PHYSICAL SPECIFICATIONS

Description: Product Types may have physical specs that describe them such as size, weight, color, etc.

Name: COMMON PRODUCT CODES (o)

Description: Standard codes used for some Product Types that have industrywide acceptance.

Name: PACKAGING SPECIFICATIONS (o)

Description: Instructions on how to prepare a Product Type for shipment and the materials to be used.

[Additional attributes describing PRODUCT TYPE would be listed]

Relationships ---

         consists of PRODUCT ITEM (10) 1:M (o)

         consists of PRODUCT TYPE (9) 1:M (o)

         is produced by BUSINESS PROCESS (19) M:M (o)

         is specified on PRODUCT ORDER (23) M:M (o)

         is acquired by CONTRACT (46) M:M

[Additional relationships would be listed here]

Figure 7.2a. Sample entity definition 1.

Entity Name: PRODUCT ITEM   Entity Number:010

Alternate Name:

Identifier: PRODUCT ITEM NUMBER

Description: A specific object or instance of Product Type that may be sold,
               leased, provided, or used by the company. Each individual
               Product Item is a uniquely trackable object that has a Product
               Item Number.

Attributes ---

Name: PRODUCT ITEM NUMBER

Description: A unique number that identifies (and may be stamped on) each
               Product Item. Also known as the Product Serial Number.

Name: PRODUCT CODES

Description: Various identifiers currently used to identify Product Items such as
               the asset number assigned by the Accounting Department, or a
               manufacturer's serial number.

Name: MAINTENANCE HISTORY

Description: The date, time, and description of the maintenance activity such
               as repairs performed on a Product Item.

[Additional attributes would be listed]

Relationships ---

        consists of PRODUCT ITEM (10) 1:M (o)

        instance of PRODUCT TYPE (9) M:1

        stored at LOCATION (14) M:1

[Additional relationships would be listed here]

Figure 7.2b. Sample entity definition 2.

entities is shown in Figures 7.2c and 7.2d. A Carrier *is a kind of*
Supplier that has additional attributes and relationships for understanding the role that a Carrier plays in the business.

The Supplier entity in Figure 7.2c has two relationships with
Equipment Type. A Supplier *supplies* Equipment Type and *repairs* Equipment Type. The toolset selected for EAP should enable multiple relationships to be defined between a pair of
entities.

Entity Name: SUPPLIER   Entity Number:011

Alternate Name: VENDOR, CONTRACTOR
Identifier: SUPPLIER NUMBER *
Description: An individual or business who supplies, could supply, or has
               supplied materials used by the division.

Attributes ---

Name: SUPPLIER NUMBER
Description: A unique number to identify each supplier.

Name: SUPPLIER NAME
Description: The official or full name of the supplier.

Name: IDENTIFICATION DATA
Description: Address, contact person, and other data that identifies the
               supplier.

Name: STATUS
Description:The current relationship with the division.

Name: PAYMENT DATA
Description: Contractual information regarding the financial arrangements with
               the supplier.

Name: EDI INFORMATION
Description: Instructions for exchanging data with the supplier.

Name: SUPPLIER HISTORY
Description: Chronological record of events with the supplier.

[Additional attributes would be listed]

Relationships ---

                consists of ORGANIZATION UNIT (2) M:M

                provides SUPPLY OR SERVICE TYPE (3) M:M

                provides SUPPLY OR SERVICE ITEM (4) 1:M (o)

                supplies EQUIPMENT TYPE (6) M:M (o)

                repairs EQUIPMENT TYPE (7) M:M (o)

                supplies EQUIPMENT ITEM (13) 1:M (o)

[Additional relationships would be listed here]

Figure 7.2c. Sample entity definition 3.

Entity Name: CARRIER   Entity Number:012

Alternate Name: SHIPPER

Identifier: SUPPLIER NUMBER *

Is-a-kind-of: SUPPLIER

Description:

Attributes IN ADDITION TO SUPPLIER   --

Name: SHIPPING DETAILS

Description: Instructions for packaging and shipping for a carrier.

[Additional attributes would be listed]

Relationships IN ADDITION TO SUPPLIER   --

                        carries OUTBOUND SHIPMENT (35) 1:M

                        approved to ship PRODUCT TYPE (9) M:M (o)

[Additional relationships would be listed here]

Figure 7.2d. Sample entity definition 4.

Task 3 Simplify complicated sets of definitions and relationships. When the set of relationships for an entity or groups of entities seems complicated or confusing, use E-R diagrams to illustrate them. Doing so may often lead to a more simple set of entity definitions and to entity names that were not on the candidate list. Consider the following kinds of actions to simplify the data architecture:

- *generalization*—merging two similar entities; for example, combining Machine Press and Fork Lift into a broader concept of Equipment Type.
- *abstraction*—relating two or more entities (often adding a temporal aspect) to form a new entity (also known as *composition*).
- *assimilation*—the elimination of a dependent entity, for example, Employee Performance Review, and making it an attribute of the independent entity, in this case, Employee.
- *separation*—splitting compound concepts into their basic concepts. For example, a freight company had a candidate entity

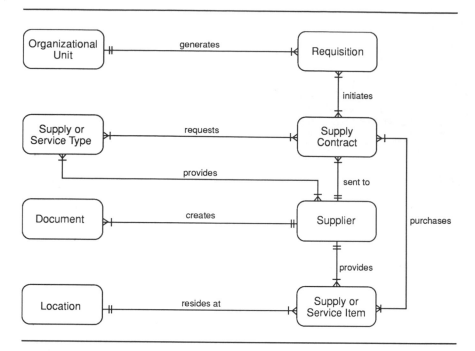

Figure 7.3.   E-R diagram for Purchase Goods and Services.

called a Weighbill. Many functions of the business used a Weighbill, and it appeared on the candidate entity list. However, defining the entity Weighbill was not easy and defied a simple consensus definition. Drawing an entity-relationship diagram did not clear up the confusion, as a Weighbill seemed to be related to so many other entities. Upon closer examination, it became evident that a Weighbill was a combination of two basic concepts—the top part of the Weighbill described the goods being shipped and the lower portion showed the routing of the goods and the carrier for each segment. The difficulty was overcome by splitting the single complicated Weighbill entity into two basic entities that became known as Shipment and Forwarding Instructions.

Task 4   Ensure that entity definitions are consistent with each other.   As each entity is defined, its definition must be consistent with the entities previously defined. Upon completing an entity definition, remove its name from the candidate entity list along with all other entities whose definitions are implied by this entity. For example, when the entity Supplier is removed from the list, any entities on the candidate list that are the same concept, such as Vendor, Carrier, Distributor, should also be removed. Continue tasks two and three above until every candidate entity has been considered and the list is empty.

Task 5   Draw E-R diagrams to illustrate* views *of the data architecture. Depending on the total number of entities, a diagram of all entities in the data architecture may not fit on a single page. Therefore, E-R diagrams may be drawn to reflect the view of the data architecture from the perspective of one business area. For example, Figure 7.3 is an example of an E-R diagram that reflects the Purchase Goods and Services view of the data architecture. Only the entities and relationships to support that business area are shown.

There are various E-R diagramming conventions, such as Chen,[13] IDEF1X,[14] Curtice-Jones,[15] and Bachman.[16] No single approach is always superior to another for conceptual data modeling. The diagramming technique selected for EAP may depend on the EAP toolset capabilities, existing standards, or the recommendations of the EAP consultant. In general, use a diagramming technique that is simple, easy to understand, and that will not consume much valuable time to draw and maintain the charts. Some products mandate a single E-R diagram be drawn for the entire data architecture. Diagrams with more than 50 entities are tedious to draw and too complicated to be shown outside of the EAP team.

Task 6   Time permitting, files and databases defined in the Information Resource Catalog can be related to the entities in the data architecture. When data redundancy has been a motivating factor for EAP, this is an important task. By relating the entities in the data architecture to the files and databases identified in the IRC, one can begin to comprehend the extent of data redundancy. This relationship could be used to show, for example, how many files contain equipment information or customer information, or how many systems maintain redundant data. These kinds of statistics will be helpful when presenting the results of EAP and determining opportunities for improvement. Every file in the IRC should "have a place" and belong in the data architecture, but not necessarily appear as an individual entity in the data architecture. Many existing files will contain data from more than one conceptual entity. By reviewing the kinds of files in the IRC, the completeness of the data architecture can be verified by ensuring that definitions for all kinds of data currently maintained have been included.

Again, it is important to remember that the purpose of this Data Architecture step is to define entities, not to design databases. Semantic data modeling and normalization are valid techniques for conceptual modeling and data design, but they are too detailed or time-consuming to define entities for Enterprise Architecture Planning. After EAP, there will be time to add detail to the data architecture.

The definitions comprising the data architecture cannot be deemed right or wrong. However, a data architecture may be of good or poor quality. A good enterprise data architecture is

- *Understandable.* The entity definitions make sense to people throughout the business.
- *Complete and Consistent.* No major data entity has been omitted and definitions do not contradict or overlap.
- *Stable.* Definitions should only be based on the business model. Stability can be attained by defining data independently from who uses the data, how the data is used, where the data is used, when the data is used, what technology is used to store the data, and how the data flows.

The criteria for a high-quality data architecture are the same as those for the business model.

STEP 3—RELATE DATA ENTITIES TO THE BUSINESS FUNCTIONS

Purpose

The purpose of this step is to determine the data entities that are created, retrieved, updated, and deleted by business functions.

Deliverables

1. Entity-to-business function lists and matrices
2. Entity-to-current application lists and matrices (optional, Task 4)

Tasks and Guidelines

Task 1   Relate each function at the lowest level of detail in the business model to the set of entities.   When short on time, divide the business model among team members and have each team member relate functions to entities. Another time saver is to relate the entities to a higher, summarized level of function in the business model rather than the most detailed functions. Since a function is defined by its parts, the numbers of relationships can be reduced. However, the tradeoff for saving time is to reduce detail and precision.

When relating the entities, note whether the data entity is

	Matrix Symbol
Created by a function	C
Updated (changed) by a function	U
Referenced (used) by a function	R

Some methodologies also mandate the use of the letter "D" when a function can delete or destroy data. But in the interest of time, the delete data usage can be implied by the update. For planning purposes, this is usually good enough (80/20 principle). The methodologies that use a D for delete refer to this table as a "CRUD matrix." Another time saver is to use an empty matrix on paper or data entry screen to facilitate recording the relationships and entering them into the toolset.

The relationship of an entity to a business function should be *significant*. Most relationships are not absolutely certain or clear because the definitions of functions and entities themselves are of only 80/20 goodness. When discussing an entity-to-function relationship, words such as "sometimes" or "occasionally" indicate that the relationship should not be considered significant (as in

ENTITY → FUNCTION	MARKET	PROMOTION-ELEMENTS	PRODUCT-ELEMENTS	PRODUCT-CONCEPTS	PRODUCT-SET	CHANNELS	CONSTRAINT	CONSULTANT	EMPLOYEE-PAYROLL	METRO-TERRITORY	TERRITORY	SALES-OPPORTUNITY	CATALOG	JOB	ACCOUNTS-DUE	PRODUCT-DUE	VENDOR	PURCHASE-ORDER	BINDERY	DESIGN	INVENTORY	PRODUCT-INTENT	INPUT-PRINT-BINDERY	RECEIPT-EXPENDITURE	PRODUCT-INVENTORY	SHIPMENT	DISTRIBUTOR-BUYER-INT	CLIENT
MONIT-COMPITION	R		R					R						R	R	R			R	R	R							R
REVISE-PRODUCTS	CUR	CUR	R	R	CUR	R								R	R	R			R	R	R							R CUR
PRODUCT-PLAN	R	CUR	R	R	UR		CUR							R							R						R	
PLN-USE-TECH	R				R																							
DEV-STRAT-BUS	R	CUR	R	R	R	R								CUR	R	R			R	R								R
ADVERTISING																	CUR											
COORD-PROD-ADV			UR	CUR	CUR	UR																						
CONSULTING			UR																									
DETRM-MKT-STRGY	R R	R		R	R																						R	
RESEARCH	UR R	R			UR							UR				R												
SALES-TRAINING			R									UR																
SERV-ENG-TSK-FS			R	R	R							R			R	R											R	R
CORD-ANN-MK-CNL			R	R	R	R						R			R												R	R
DIST-SLS-RPTNG		R	UR	UR	UR	R	UR	R	R	UR	UR	UR	UR	UR														
RGNL-SLS-RPTNG		R	R	R	R	R	R	R	R	R	R																	
BUSINESS-RPTNG		R	R	R	R	CUR	R	R	R	R																		
PREP-CHG-SCL-PROB			CUR	CUR	R	R	R	R	R																			
RESOLV-SLS-PROB		R	CUR	CUR	CUR	R	UR		R																			
GEN-NEW-SALES	R	UR	CUR	CUR	CUR		R																					
LEAD-IDENT	R		R	R			R																				CUR	R
SUSPECT-IDENT	R		CUR	CUR	UR																							R CUR
FILE-SALES	R		R																		UR							R

MONIT-COMMISNS			UR						UR	UR	CUR	UR	UR	UR	R																					
PROC-COMPLAINTS		R	R		R	UR			UR	UR			R	R	R	R	R	R	R	R	R	UR		UR	UR		UR	R								R
SLS-CALL-ACTVTY	R		R	R	CUR	UR	UR		CUR	CUR		CUR	CUR	CUR	R																					
WRT-CONTRACT-CPI		R	UR		CUR	UR	UR	R	R	UR			UR	UR	CUR	CUR	CUR	CUR	CUR						UR											
ESTB-CLS-POLICY			R						R	R					R		R	UR	UR	CUR				R	R											
DEVELOP-INDEXES		R	R		R				R	R					R		R	R		R	CUR			R	R											
PREP-SEL-DATA		R													R		R			R	R	CUR	CUR													
BINDING		R			UR												R	R	UR			CUR	CUR	UR	R	CUR	UR		R	UR	CUR					
CLNT-SVCS		R			UR	R			R	R					R	R	R	CUR	UR			R		R	R			R								
PREP-REVNU-RPTS																R	R	UR	R			R	R		R		R									
CATALOG-DESIGN					R				R	R							R	UR	CUR						R			R								
CATALOG-PROD					R				R	R							R	UR	CUR			CUR			R			R								
DES-PROD-RPTS					R				R	R							R	UR	CUR						R			R								
MONIT-COSTS					R					R						R	R	UR	UR			R	CUR		R		UR	R								
MAN-CLI-CONTACT					UR					R					R	R	R	UR	UR			R			R		R									
MONT-MFG-ACTVTY																R	R	R	R			CUR	CUR	CUR	CUR		CUR	CUR		R						
PAPER-CTL																						CUR	CUR				R		CUR	CUR	R					
CUSTOMER-SVCS															R											R						CUR		UR	R	
DISTRB-FILES		UR			R										R									R		UR						R	CUR	CUR	CUR	
ESTB-RCPNT-QUAL		R																														UR				
IDFY-QUAL-RCPNT		R																														UR				
MKTLST-CPY-DIST		R			R										R							R										UR				
BUYLINE																						CUR														
BUYLINE-OPERAT					CUR	R									R		R				R															CUR
PRODUCT-LINE					UR	R																CUR										R				
VERIFY-WHOS-NEW					UR	R																CUR										R				
EXT-COUNCILS					R	R																CUR										R				
CONTRACT-PROCSS			R		CUR	R		R		R	R				UR		R			R																
CREDIT-COLLCTNS			R		R	R				R					R																					
NON-CNTRCT-CHGS					R	R										R	R		R			R		R	R		R		R		UR					
PAID-DISTRB		R																														UR	R			

Figure 7.4. Database entity-to-function relationship.

"Business Function F sometimes creates entity E"), whereas words like "usually" or "frequently" indicate the relationship is significant.

With some EAP toolsets, only the predominant data usage can be recorded in the relationship. In this case, Creates (C) implies Updates (U) and References (R), and Updates (U) implies References (R).

Consensus and compromise also apply to this task. There can be thousands of potential data usage relationships, so there is little time to dwell on particular relationships.

Task 2 ***Enter the function-to-entity relationships into the toolset and generate matrices.*** By convention, the functions are the rows of the table and should be sequenced hierarchically by major functional area. The entities form the columns and are grouped according to the major functional area to which they are most associated, usually the area that creates them.

In Figure 7.4, the heavy lines that form boxes along the diagonal of the matrix identify the entities that are most associated or belong with the functional area of the business. Those usage relationships that are outside those boxes and the overlap of some boxes represent data that is shared from one business functional area to another. These matrices are used to develop the scope of applications in the next phase and to demonstrate the extent of data sharing in the business. The large number of matrix entries outside of the boxes demonstrate the importance to the business of a shared data environment.

The literature on Information Engineering discusses an approach, called entity affinity analysis, which clusters entities into the groups for this matrix. Figure 7.5 shows the formulas used for affinity analysis.

However, affinity analysis often produces erroneous results for the following reasons:

1. Affinity analysis uses mathematical formulas that presume precise numbers for data usage, but in EAP we have been following the 80/20 principle—not trying to be perfect—and we have accepted some degree of inaccuracy and imprecision to save time. Applying a mathematical formula to estimates

---

ENTITY AFFINITY ANALYSIS FORMULAS

$$\text{AFFINITY OF } E_1 \text{ TO } E_2 = \frac{a(E_1, E_2)}{a(E_1)}$$

$a(E_1)$ = number of functions using entity E_1

$a(E_1, E_2)$ = number of functions using both E_1 and E_2

Weighted Affinity of E_3 to the Cluster E_1, E_2 =

$$\frac{(\text{Affinity of } E_3 \text{ to } E_1) \times a(E_1) + (\text{Affinity of } E_3 \text{ to } E_2) \times a(E_2)}{a(E_1) + a(E_2)}$$

Figure 7.5. Affinity analysis formulas (from Martin[17]).

that have an unknown variance or distribution can lead to statistically insignificant results.

2. The definitions upon which these relationships (affinities) are based are subjective from the perspective of the planning team.

3. The scope and detail of the business functions will vary. Some aspects of the business model will have many levels of detail in order to define a complicated function, other areas will have less detail. The amount of detail affects the usage numbers.

4. These formulas do not consider data that may need to be grouped together for reasons of security, geographical distribution, legal requirements, or existing systems.

If your toolset for EAP will automatically and quickly generate an entity affinity grouping, then do so. But use the results only for ideas or suggestions. Don't simply accept the results of the formulas.

The grouping of entities into meaningful clusters that can be related to functional areas can be done manually, usually taking one hour or less. The EAP team can determine the groups subjectively by examining the matrix visually and generalizing entities under a meaningful title.

Task 3 In full team meetings, review the entity-to-function relationships by relating each entity to the set of business functions.   Verify that each entity is created by at least one function, and that each entity is updated or referenced by a function other than the one that created it.

Task 4 Time permitting, entities may be related to existing applications or inputs/outputs/files/databases and information sources.   When generating a matrix to display the relationship of entities to existing applications, the existing applications are conventionally listed on the rows and the entities listed in the columns. The C, U, and R are assigned to those applications that currently create, update, and reference a specific entity. Determining these relationships can be difficult because data in current files may use different names and may be derived from combinations of the basic entities defined in the data architecture.

Tabulate the extent of overlap between existing systems and entities. Formulate opportunities for improvement based on the redundant storage and usage of data. If the magnitude of the cost of redundant data can be determined, such figures may justify the acceptance of the architecture and plans.

STEP 4—DISTRIBUTE THE DATA ARCHITECTURE

In this step, the data architecture document is produced and distributed, a presentation developed, and comments to improve the data architecture are collected.

Deliverables

1. Data architecture document
   - Introduction
   - List of entity names
   - Complete entity definitions
   - Entity relationship diagrams
   - Entity usage matrices
2. Presentation material is developed.
3. Comments from users (information consumers) are solicited.

Tasks and Guidelines

Task 1   Write an introduction to the data architecture document with an explanation of how to interpret the reports.   Generate reports from the toolset such as an alphabetical list of entity names, complete entity definitions, E-R diagrams, and entity usage matrices. Write an introduction to each section of the document explaining how to use and interpret the reports. These reports and presentations, as with all EAP reports and presentations, should be in plain, nontechnical language. The audience for this document consists of people of diverse business backgrounds.

Business policies and procedures affected by data ownership or sharing, data integrity, and the use of standard identifiers should be addressed in the document. See Appendix F for a sample data architecture document.

Task 2   Prepare presentation material.   Use appropriate props when making the presentation. For example, if the data architecture is for an insurance business, then hold an insurance policy and explain the appropriate entities and relationships from the data architecture, such as Coverage, Terms, Insured, and how a document such as a policy can be a combination of basic business concepts that have data associated with them.

Present the data architecture to management and distribute the document to those attending the presentation. The presentation should be about 20 to 30 minutes, and it should prepare the audience for reading the document and making comments (Figure 7.6). Describe the changes to the business resulting from standard enterprisewide data and identifiers.

Do not stimulate a discussion during the presentation about the entity definitions. Questions aimed at understanding and clarification are acceptable, but discussions, opinions, and points of view that the team has already considered will not be useful. Avoid justifying definitions. At the beginning of the presentation, explain, in general, the procedures and rules for defining entities used by the team. Be sure to cover the goodness criteria for a data architecture.

Task 3   Collect written comments from people throughout the business.   Make arrangements for receiving the comments

---

**OUTLINE FOR
DATA ARCHITECTURE PRESENTATION**

I. PRESENTATION INTRODUCTION
   A. Agenda
   B. EAP project phases
   C. Status of current phase
   D. Significant changes to the business model
II. DATA ARCHITECTURE CONCEPTS
   A. What is an entity? What are its components? Goodness criteria
   B. Data architecture reports and their interpretation
   C. Examples of data reports
   D. Impact to the business
III. Next Steps
   A. Review and comments to data architecture
   B. Applications architecture

Figure 7.6.   Presentation outline for data architecture.

promptly. One method, discussed previously in the Business Model Phase, is to have the comments sent to the attention of a person in upper management. This will often motivate people to respond promptly.

The team should review the comments and decide which are applicable. It is possible that 70 percent of the comments will be judged to be *non*-applicable. The reason is that the reader has misunderstood the entity definition or has a perspective that is too narrow or specific. Revise the data architecture accordingly. Redistribute the document only if it is reasonable to do so or is expected.

DISCUSSION QUESTIONS

1. How many entities would you expect to be in your candidate entity list? In your data architecture?

2. Are there internal or external data models that are available to the EAP team? Can you obtain a data architecture from another company?
3. Who on the team should lead the entity definition discussions?
4. Will data administration or other experienced data modelers supplement the EAP team for this phase?
5. What actions might you consider if the definition and usage steps (2 and 3) of this phase begin to consume too much time?

REFERENCES

[1]*Reference Model for DBMS Standardization*. Database Architecture Framework Task Group (DAFTG) of the ANSI/X3/SPARC Database System Study Group.

[2]Nijssen, G. M., and T. A. Halpin. *Conceptual Schema and Relational Database Design: A Fact-Oriented Approach*, Prentice-Hall, Englewood Cliffs, NJ, 1989.

[3]Ross, Ronald. *Entity Modeling: Techniques and Applications*, Database Research Group, Boston, MA, 1987.

[4]Thompson, J. Patrick. *Data with Semantics: Data Models and Data Management*, Van Nostrand Reinhold, New York, 1989.

[5]Spewak, Steven H. "The Three-Dimensional Data Model," *Data Base Newsletter*, Vol. 10, No. 2, March 1982.

[6]Flavin, Matt. *Fundamental Concepts of Information Modeling*, Yourdon Press Monograph (now Prentice-Hall), New York, 1981.

[7]Flemming, Candice C., and Barbara von Halle. *Handbook of Relational Database Design*, Addison-Wesley, Reading, MA, 1989.

[8]Coad, Peter, and Edward Yourdon. *Object-Oriented Analysis*, Prentice-Hall (Yourdon Press), Englewood Cliffs, NJ, 1990.

[9]Shlaer, Sally, and Stephen J. Mellor. *Object-Oriented Systems Analysis: Modeling the World in Data*, Prentice-Hall (Yourdon Press), Englewood Cliffs, NJ, 1988.

[10]Chen, Peter P. "The Entity-Relationship Model—Toward a Unified View of Data," *ACM Transactions on Database Systems*, Vol. 1, No. 1, March 1976.

[11]*ICAM Definition (IDEF) Method for Function Modeling*, IDEFUG-M-1X-8511, IDEF Users Group Secretariat, Ann Arbor, MI, 1985.

[12]McKee, Richard, and Jeff Rogers. "Data Modeling Techniques: A Matter of Perspective," *Data Resource Management*, Vol. 3, No. 3, Summer 1992.

[13]Chen, Peter P. "The Entity-Relationship Model—Toward a Unified View of Data," *ACM Transactions on Database Systems*, Vol. 1, No. 1, March 1976.

[14]Bruce, Thomas A. *Designing Quality Databases with IDEF1x*, Dorset House Publishing, New York, 1992.

[15]Curtice, Robert, and Paul Jones. *Logical Data Base Design*, Van Nostrand Reinhold, New York, 1982.

[16]Bachman, Charles, and Chris Gane. "The Bachman Approach to the Lou's Slips Marina Problem," *Data Base Newsletter*, Vol. 17, No. 2, March/April 1989.

[17]Martin, James, *Information Engineering: Planning and Analysis* (Book 2), Prentice-Hall, Englewood Cliffs, NJ, 1990. pp. 157–160.

8

Applications Architecture

INTRODUCTION

The purpose of the *applications architecture* is to define the major kinds of applications needed to manage the data and support the business functions of the enterprise. The applications architecture is *not* a design for systems, nor is it a detailed requirements analysis. It is a definition of what applications will do to manage data and provide information to people performing business functions. The applications enable the I.S. function to achieve its mission, that is, provide access to needed data in a useful format at an acceptable cost.

Applications are the mechanisms for managing the data of the enterprise. The term "managing the data" includes such activities as entering, editing, sorting, changing, summarizing, archiving, analyzing, and referencing data.

The applications architecture corresponds to the Owner's View of the Process column of the Zachman Framework for I.S. Architectures (Figure 1.6). It is the second of the three architectures for EAP.

Five Steps to Applications Architecture

There are five basic steps in managing the process to create the applications architecture:

1. List candidate applications.
2. Define the applications.
3. Relate applications to functions.
4. Analyze impact to current applications.
5. Distribute the applications architecture.

With the exception of step 4, if these steps seem familiar, it is because they are similar to the previous phase. The process of defining an applications architecture is essentially the same as defining the data architecture. The data architecture is also known as a conceptual data model, so it is entirely appropriate to refer to the applications architecture as a conceptual applications model.

Since the processes for creating these two architectures are essentially the same, the skills required of EAP team members are also the same for these two phases. Experience has shown that, upon completing the definition of a good data architecture, EAP team members are capable of defining a good applications architecture. The team can be supplemented with individuals having extensive applications definition and systems analysis experience.

The Applications Architecture Phase consumes about the same amount of time as the Data Architecture Phase—about 15 percent of the total EAP effort. For most EAP projects, this phase will be completed in less than six weeks. The time allocated to the steps in this phase is

Step 1 = 10 percent
Step 2 = 50 percent
Step 3 = 15 percent
Step 4 = 15 percent
Step 5 = 10 percent
_____
100 percent

STEP 1—LIST CANDIDATE APPLICATIONS

Purpose

The purpose of this step is to identify every possible application needed to manage data and support the business. Applications will be given appropriate names that describe their purpose and function. The EAP team will consider the strategic use of information and technology for competitive business advantage. This first step can be divided among team members, in which case the separate lists of candidate applications will be combined into one in the final task. Do not spend time in this step trying to define the applications, as that will be done in the next step.

Deliverable

1. List of the names of possible applications, which may include a brief preliminary definition, an indication of the business functions supported, and the information managed

Tasks and Guidelines

Task 1 Identify candidate applications. EAP team members should understand the contents of the data architecture definitions, the data usage matrix, functional business model, and the information resource catalog. Use this material to propose applications.

The data usage (CRUD) matrix can be used to propose both data-oriented and function-oriented applications. Take the data usage (CRUD) matrix and scan down each column corresponding to a data entity, and examine the business functions that reference, update, or create new instances of that data. Propose applications that will perform these data management activities. After scanning the columns, look across the rows of the matrix that correspond to business functions, and propose applications that will automate or provide data to those business functions.

Examine the opportunities that were collected during the Enterprise Survey interviews and documented as part of the business model. A report containing the function improvement opportunities can be distributed to each team member. The Information Resource Catalog contains descriptions of current applications that can also provide ideas for the applications architecture. Consider the findings of user-satisfaction ratings compiled during the Enterprise Survey or Information Resource Catalog.

A good name for an application will convey the primary purpose or focus of the application. Avoid names that are similar to those for existing applications. By convention, the word "system" can be part of most application names. The phrases "information system" or "administration system" may also be commonly used. Some candidate applications will be focused on managing a particular kind of data, having names such as

Customer Information System
Facilities Administration System
Vehicle Management System
Human Resources Information System
Account Management System
Material Inventory System

Other candidate applications will focus on supporting a particular set of business functions or a business procedure. These may have names such as

Order Processing System
Advertising and Promotion System
Production Tracking System
Employee Benefits System
Accounts Receivable System
Training and Development System

Texts on information engineering such as Martin[1] and Finkelstein[2] state that cluster analysis and matrix manipulations can automatically determine the "business systems" architecture. Applications will follow "subject database" boundaries and form "business areas" for subsequent analysis. However, to repeat from the previous chapter, cluster analysis often produces erroneous results because the data about architectures is of questionable accuracy, completeness, and unknown variance, is based on subjective perspectives, the scope and detail of business functions is inconsistent, and does not consider the validity and stability of strategic business objectives and plans. The lesson, therefore, is not to rely solely on those results for defining applications. If such analyses are available with little cost or time consumed, then the results may provide useful ideas to the planning team.

Task 2 Identify applications that could improve the business or provide a competitive advantage. There is a rapidly growing body of literature on strategic systems for competitive advantage. Authors such as Synott,[3] Marchand and Horton,[4] Wiseman,[5] Ives and Learmouth,[6] and Rachoff[7] offer valuable ideas to spark creative thinking. Executive information, decision support, and expert systems fall into the category of strategic systems.

In the book *Computers and Strategy*, Charles Wiseman describes a "Strategic Option Generator" to identify information system opportunities based on the "strategic target" (supplier, customer, competitor), the "strategic thrust" (differentiation, cost, innovation, growth, alliance), the mode of the strategic thrust (offensive, defensive), and the user of the application (internal, external targets). Porter,[8] Atkinson,[9] and Curtice[10] suggest analyzing the value chain of the business to determine the most significant opportunities. By following the guidelines in Chapter 4 on the use of value-added concepts for defining the major business functions, the business model can support the analyses suggested by these authors and be used to conceive opportunities and evaluate their contribution. Team brainstorming will also generate many good ideas for applications.

Use the function-to-entity data-usage (CRUD) matrix to ensure that every kind of data is managed—that is, created and updated by at least one application. Consider how the quality of business functions could be improved—better efficiency, accuracy, reliability, or cost reduction—by having access to data.

Many of the ideas generated at this point are referred to as "business reengineering" because having access to data via applications can lead to significant business function changes; the innovative use of information systems and technology can improve the way that business is conducted.

Reengineering the business means that new functions will be proposed, some may be eliminated, and others will be moved in the hierarchy of the business model to reflect the change to the definition of the business. The names below are examples of candidate applications that would be in the category of strategic systems:

Price/Rate Determination System
Delivery Route Optimization System
Customer Qualification System
Manpower Planning System
Performance Management System
Purchasing Pattern System

Task 3 If team members have proposed potential applications in separate lists, combine them into a single list. Record the name or initials of the team member that provided each application in the combined list. In a team meeting, review the combined list and remove any obvious duplicates. The number of candidate applications may range from 50 to more than 200.

STEP 2—DEFINE THE APPLICATIONS

Purpose

The purpose of this step is to provide a standard definition for each application in the applications architecture.

Deliverables

1. Applications definitions
2. Schematics of the applications architecture (optional)

Tasks and Guidelines

Task 1 Assign applications to team members for definition. Unlike the previous phase in which it was suggested that every data entity definition be formulated in meetings of the entire team, the writing of the application definitions can be divided among individual team members. The time saving that results from this step can be significant and worthwhile.

Divide the candidate applications into groups of "related" applications, in the sense that a group involves the same kinds of data or supports the same functional area of the business. Prior to writing, the team should discuss the definition of each application within each group. The responsibility for writing the definition of an application can be assigned to a particular team member after the team has verbally agreed on some of the capabilities of that application.

Task 2 Define each application. Team members should define the applications that have been assigned to them. An application definition should describe *what* an application does, not *how* it works. Application definitions should include

- a brief purpose,
- a general description and capabilities, and
- the business opportunities and benefits, both tangible and intangible.

Each definition should be stated in nontechnical, plain language. Use terms that are defined in the data architecture and business model, and avoid terms not defined there.

The definitions should be as independent of technology as *possible*. However, some capabilities of an application may be dependent on technology platforms. Be reasonable when proposing the capabilities of new applications. Subsequent technological and cost/benefit analysis may show some application components to be infeasible, in which case some definitions in the architecture will be modified so that the applications can be implemented reasonably.

Three examples of applications definitions are provided in Figures 8.1, 8.2, and 8.3. Assume that the terms for data (Lead, Facility, Organization Unit, and so on) have been defined in a data architecture.

To the casual reader, these applications may not appear as profound innovations. Indeed, they should seem as simple and understandable as the examples of entity definitions in the previous chapter. However, a review of the lengthy documents con-

---

APPLICATION ARCHITECTURE

Application Name: Sales Lead Tracking System

Application Number: 114

Description: Sales Lead Tracking will enable the sales groups to track sales leads. This application's primary use would be to inform field sales representatives about potential sales. A sales lead for potential or existing customers could be initiated by a customer phone call, an employee, walk-in, response card, and so on. If the lead was for an existing customer, this application will create lead data with specific information about the type of lead, reason for the call, calling data and time, follow-up actions, equipment involved, and lead status. The lead would be queued and routed to a specific sales representative for follow-up. The routing would be based on the type of lead and sales territories. This application will maintain the follow-up and status information for leads. If the lead resulted from an employee, the application will initiate an employee compensation transaction. This application will also produce summary and performance reports for sales leads.

Figure 8.1. Sample application description 1.

APPLICATION ARCHITECTURE

Application Name: Facility Maintenance Planning

Applications Number: 44

Description: Identifies and plans recurring preventative maintenance for buildings, structures, utility systems, and equipment. The application identifies scheduling constraints and other repairs or maintenance to eliminate duplication of effort. Facility repairs will be identified through inspection, external studies, analysis of prior repairs, manufacturer's suggestions, and technical advances that could reduce the current amount of maintenance. Maintains facility maintenance records for up to ten years. Authorization and notification requests are prepared and routed to appropriate individuals and departments. The application keeps maintenance history and costs by type of facility and repair.

Figure 8.2. Sample application description 2.

APPLICATION ARCHITECTURE

Application Name: Production Control System

Application Number: 138

Purpose: To monitor and access real-time production information and performance indicators related to the manufacturing process. Management will use this information to oversee production.

Description:
1. Report actual measurements as well as targets in both graphical and text displays covering specific time periods
2. Quality reports will include shipped product quality, internal and external quality measurements by work group, test results for a given period, incidents occurrences, quality history by product line, product item, and production process
3. Service reports will include cycle time of products and product item for any organization unit, performance or organization units to their target
4. Cost reports will measure efficiency by the hours earned versus worked for each organization unit and total expenses

Benefits:
1. Enables organization units to track and easily report quality, service, and cost metrics.
2. Efficient, timely management of manufacturing by access to real-time data.
3. Production equipment utilization can be optimized.
4. Supports corporate objectives for product quality by reducing and correcting defects.

Figure 8.3. Sample application description 3.

taining the business models and architectures from these EAP projects would show that the above applications do offer substantial benefits to these organizations over their current application portfolio.

Task 3 Enter definitions into the toolset. The EAP team should review and edit every application definition. Enter the definitions into the toolset as soon as possible after they are written. Depending on the toolset being used, team members may directly enter the definitions, or they will write the definitions and pass them to the toolset administrator or EAP project librarian for data entry. Produce application definition reports for the team to review at each meeting.

Task 4 Simplify complicated applications and eliminate redundancy. If an application seems to be particularly complex, lengthy, indistinguishable from another application, or difficult to describe, it may indicate that multiple applications are being combined into one. To simplify a complicated application, split it into two or more separate applications with distinguishable features that are more easily defined. Examine the entire applications architecture to combine similar or like applications into a single application, and to eliminate duplicate applications and overlapping capabilities.

Task 5 Note preliminary ideas for external software packages and critical technology platforms. It is *not* a presumption that all applications are going to be developed internally by the I.S. organization. Indeed, many companies purchase applications software and may continue to do so. When the EAP team recognizes that a conceptual application could be fulfilled by purchasing a software product, this should be noted in the architecture documents. The definition of application may be used in part as the basis for software package selection. Also, where an application description mentions a critical technology dependence, this too should be highlighted for consideration in the Technology Architecture Phase.

Task 6 Time permitting, draw schematics or blueprints of the applications architecture (optional). This task is optional depending on available time, and whether schematics were drawn in the Current Systems & Technology Phase. If the Information Resource Catalog has schematics showing the input-output flow of applications and how they fit together, then similar schematics may be created showing how applications fit together in the application architecture. Figure 8.4 is one example of how a schematic may appear.

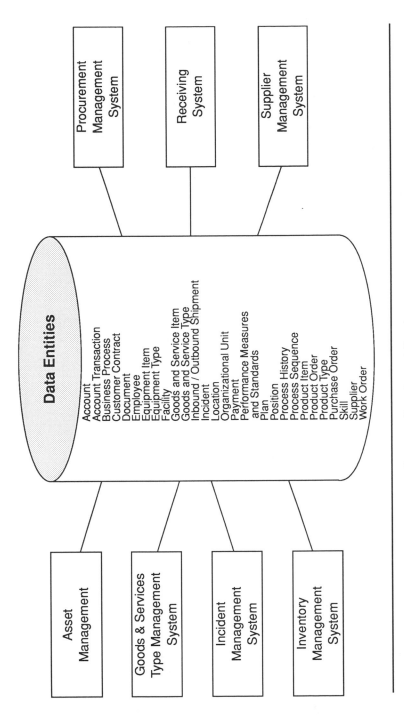

Figure 8.4. Applications supporting Procure Goods and Services.

Data Entities

Account
Account Transaction
Business Process
Customer Contract
Document
Employee
Equipment Item
Equipment Type
Facility
Goods and Service Item
Goods and Service Type
Inbound / Outbound Shipment
Incident
Location
Organizational Unit
Payment
Performance Measures
  and Standards
Plan
Position
Process History
Process Sequence
Product Item
Product Order
Product Type
Purchase Order
Skill
Supplier
Work Order

Procurement
Management
System

Receiving
System

Supplier
Management
System

Asset
Management

Goods & Services
Type Management
System

Incident
Management
System

Inventory
Management
System

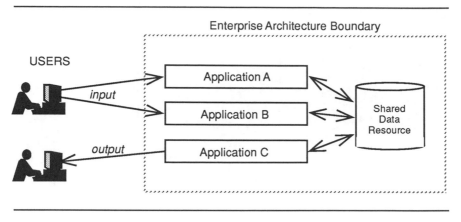

Figure 8.5. Concept of shared data resource.

An enterprisewide shared data environment differs from the traditional applications-oriented environment. Dataflow diagrams, used to show that the output of one system may be the input to another, are not appropriate to illustrate the applications architecture in which data does not "flow," but is shared. Conceptually, the sharing of data along with external inputs and outputs are illustrated in Figure 8.5.

Task 7 Assure the quality of the applications architecture. An applications architecture consists of definitions of applications. As with the other products of EAP, definitions are not necessarily right or wrong, but there are applications architectures that will prove to be good over time and those that will not be so good. There are three criteria for a good applications architecture:

1. It should be *understandable*: the application definitions make sense and are easily understood by people throughout the enterprise.
2. It should be *complete*: applications support most business functions and every data entity is being managed; and it should be *consistent* with no overlap or duplication of application capabilities.

3. It should be *stable*: each application definition is based solely on the business model and data architecture and is independent of who uses the application, how the application works, where the application is located, or when the application is operated.

STEP 3—RELATE APPLICATIONS TO FUNCTIONS

Purpose

The purpose of this step is to identify the business functions that are directly supported or performed by applications. This step is often done at the same time as step 2, that is, as an application is defined, the business functions supported can be identified.

Deliverables

1. Application-to-function cross-reference lists and matrices
2. Application-to-organization unit cross-reference lists and matrices

Tasks and Guidelines

Task 1   For each application, identify the business functions supported.   Use the applications definition (step 2) and the functional business model for this task. Business function support should be considered significant, that is, necessary and worthwhile. Again, the 80–20 principle can be used subjectively to determine significance. If support is not readily apparent, then do not list it. Significant support includes information provided to the function or the actual work of that function being automated or performed by the application. The functions supported should be at the lowest level of detail in the business model.

Enter the application-to-business function relationships into the toolset. Generate cross-reference lists—functions supported for each application and applications that support each function. The second cross-reference list can be more informative for summarized business functions. Examine situations where functions are being supported by two or more applications to determine whether there is an overlap or duplication of applications. Eliminate duplicate application capabilities so there is no overlap. Matrices can be used instead of cross-reference lists for completeness and consistency analysis.

The business functions supported by applications should be listed directly on the application definitions reports. For example, some of the business functions that are supported by the three sample application definitions from the previous step are shown in Figures 8.6, 8.7, and 8.8. The business functions were defined in their respective business models, and the internal function numbers are shown in parentheses. The order of the functions supported has no significance; the first function listed is not the most important nor is it the first function supported by the application.

Task 2   List functions not supported by any application, and explain why.   Figure 8.9, from an application architecture report, is a list of business functions not directly supported by any application.

Application: Sales Lead Tracking
Functions Supported:

> Handle walk-in traffic (239)
> Identify new markets (309)
> Handle sales leads (323)
> Handle customer calls (324)
> Perform sales follow-up (325)
> Close a sale (333)
> Identify new opportunities and expand existing markets (530)
> Sales administration (780)
> Direct sales into new market areas (1167)
> Develop and maintain local sales leads (1174)
> Liaise with environment department (505)

Figure 8.6.   Functions supported by Sales Lead Tracking.

Application: Facility Maintenance Planning
Functions Supported:

>Gather facility maintenance history
>Identify items that require preventative maintenance
>Identify other maintenance, repair, or alteration
>Determine schedule constraints, eliminate duplication
>Identify inspections to perform
>Schedule inspections and generate orders
>Analyze findings from inspections
>Prepare work request

Figure 8.7. Functions supported by Facility Maintenance Planning.

Application: Production Control System
Functions Supported:

>Analyze and improve existing products and processes (221)
>Calculate equivalent unit of output (187)
>Ensure conformance to process standards (241)
>Ensure conformance to product standards (242)
>Identify cause of failure (247)
>Manage production capacity (236)
>Machine insertion of components (217)
>Manage progress of customer order (210)
>Perform inspections (245)
>Repair defects to meet specifications (219)
>Test functionality of product (246)

Figure 8.8. Functions supported by production control system.

Every function in the business model does not have to be supported by an application, but when it is not, a reasonable explanation should be documented. There are several reasons a function might not be supported by any application. For example, the functions in Figure 8.9 preceded by an asterisk (*) are considered to be outside the scope of EAP, and therefore no applications are intended to support those functions. Another explanation might be that a function is indirectly supported by receiving data from other functions, people, or organization units rather than directly from an application.

PARTIAL LIST OF FUNCTIONS NOT SUPPORTED BY APPLICATIONS

* Demonstrate technology (880)
* Set policy (26)
Administer stock option plans (1072)
Conduct internal and external investigations (1127)
Coordinate company functions (687)
Develop career programs (241)
Establish budget timetable (116)
Liaise with customer accounting (502)
Liaise with engineering (500)
Liaise with legal department (505)
Maintain existing markets (335)
Maintain photocopy equipment (62)
Maintain sales display area (307)
Perform first aid (778)
Serve as company spokesperson (680)
Mediate lunch-hour discussions (1111)

Figure 8.9. List of functions not supported by applications architecture.

Task 3 Relate applications to organization units via business functions. As part of the business model, functions were related to the organization units that performed those functions. Task one, above, related applications to business functions. Cross-reference lists or matrices can therefore be created to show the relationship of applications to organization units. Since the 80/20 principle has been used, the inference of organization unit support will not be completely accurate, but the extent of applications that span multiple organization units, nevertheless, can be reasonably determined.

Figure 8.10 shows part of a report that relates applications to organization units via business functions.

This figure is for one application named Miscellaneous Billing. The first column lists the full name of the function being supported by this application. The second column lists the organization units that perform those functions and are therefore also assumed to be supported by this application. Figure 8.10 shows that the application Miscellaneous Billing supports three different organization units: manufacturing, distribution, and accounting. *This is a common result of EAP*—applications will

---

APPLICATION: MISCELLANEOUS BILLING

FUNCTION FULL NAME	ORGANIZATION
Manufacturing revenue forecasting (250)	Manufacturing
Prepare manufacturing revenue Report (157)	Manufacturing
Market list label Sales (84)	Distribution
Receive and bill sundry sales cards (184)	Accounting
Appr billing of client product changes (39)	Manufacturing
Prepare supplementary order (93)	Accounting
Receive S.O. and batch for billing (171)	Accounting
Receive/file supplemented charges/orders (169)	Accounting
Report revenue/expenses for suppl orders (182)	Accounting
Reconcile work-in-process (190)	Accounting

Figure 8.10. List of organizations supported by Miscellaneous Billing.

span more than one major organizational unit. *A shared data environment also implies a shared applications environment.*

A shared applications environment is of particular significance to organizations that have funded I.S. efforts through a "charge-back" method that allocates the cost of developing, operating, and maintaining an application to the organization unit (department or budget center) that uses it. The question becomes "Who pays for applications that are used by more than one organizational unit?" A shared applications environment can therefore bring about budgetary and political changes. A "charge-back" method can be a major obstacle for achieving a shared data and applications environment, because it is intended for environments in which applications are implemented for a particular organization unit.

Historically, the I.S. organization has been managed as a job-shop. That is, when an order (requests and requirements) is received by I.S. from a department, a system is custom-made (designed and implemented) for that organization unit who pays for it, directly or indirectly, out of their budget. Though I.S. may operate the system, the department feels that they own it. All of the parts (code, modules, data, files) are tailored to fit that application only. The application development area within I.S. may be organized along the departmental lines served.

The industrial revolution brought about a fundamental change in manufacturing from job-shop to assembly-line production. The I.S. function will undergo a similar change as systems development will use interchangeable standard parts from the definitions of applications and entities that will serve the enterprise, not a single organization unit. Development costs will be allocated to the business, and an organization unit will not own applications and will not own data. Instead, there will be responsibilities for managing these resources as there are for the other business resources such as personnel, capital, facilities, equipment, and so on.

Providing data to business functions that need it *when* it is needed is similar to providing electricity, gas, and water to people during daily life. Who pays for the initial construction and installation of the facilities of a utility company? The general public and the areas served are assessed for the cost of initial development. Thereafter, a customer's payment is based on usage, with rates intended to cover maintenance and other costs. Data is a resource, a commodity of value, and the I.S. organization is like a utility company. For the "I.S. utility," data is the commodity and applications are the mechanisms that pump the data to the customer. The cost of the initial applications development, as the architectures are implemented, must be shared by the business community, then each consumer "user" will be charged based on measurable usage. For some companies this means a significant change in I.S. financial accounting policies and political changes, too, as applications will not be "owned" by a department or single group of users. The sharing of enterprise applications should be understood and accepted *prior to commencing EAP*.

STEP 4—ANALYZE IMPACT TO CURRENT APPLICATIONS

The purpose of this step is to determine the impact of the integrated, enterprisewide applications on the existing applications defined in the Information Resource Catalog. As with step 3 above, this step can also be performed concurrently with step 2. This step is sometimes performed as part of the Implementation/ Migration Phase (Chapter 10) in some EAP projects, because it compares existing applications (today) to the conceptual applications (future).

Deliverable

1. Impact statement of applications architecture to existing systems

Tasks and Guidelines

Task 1 Relate each application in the applications architecture to existing systems defined in the Information Resource Catalog. Note whether each existing application is expected to be

- *completely replaced* by the application in the applications architecture,
- *partially replaced* and/or modified to be in a shared data environment, or
- *retained* with minimal enhancement.

The time allocated for this step in your EAP workplan and the current status of the project with regard to the schedule will determine the extent of the impact analysis, including

- no impact analysis—this step is skipped due to insufficient time,
- partial impact analysis—there is enough time to provide a simple yes/no answer, with a yes answer assumed to mean "replace" the existing application, or
- full-impact—analysis examine each existing application to determine whether it should be completely replaced, partially replaced, or essentially retained. Codes can be used to represent these three conditions. Alternatively, the impact of existing applications may be rated on a scale (or percentages) from 0 to 10 (or 100), with 0 being full replacement, 10 meaning retain the application as is, and 5 to assume that about half of the existing application will be replaced when the conceptual application is implemented.

There is a many-to-many relationship between existing applications and the conceptual applications defined in the architecture. A detailed impact analysis would describe at the relationship level the extent of the changes expected. But there is usually not enough time in the EAP workplan to perform a detailed impact assessment, and the 80/20 principle will again enable the team to arrive at an acceptable balance between the level of detail and the time and resources to devote to this step. Since one existing application may be replaced by several conceptual applications, the EAP team should verify that the parts of the existing application are replaced consistently and without redundancy.

The EAP team that defined the Sales Lead Tracking System recognized that, over time, the implementation of the architectures would eventually result in the replacement of most existing applications. Thus, within the 80/20 principle, the yes-no impact assessment was sufficient for their planning purposes. Departments in different company locations had independently and redundantly developed similar sales lead tracking applications that would be replaced by one that would provide greater capabilities and consistency across the enterprise. The "new" Sales Lead Tracking application impacted (i.e., replaced) the following existing applications:

Reporting and Tracking Sales Work
[Location A] Sales Reporting
[Location B] Sales Reporting/Tracking
[Location C] Sales Reporting/Tracking
Commercial/Industrial Marketing
[Location D] Sales Productivity
[Location D] Sales Analysis and Tracking

The EAP team that defined the Production Control System faced a different situation, because some of their existing applications were expected to be retained or be partially replaced. For the Production Control System, 19 existing applications involving several product types and production stages were identified as complete replacements. One existing application, named the Dynamic Sequencing System, was expected to require significant modification. Another, the Customer Service Module, was expected to be retained and incorporated into the Production Control System.

Task 2 Check that the impact assessment is complete. Every existing application in the IRC should be related via impact to at least one architecture application. An existing application that is to be retained should be defined as an architecture application or as part of one.

STEP 5—DISTRIBUTE THE APPLICATIONS ARCHITECTURE

The purpose of this step is to inform people throughout the enterprise of the applications that have been defined and to ask for their comments and suggestions. For some EAP projects, this step may be combined with the step to distribute the technology architecture report (see Chapter 9). People may better understand the two architectures when they are combined, because the physical technology—computers, workstations, screens, reports—may be perceived as being the applications themselves. Recognize that some people may have difficulty distinguishing "what an application will do" from "what the application appears to be."

Deliverable

1. Applications architecture document is completed and distributed

Tasks and Guidelines

Task 1 Write an introduction to the applications architecture. Order the applications alphabetically in lists and reports. Make sure that this document and presentation, as with all EAP documents and presentations, are in plain, nontechnical English. See Appendix G for a sample introduction from an applications architecture document.

Task 2 Generate reports, with an introduction for each section to explain the report and discuss significant results or business impact. The EAP toolset should generate definition reports, cross-reference lists, and matrices. Include schematics and diagrams to explain the sharing of data. One of the reports in Appendix G describes the usage of data by applications. Relating applications to entities can be performed as part of the Applications Architecture Phase of EAP, or as part of the Implementation/ Migration Planning Phase. In this book, the usage of data by applications is discussed in the first step of Chapter 10.

Task 3 Prepare presentation material using appropriate props. Use business analogies to explain the applications. Scenarios and demonstrations can be used to illustrate the impact of applications for particular business functional areas.

OUTLINE FOR APPLICATIONS ARCHITECTURE PRESENTATION

I. INTRODUCTION
    A. EAP project phases
    B. Status of current phase
    C. Update the business model and data architecture
II. APPLICATIONS ARCHITECTURE CONCEPTS
    A. What is an application? Components of Applications
    B. Goodness cirteria
    C. Sample applications architecture reports
    D. Business impact of applications architecture
III. NEXT STEPS
    A. Review comments to applications architecture
    B. Technology architecture
    C. Implementation planning phase

Figure 8.11. Outline for applications architecture presentation.

Task 4 Present the applications architecture to management and distribute the report. Figure 8.11 contains an outline for an applications architecture presentation. Solicit comments and suggestions from the business community regarding the capabilities of applications and support for their respective business functions.

Task 5 Collect written comments from management. The team should review the comments and decide which are applicable and which are not. Revise the applications architecture accordingly.

DISCUSSION QUESTIONS

1. How many applications would you expect to manage data and to support the business functions of the enterprise?
2. Who on your EAP team should lead the discussions about applications?

3. Will additional applications experts (i.e., systems analysts) be employed to supplement the EAP team?
4. How can bias and traditional "old way" thinking be avoided by EAP team members for conceiving applications in this phase?
5. What actions might you consider if the steps in this phase begin to consume too much time?
6. What tactics can be used to avoid the tendency of team members to design how applications will work and keep the focus on what applications should do?

REFERENCES

[1]Martin, James. *Strategic Data Planning Methodologies* (1st ed.), Prentice-Hall, Englewood Cliffs, NJ, 1982.

[2]Finkelstein, Clive. *An Introduction to Information Engineering: From Strategic Planning to Information Systems*, Addison-Wesley, Reading, MA, 1989.

[3]Synott, William. *The Information Weapon: Winning Customers and Markets with Technology*, John Wiley & Sons, New York, 1987.

[4]Marchand, Donald, and Forest Horton, Jr. *Infotrends*, John Wiley & Sons, New York, 1986.

[5]Wiseman, Charles. *Strategy and Computers: Information Systems as Competitive Weapons*, Dow Jones-Irwin, Homewood, Illinois, 1985.

[6]Ives, Blake, and Gerald Learmonth. "The Information System as a Competitive Weapon," *Communications of the ACM*, Vol. 27, No. 12, December 1984.

[7]Rachoff, Nick, Charles Wiseman, and Walter A. Ullrich. "Information Systems for Competitive Advantage: Implementation of a Planning Process," MIS Quarterly, December 1985.

[8]Porter, Michael, and Victor E. Millar. "How Information Gives You Competitive Advantage," *Harvard Business Review*, July–August 1985.

[9]Atkinson, Robert A. "The Real Meaning of Strategic Planning," *Journal of Information Systems Management*, Vol. 8, No. 4, Fall 1991.

[10]Curtice, Robert M., and Dave Stringer. "Visualizing Information Planning," *Computerworld* (In-Depth), January 14, 1991.

9

Technology Architecture

INTRODUCTION

The purpose of the *technology architecture* is to define the major kinds of technologies needed to provide an environment for the applications that are managing data. The aim of this chapter is not to teach technology concepts—distributed computing, networks, communications, and so on—but to describe how to manage this phase as one component of an overall enterprise architecture.

The technology architecture is not a detailed requirements analysis or a design of enterprise computing networks and software. It is a definition of the kinds of technologies—referred to as platforms—that will support the business with a shared data environment. For the data management business, technology platforms provide the means for collecting data from suppliers, transporting, storing and processing data, and delivering data to customers. Technology platforms are the pipeline and physical facilities of a data utility.

The technology architecture corresponds to the Owner's View (second row) of the Network column of the Zachman Framework for I.S. Architectures (see Figure 1.6). Some people may say that the identification of technology platforms goes beyond the business logistics network of the second level in the framework. However, the framework has been evolving since 1987, and the cell

223

boundaries are subject to interpretation. Most business executives expect technology platform decisions as part of a strategic plan.

The data architecture is a conceptual model that defines entities, and the applications architecture is a conceptual model that defines applications. Similarly, the technology architecture is a conceptual model *defining* platforms, not *designing* them. The technology architecture should not be confused with the fourth level or row of the Framework for I.S. Architecture, the Technology Model. The Technology Model of the framework consists of the physical designs for data in a DBMS, applications in a programming language, and technology with particular equipment.

Technology expertise is needed for this phase. Therefore, this phase, more than any other in EAP, may have additional people with appropriate technological backgrounds to supplement the EAP team. In some EAP projects, a separate team or subcommittee is established to perform this phase. This team is comprised of technology experts plus some members of the EAP team. The EAP project manager should lead the technology team to ensure consistency with the applications architecture, data architecture, and business model. This second team should *not* define the technology architecture independently from the other architectures. It should be defined *after* the data and applications architectures to ensure that the technology platforms are reasonable, feasible, and consistent with the other architectures. Though it may be defined by a separate team, the technology architecture is one component of three interrelated architectures to support the enterprise and should not be viewed or presented as an independent architecture.

Four Steps to Technology Architecture

There are four steps for the Technology Architecture:

1. Identify technology principles and platforms.
2. Define the platforms and distribution.
3. Relate the technology platforms to applications and business functions.
4. Distribute the technology architecture.

The Technology Architecture Phase consumes about 10 percent of the total EAP effort. For most EAP projects, this phase can be completed in less than four weeks. The time allocated to the steps in this phase are

Step 1 = 15 percent

Step 2 = 50 percent

Step 3 = 20 percent

Step 4 = 15 percent

100 percent

STEP 1—IDENTIFY TECHNOLOGY PLATFORMS AND PRINCIPLES

Purpose

The purpose of this step is to identify the underlying principles for technology platforms and the potential platforms needed to support an enterprisewide, shared data environment. The principles will determine the kinds of platforms to be defined in step 2 and set the direction for technology acquisition.

Deliverables

1. Technology platform principles
2. List of candidate technology platforms

Tasks and Guidelines

Task 1 Formulate technology platform principles. Assess trends and changes in technologies regarding computers, communications and networks, storage, software, input and output devices, and so forth. Obtain descriptions and predictions about technology trends from technical information services, consulting companies, books, and articles. Formulate principles that will serve as the basis for the technology architecture. Consider the business model, data architecture, applications architecture, and the opportunities identified by the Information Resource Catalog, and by business people in the Enterprise Survey. Examples of technology platform principles adopted by EAP teams in recent years have included the following:

- Client/server technology will be used for applications and database implementation.
- A common graphical user interface (GUI) will be used by all applications.
- Data storage will use relational technology, and data access will employ SQL.
- Adhere to national and international standards for network protocols and messages (ISO, ANSI, IEEE, CCITT). Employ the seven-layered OSI network management framework.
- Apply open-systems concepts, meaning that operating systems should be
  —portable: run across multiple vendor platforms;
  —scalable: run across a wide power range from small to large computers;
  —interoperable: run in a heterogeneous environment; and
  —compatible: preserve the investment in existing software and enable technology advances to be integrated with other components.
- System development methodology should employ object-oriented techniques, information engineering methods, and be supported by CASE and repository tools from requirements analysis through code generation.
- Data should be captured once at its source.
- Data should be administered centrally and maintained for shared access. Implement the data warehouse concept.
- Information that is stored online will be continuously available.
- Implement distributed data and application systems. Downsize systems such that data and applications are located near the business users.
- Maintain the security of data, software, and hardware assets at all levels of the technology architecture, with security being as transparent as possible.
- Ensure recoverability to protect the continuation of business by having

—adequate and appropriate backups of all data;

—software with built-in error checking and recovery capabilities; and

—integration and compatibility of hardware with redundancies for critical operations.

- Integrate diverse forms of data from multiple sources using multi-media technology.

When the team has reached a consensus agreement on the technology platform principles, one or two team members should formally write the principles and their supporting rationale or justifications. All team members should review and edit this document to produce a compromise statement of technology platform principles.

Task 2   List the potential technology platforms.   A hierarchical decomposition of technology platforms was produced as a part of documenting the current applications and technology architectures (see Chapter 6, step 2, task 3). Update that technology platform decomposition by removing obsolete platforms and adding new categories and technology platforms, consistent with the principles of task 1. The list should identify the kind of platform to be used without specifying a particular vendor or brand name, unless the product has already been acquired from a vendor and the use of that product would be mandatory.

Compile definitions or descriptions of the technology platforms into a glossary. The glossary will explain the platforms to business people who will be reading the technology architecture and should therefore be written with that audience in mind.

STEP 2—DEFINE THE TECHNOLOGY PLATFORMS AND THE DISTRIBUTION OF DATA AND APPLICATIONS

Purpose

Having defined the principles for the technology architecture, the purpose of this step is to determine a strategy for distributing applications and data, and to define the technology platforms that will become an environment for the applications and data to support the business.

Deliverables

1. Data and application distribution tables and lists
2. Configuration of technology platforms
3. Conceptual architecture evaluations (optional)

Tasks and Guidelines

Task 1 List business locations. The location of business functions was identified as part of the business model. Location was documented either as an attribute of an organization unit or as a separate hierarchical structure related to both organization units and business functions. Technology networks generally link department-level organization units, and the structure of the networks usually mirrors the organization unit structure. List the business locations, and for each location, show the organization units and functions performed.

Task 2 Define the data and application distribution. Determine the conceptual locations for storing data and executing applications. A conceptual location may be a specific physical place, or it can be a category or group of places. Examples of conceptual locations are an assembly plant, executive office, or (the current location of) a service vehicle. Relate the entities in the data architecture to business locations by way of the relationship with the business functions that create, update, and reference entities. This will identify the locations that need data. Consider the quantity and form of the data—text, graphics, video, audio, image—to be used by the functions at each location. Applications in the applications architecture can also be related to business locations via the business functions supported by the applications. Consider the primary purpose of the application that should be needed at each location.

For most conceptual technology architectures, the information provided by the relationships of the data entities and applications to business locations is sufficient for describing where the data and applications should reside. Detailed procedures and criteria for distributing data and applications can be found in books by Martin,[1] Gunton,[2] Ceri and Pelagitti,[3] and Coulouris and Dollimore.[4] After following these procedures, cross-reference lists or matrices should be produced from the toolset that show

1. for each conceptual location, the data and applications to reside there;
2. for each entity, the locations for that entity; and
3. for each application, the locations for that application.

For this task and the following one, the team members may tend to go into more detail or thoroughness than required for planning purposes. The 80/20 principle should be judiciously applied to these tasks to ensure that the EAP project is not delayed. Be certain that every team member is aware of the time constraints for these tasks and can arrange his time to be most productive.

Task 3   Define a configuration for the technology platforms.   A vision for the technology environment is created in this task using the platform decisions and principles of step 1 and the data/applications distribution requirements. The conceptual technology architecture should address three levels: the conceptual workstation, the conceptual enterprise network, and the business systems architecture.

The Conceptual Workstation

The conceptual workstation is the facility employed by users to access data directly or provide data to applications or other users. Components of a conceptual workstation are shown in Figure 9.1. All workstations throughout the enterprise should have this structure. A workstation consists of storage locations and compartments.

Storage locations.   A repository or facility that holds applications or data. Lists and directories display the contents of storage locations, and the contents can be transferred from one location to another. Examples of storage locations are desktop, desk drawer, tool box, file cabinet, tool shed, and wastebasket.

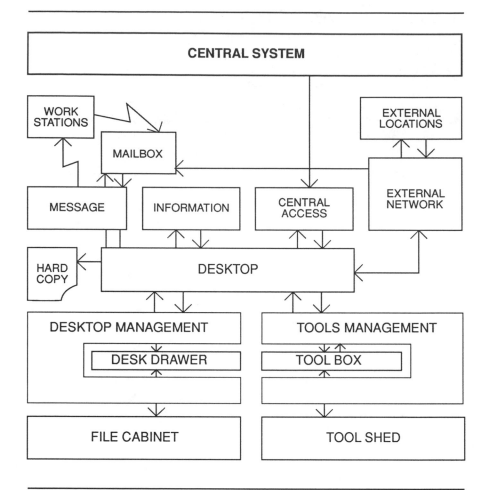

Figure 9.1.   Components of the conceptual workstation.

Compartments.   The compartments of the conceptual workstation provide a wide range of facilities, such as electronic mail, personal information management, input/output services, browsing
and editing. The following are the six compartments of the conceptual workstation:

1. Business systems access compartment
2. Information compartment
3. Message compartment

4. Desktop management compartment
5. Tools management compartment
6. External access compartment

The Conceptual Enterprise Network

The enterprise network consists of computing, input, output, storage devices, and telecommunications facilities. It is called *conceptual* because it is independent of the actual choice of equipment, software, and communications services that will be used to implement it.

An example of a conceptual enterprise network is shown in Figure 9.2. Each of the elements shown in this figure plays a role in providing some form of information support to the functions of the business.

In the conceptual enterprise network, all computing elements are connected directly or indirectly. A direct contact is one in which two network elements interact directly with each other. An indirect connection is one in which they communicate through another network element.

The actual quantities and locations of the network elements are not fixed. They will change over time depending on usage patterns, priorities, and business practices. The conceptual enterprise network should also be flexible and adaptable and accommodate changes with no disruption of operations.

The Business Systems Architecture

The business systems architecture is the technology for implementing and maintaining the applications and databases of the enterprise. One illustration of a business systems architecture is in Figure 9.3. Such illustrations usually show multiple layers through which the data of the business can be accessed.

Access to business systems from the conceptual workstation can be for five purposes:

1. Operational information update creates, changes, or deletes operational data interactively. Applications provide dialogues and screens for this purpose.
2. Operational information inquiry enables applications to ac-

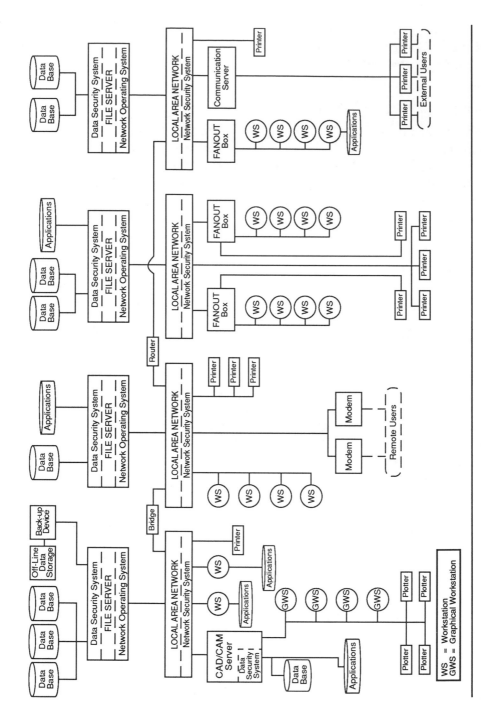

Figure 9.2. Example of conceptual enterprise network.

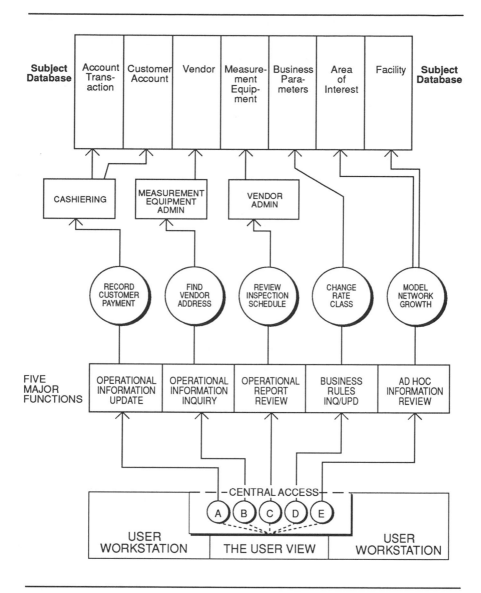

Figure 9.3.   Example of business systems architecture.

cess data interactively and view data in a variety of formats and media that have been prepared in advance. For example, a user can view payment history data about a customer via a unique customer number (the entity identifier) or, alternatively, the user can search all customers using criteria such as customer last name.

3. Operational report review helps users to locate and view batch-generated and scheduled reports.
4. Ad hoc information review provides facilities for accessing enterprise data with SQL or some other convenient language.
5. Business rules inquiry and update enables authorized users to edit rules that govern the operation of business systems. Rules fall into several general classes:
   - edit rules for data,
   - authorization rules covering access and privileges,
   - tables such as price lists, distribution lists, approved suppliers,
   - triggers that cause subsequent actions to be taken when events occur,
   - algorithms and procedures performed as part of applications, such as price determination, payroll deductions, vendor selection, reordering, and
   - decision-making rules and criteria to determine, for example, credit worthiness, risk, and so on.

At the conclusion of this task, draw diagrams to illustrate the conceptual technology configurations and concepts. Define each technology platform in common language so that the concepts can be understood by people throughout the enterprise. Again, use analogies to business facilities to explain technical concepts in familiar terms.

Task 4 Evaluate the conceptual technology architecture (optional). For those businesses that have extremely critical performance requirements regarding technology, use functional performance modeling to determine that the conceptual technology architecture will likely satisfy the requirements. The estimates and assumptions at this stage are quite rough. High-performance requirements may specifically involve the number of transactions, volumes and flows of communications, or response times.

Functional performance modeling may employ mathematical formulas, iconic models, simulations, or situation comparisons. For this task, the EAP team is usually supplemented with people who have this kind of modeling experience.

STEP 3—RELATE THE TECHNOLOGY PLATFORMS TO APPLICATIONS AND BUSINESS FUNCTIONS

Purpose

This step will begin to establish a justification for the technology platforms by relating them to the business functions that will directly utilize them.

Deliverables

1. Technology platform-to-application cross-reference list and tables
2. Technology platform-to-business function cross-reference list and tables

Tasks and Guidelines

Task 1 Relate technology platforms to applications. Relate the technology platforms identified in the previous step to the applications in the applications architecture that will require that technology. The degree of dependency of an application for a technology platform can be indicated with a Yes–No, High–Moderate–Low, or numerical scale. The relationship can be displayed as a table or matrix, or as a cross-reference list. When compared to the matrix relating existing applications to technology platforms (Chapter 6), the matrix from this task will show new platforms to be utilized by the architecture applications and existing platforms that will be replaced or discontinued. These two matrices, current and future, are among the most valuable products of EAP that show architectural decisions.

Task 2 Relate technology platforms to business functions. Applications were related to business functions in Chapter 8, step 2. Combining that relationship with the result of task 1 above will result in an approximate relationship of the technology platforms to be used by business functions and organization units (via that relationship established in Chapters 4 and 5). For presentation purposes, the combined relationships may be good enough. Time permitting, however, the EAP team should review those implied relationships for reasonableness due to the compounding of the 80/20 principle.

STEP 4—DISTRIBUTE THE TECHNOLOGY ARCHITECTURE

The purpose of this step is to confirm that the enterprisewide technology architecture is reasonable and acceptable. The application architecture may be issued concurrently with the technology architecture as a single document covering both architectures.

Deliverables

1. Technology architecture document
2. Presentation or meetings with the business community
3. Revisions to technology platforms based on user feedback

Tasks and Guidelines

Task 1 Prepare the technology architecture document. Write introductions explaining each section of the document. The glossary of technology terms should be included with the document. Also include the diagrams that illustrate the technology platform concept and the layered configuration. The EAP team should edit drafts of this report to ensure that it is suitable for general distribution. Example tables of contents from technology architecture documents are presented in Appendix H.

Task 2 Prepare presentation materials. Include examples and illustrations of the technology architecture in the presentation. Present/future comparisons can be useful for conveying the impact of new technologies. Create demonstrations of new capabilities to further convey the vision of the future. When creating demonstrations, be mindful of the razzle-dazzle effect; show capabilities that are most useful for management and use glitzy displays with color, windows, tutorials, and graphics.

Task 3   Present the technology architecture (and applications architecture) to the business community emphasizing the benefits and the achievement of business opportunities and success factors.   As with the other prior architectures, solicit the opinions and suggestions from the business community regarding the technology architecture decisions. Ensure that the technology architecture is generally acceptable before proceeding with the Implementation Plan Phase.

Presentations and meetings at this stage should be informal. This is a suggested agenda for a meeting with a business executive:

1. Describe recent business model changes related to their function,
2. Review the data and applications architectures and their influence on the technology architecture,
3. Describe the technology principles and opportunities,
4. Present the technology architecture and discuss the tradeoffs of decisions,
5. Discuss additional business requirements and their implications,
6. If necessary, agree on changes to make the architectures acceptable,
7. Indicate when further comments and suggestions are to be returned,
8. Describe the steps of the Implementation Plan Phase.

Discuss the implications and potential changes to the organization, policies, and procedures for a shared data environment. Review the data integrity and security requirements for the business. Explain that the implementation plan devised in the next phase will answer questions such as "When will the architectures be implemented?" "Who will implement them?" and "How much will they cost?"

Task 4   Revise the technology architecture to accommodate suggestions and comments from the business community.   The EAP team should review all of the comments and suggestions regarding the technology architecture. Revisions may be incorporated to make the architectures acceptable, providing it remains feasible at a reasonable cost.

DISCUSSION QUESTIONS

1. Considering the people and standards of your organization, is it better to separate the reports for the applications and technology architectures, or to issue a single, combined report?
2. What actions can be taken to avoid spending too much time for this phase?
3. What security requirements will influence the technology architecture?
4. Are there corporate missions or goals statements that can be incorporated into your technology vision and principles?
5. With respect to timing or volume, do you expect to have areas of your architecture where the technology performance is critical? How could you show that the architecture should satisfy performance requirements?
6. Is there sufficient industrywide technology knowledge and experience within your organization, or will external support be needed for this step?

REFERENCES

[1]Martin, James. *Strategic Data Planning Methodologies* (1st ed.), Prentice-Hall, Englewood Cliffs, NJ, 1982.

[2]Gunton, Tony. *Infrastructure: Building a Framework for Corporate Information Handling*, Prentice-Hall, Englewood Cliffs, NJ, 1989.

[3]Ceri, S., and G. Pelagitti. *Distributed Databases: Principles and Systems*, McGraw-Hill, Inc., New York, 1984.

[4]Coulouris, George, and Jean Dollimore. *Distributed Systems: Concepts and Design*, Addison-Wesley, Boston, MA, 1989.

Implementation Plan

INTRODUCTION

The purpose of this phase is to formulate and prepare a plan for the implementation of the architectures. As discussed in Chapter 1, architectures without implementation plans usually end up on a shelf with little benefit to the business. The methodology in this book is called Enterprise Architecture *Planning* because the deliverable of most significance to the business is the implementation plan.

The previous phases of EAP have been directed at better understanding the business and defining the architectures that are a vision of the future. In this phase, the business model, Information Resource Catalog, and the three architectures are used to produce an implementation plan.

In some EAP projects, this plan is called a migration strategy to emphasize the strategic move from where the business is today to where the business wants to be in the future. The plan is long term—usually five years or longer. Over that period of time, the architectures will be implemented incrementally, like an office building that is built one floor at a time.

Implementation Plan Steps

There are four steps in creating the implementation plan for architectures.

1. Sequence the applications.
2. Estimate the effort, resources, and produce a schedule.
3. Estimate the costs and benefits of the plan.
4. Determine the success factors and make recommendations.

STEP 1—SEQUENCE THE APPLICATIONS

Purpose

In the Applications Architecture, perhaps more than a hundred applications have been defined. The purpose of this step is to establish priorities and formulate a sequence in which the applications should be implemented.

Chapter 1 stated that EAP was different from traditional systems planning approaches because data would be used to drive the implementation sequence. EAP follows a fundamental application sequencing principle:

*Applications that **create** data should be implemented **before** applications that **use** data.*

This principle is the most important criterion for determining the sequence priority of application development for an architected, shared data environment. Though this principle may seem like common sense, traditional approaches for setting application priorities rarely apply it because the systems are usually large, independent, and contain all the data they need internally. Setting implementation priorities for building and maintaining a shared data resource requires a different approach from traditional systems planning.

Consider the following analogy to constructing a multistory office building from architectural blueprints. Which floor or office of the building should be built first—the basement and foundation that will house the maintenance staff or the executive penthouse suite? There are several technically possible alternatives for constructing each floor of the facility:

1. Build the executive suite first, then elevate it and build the floor beneath it, and in turn, build the desired lower floors by lifting the building to insert each floor.

2. Have the executive suite be in the basement or on the first floor and not at the top.
3. Initially, have the executive suite on the first floor while constructing the floor above it. As each floor is completed, move the executive suite up and redo the interior of the lower floors for another office or purpose. Other offices could similarly shift internally as each upper floor is added, which increases maintenance and eventually retards progress.
4. Start construction with the foundation and basement and continue to add floors with each floor serving its original, intended purpose. The executive suite at the top of the building is constructed last. Obviously, this approach is the one usually followed for constructing an office building.

Compare the alternatives above to how organizations traditionally set priorities for constructing their systems facility. Which system will be built first? The executive information system (EIS) for supporting decisions may be given top priority because executives approve the budget, have substantial influence, and may control the decision itself. Moreover, the I.S. staff will generally strive to fulfill a request from the president or a senior officer.

Alternatives corresponding to the four above for constructing the office facility could be considered for implementing the systems facility:

1. Build the EIS first, connecting it via temporary interfaces to transfer data from existing files and databases to the internal EIS database. When a new application adds to or changes the shared data resource, the interfaces will be modified and the EIS will be enhanced to accommodate the underlying structural changes. This is the most expensive alternative. The real-world complexities and differences between the old files and the databases to a new shared data resource make this approach impractical. Many EISs have been abandoned that have, in essence, attempted to be constructed in this fashion.
2. The EIS is implemented first with its own internal database fed by existing systems, but it is not modified as new applications are developed. This alternative is the fastest, but it is a

short-term solution as the use of the EIS will diminish as better data becomes available from new systems.

3. The traditional approach for setting priorities is to construct applications in order of their perceived importance. The EIS would be among the first to be implemented. Adding a subsequent application that changes or supports the data structure would cause a ripple effect of changes and enhancements to previous applications and their interfaces to existing data. Eventually, the enormous amount of maintenance and enhancements to the systems and the multitude of interfaces would severely limit the amount of new construction, and there would be little ability to satisfy new requirements for data or to adapt to changing business conditions.

4. Construct what Leo Cohen refers to as "source data" applications that create data first.[1] The data resource will grow over time. When an appropriate portion of the data resource has been created, an EIS can be built to work directly from it. This approach is the least expensive and most stable over the long term. Like constructing an office building, this approach to sequencing applications is sound business practice.

Deliverables

1. Application to data entity tables and split matrices
2. Priorities for sequencing
3. Applications in implementation order
4. A plan for converting and/or replacing existing systems
5. Applications grouped into projects
6. Technology implementation sequence

Tasks and Guidelines

Task 1 Relate the applications to data entities via business functions. A matrix relating data entities to business functions was produced in step 3 of the Data Architecture Phase. The relationships in this entity usage matrix noted whether the data was Created, Updated, or Referenced (C, U, R) by each function. In step 3 of the Applications Architecture Phase, the applications were related to the business functions. Applications that would span organization unit boundaries were identified at that point.

These two relationships, applications to functions and functions to entities, can be combined using a process tantamount to matrix multiplication in linear algebra. The resulting matrix relates applications to entities with an entry noting whether an application will create, update, or reference an entity. By convention, applications form the rows of the matrix, and the columns are for the entities. Though this tedious process can be performed manually in about two to four hours, there is an increasing number of products that can combine these relationships or matrices automatically to save some time.

The combined application-to-data matrix is raw or preliminary. The EAP team should review each cell of the application-to-data matrix and verify an entry or lack thereof. The reason for performing this verification is the 80/20 principle. We have accepted that an accuracy or completeness of 80 percent is good enough for planning purposes. However, the result of combining two 80/20-level matrices is significantly less than 80/20—not good enough. An empty cell may require an entry. A cell entry relating an application to an entity may need to be changed or may be eliminated.

Do not accept a combined matrix from the toolset simply because it was generated automatically. Each cell must nevertheless be reviewed to ensure a reasonable degree of accuracy.

Task 2   Rearrange the application-to-data matrix to determine the data-driven sequence.   The rows and columns of the verified matrix need to be rearranged to have the structure illustrated in Figure 10.1. Rows corresponding to applications will be moved up or down, and columns corresponding to data will shift to the left or the right. The aim is to place most of the **C** entries for the Creates along the diagonal of the matrix from the upper left to the lower right, with little or nothing above the **C** entries, and most of the **R** and **U** entries below the **C** entries. The area above the diagonal should be made as empty as possible.

This is an optimization procedure. Rows with the fewest entries will be moved toward the top, and rows with the most entries will sink to the bottom with the **C** entries toward the right

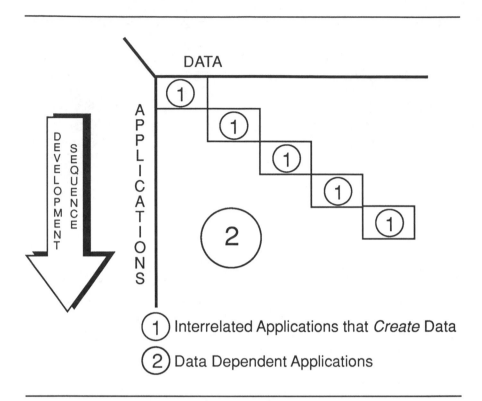

Figure 10.1. Implementation/migration plan application sequencing matrix.

side. Columns with the most entries will shift toward the left, and columns with the fewest entries will shift toward the right with the **C** entries toward the top.

Rearranging the matrix into this form will result in the applications listed on the rows in the data-driven development sequence. That is, the applications at the top of the matrix should be implemented first because they create data used by the applications beneath them.

Figure 10.2 shows an actual matrix that has been rearranged into this format. There are several aspects about the matrix in Figure 10.2 worth noting. The five columns farthest to the left have *no* Creates. This happened because those five kinds of data are static and are updated so infrequently that there were no

APPLICATION / ENTITY-->	MARKET	FILE	SALES REGION	DESIGN REGION	PRODUCTON AREA	CONSULTNT	DISTRICT MANAGER	EMPLOYEE	CHARGE SCALE	CLASSIF CODES	CLIENT CONTACT	CLIENT PROSPECT	SERVICE CONTRCT	CATALOG	JOB	JOB PROD INFO	CASE	TERRTRY ASSGNMT	TERRITORY	VENDOR	BINDERY	PRINTER	CARRIER	DISTRIBUTOR	FILE INVENTORY	PURCHASE ORDER	PRINT & BIND ORDR	PAPER	PAPER INVENTRY	SUPPLMTY ORDER	RECIPIENTS	SHIPMENT	COMP PLAN	PROMOTION	CLIENT REP	PRODUCT TERM
EMPLOYEE-INFO						CUR	CUR	CUR																												
CONTR-PRIC-TBL		R							CUR																											
CLASSIFICATION										CUR																										
CLIENT-PROSPECT	R	R	R	R		R	R	R	R	R	CUR	CUR	R	R	R	R	R	UR	R															R		
ORDER-PROCESS		R	R	R		R	R	R	R	R	R	R	CUR	CUR	CUR	CUR	UR	R	R														R			
ASSIGNMENT-LIST		R	R			R	R	R	R	R	R	R	R	R			CUR	R	R															R		
TERRTY-ALIGNMNT		R	R				R	R				R	R				R	CUR	CUR																	
ACCNTS-RECVBLE		R	R		UR		R				R	R	R	R	R			R																		
SLS-FORECSTNG		R	R				R	R				R	R	R	R		R	R	R																	
CALL-ACTIVITY	R	R	R			R	R	R		R	CUR	UR	R	R			UR	R	R															R		
SALES-RPT-NEW	R	R	R			R	R	R		R	R	R	R	R	R		R	R	R																	
CONSULT-ACTIV		R	R	R	R	R	R	R		R	R	R	R	R	R	CUR	UR	R																		
SUSPECTS	R	R	R				R			R	R	CUR						R	R															R		
VENDOR-INFO		R		R	R		R							R	R	R				CUR	CUR	CUR	CUR	CUR	R	R	R	R	R			R		R		
PRODUCTION-TRACK		R	R	R	R	R	R	R			CUR	R	R	R	UR	CUR				R	R	R			CUR	R	R	R	R	R						
PRODUCTION-EST		R	R	R	R		R	R			R	R	R	R	UR	UR				UR	R	UR				CUR	CUR	R	UR	R						
PAPER-INVENTORY																				UR		R				CUR	R	CUR	CUR							
ACCNT-PAY-INTFC				R	R		R						R	R	UR	UR			R	R	R	UR	R	R		CUR	R	R		R						
MISC-BILLING		R	R	R	R		R				R	R	R	R	R	R			R	R		R				R	R	R		CUR						
COMPLAINT-PROC		R	R	R	R	R	R	UR		R	R	UR	R	R	R	R			R	UR	UR	UR								R						R
RECIPIENT		R																		UR				R	R						CUR	UR				
PAID-DISTRIB		R																		R											UR					
DELIVERY-TRCKNG		R																			R		UR	UR	UR						R	CUR				
DISTRB-RTE-ANYL		R																			R		UR	UR	UR						R	R				
MARKET-COVERAGE	R	R								R																					R					
COMP-PLAN		R	R			R	R	R				R	R					R															CUR			
ADVERTSNG-MKTNG	R	R	R			R	R	R		R	UR	R	R	R				R		UR						CUR					R			CUR		
BUYLINE-MAINT			R				R			R	CUR	R	R	R				R		R															CUR	R
INDEXING		R	R	R		R	R	R		R	UR	R	R	R	R	UR		R		UR	R					CUR										CUR
BUYLINE-INQUIRY										R		R		R						R															R	R

Figure 10.2. Database entities-to-applications relationships.

applications or business functions defined to create them. Situations such as this are apt to occur as a result of the 80/20 principle. The solution for this business was to insert a new application at the top of the list with the purpose of creating and maintaining these five entities.

Notice the boxes that have been drawn diagonally through Figure 10.2. These groups form naturally because of the data shared among applications. One application creates data used by another application, and the second application may create data for the first. Look at the box in the middle of Figure 10.2 that begins with the application called VENDOR-INFO. The VENDOR-INFO application creates VENDOR information that the PAPER-INVENTORY application needs to update and reference. However, the PAPER-INVENTORY application creates PAPER information that the VENDOR-INFO application needs to reference. These applications depend on each other to create data, and therefore should be developed concurrently. Some EAP teams refer to this group of applications as a *project.*

There is another important aspect of the matrix that may not be immediately apparent because the abbreviated names were used for the applications. Some of the applications in the first group support product-planning functions. Those in the second and third groups primarily support sales and marketing functions. The middle group supports production functions, the next supports distribution functions, and the last group supports some of the functions for customer services. If that sequence seems familiar, it is not coincidental. It is a general result of EAP that *the sequence of implementing applications will follow the value chain of the enterprise.* Upon reflection, this seems to be reasonable—each stage in the product or service lifecycle creates data that is used in subsequent stages.

There are two perspectives for the matrix in Figure 10.2. We have seen that the rows show the sequence for implementing applications. The columns on the other dimension from left to right show *the sequence of the creation of the shared data resource.* The entire data resource is not created all at once but rather grows over time to serve the business.

Task 3   Adjust the data-driven sequence to accommodate business needs.   The data-dependency principle used to se-

DEMAND
- Need and importance
- Political issues and pressures

EXISTING SYSTEMS
- Value / adequacy / quality
- Maintenance costs

LIKELIHOOD OF SUCCESS (Risk)
- Resources required
- Resources available
- Length of development
- Technical difficulty and complexity

POTENTIAL BENEFITS
- Return on investment
- Achievement of goals and objectives

ORGANIZATIONAL IMPACT
- Departments and people affected
- Current commitments
- DRM, standards, and procedures

Figure 10.3. Additional sequencing priority criteria for applications.

quence applications in the previous task is the most important criterion. However, there are additional business requirements that must be addressed in setting priorities for the implementation sequence. Figure 10.3 is a list of criteria, in addition to data dependency, to be considered for setting priorities that can influence the implementation sequence.

Demand measures how much an application is needed. The more importance attributed to an application and the more political pressure there is to have it, the sooner it should be developed.

If an existing application is adequately supporting a set of business functions, there is little incentive to modify that application to operate in a shared data environment. Conversely, the more expensive an existing application is to maintain, the sooner another application should replace it.

The likelihood of successfully implementing an application depends on the amount of resources required, the amount of resources available, the time to develop an application, and its technical difficulty and complexity. Generally, a risky application should be pushed back in the sequence. Applications that can be implemented quickly and have a high probability for success should be implemented as soon as possible.

Applications with the highest payback or rate of return should be implemented sooner. Applications having the least amount of impact to the organization, commitments, and standards should be the easiest to implement and could be completed sooner. In short, important business conditions could and should affect the sequence of implementation determined by data dependency.

The EAP team should examine the general list of priority criteria, define in writing specific criteria for their situation, and set a *relative* weight or importance to each criterion by evaluating the tradeoffs among them. If goals and objectives were documented with the business model, consider them to determine the cirteria and weights. Demand, for example, may be considered equal in weight to all other criteria combined. Return on investment may be considered twice as important as risk.

Then the team should rate or score every application individually for each criterion. Multiply the rate times the weight and add the scores for each application. Applications scoring the highest should be moved to an earlier position in the sequence than those with a low score.

Use the application-to-entity matrix to determine the impact from the data resource perspective for each adjustment to the application sequence. Some applications can be easily moved in the sequence, particularly within a natural project group, but moving others can have serious consequences. Moving an application up or sooner in the sequence may cause it to require data that may not have been created by a prior application. In that situation, there are several alternatives available:

1. Move the application up in the sequence and construct temporary interfaces to existing files and databases for needed

data that would not be part of the shared data resource at that time. Building and maintaining bridges, as they are sometimes called, can substantially increase the cost of an application, with 200 to 300 percent increases possible. Nevertheless, if the benefits of having the application sooner are significantly greater than the costs, then implementing the application earlier may be an acceptable business decision.

2. Move the application up in the sequence and add to it the capabilities of creating and maintaining all required data—capabilities that would otherwise be part of other applications. The cost increase of the added capabilities can be as much as, if not greater than, the first alternative above but may be preferred because temporary bridges would not be constructed. This alternative may require significantly more resources than current levels during the first years of implementation.

3. Split the application. Portions of the application that would only use available data can be moved to an earlier position in the sequence. The capabilities of the application that require other kinds of data can be implemented later in the sequence.

Task 4 Make nonquantifiable adjustments to the sequence.   Data dependency was used to determine the initial application sequence in task 2. In task 3, measurable or quantifiable criteria were used to adjust that sequence. There will usually be another factor to consider that will not be quantifiable but will, nevertheless, affect the sequence.

For example, because the sequence of applications tends to follow the value-added chain of the business, the functions at the end of the value-added chain, such as Customer Service, would not be supported until late in the implementation plan. The wait could be five years or longer for those applications. In this case, how much political support for the architectures and plans could be expected from the Customer Service department? No support at all, and probably worse, this situation would provide incentive for that organization unit to discredit the plan and have it rejected. If the plans are rejected, EAP will not be viewed as successful and the architectures would remain on the shelf. Therefore, it is necessary for EAP to *provide every organization unit as much benefit as soon as possible* in order to maximize political support for the architectures and plans. Such unquantifiable criteria can cause some applications to be moved up in the sequence and others to be moved down.

Another reason for nonquantifiable adjustments is to accommodate environmental changes outside the control of the business. These include legislative directives, taxes, industry rules and regulations, currency valuations, wars, competitive moves, and so forth. New applications or enhancements borne from these kinds of events have to be implemented first—there is no choice. Sometimes, the necessity for an application is sudden, other times the need may be known well in advance. Regardless, criteria of this kind can affect the implementation sequence.

Avoid major departures from the natural data-driven sequence to accommodate the quantifiable and nonquantifiable criteria. As a general rule of thumb, avoid moving an application in the sequence more than 20 percent of the length of the data-driven sequence. For example, if there are 100 applications in the sequence, avoid moving an application more than 20 positions in either direction in the sequence from its data-driven position determined in step 2. Doing so usually means making major changes to that application—rearrangement of components, construction of interfaces and bridges—that will substantially increase the cost of development and maintenance.

The EAP team will discuss and evaluate the tradeoffs of the sequencing decisions to arrive at a compromise. The result of using the application-to-data matrix to balance these three criteria categories—data dependency, quantifiable business considerations, and nonquantifiable adjustments—is a *split matrix* showing the overall implementation sequence for applications and data. Figure 10.4 is an example of a split matrix.

The split matrix has two parts. The upper part is from the top to the dotted line and usually includes about 30 to 40 percent of the applications portfolio in an arrangement similar to the matrix in Figure 10.2. This upper part contains *the most important* applications, considered so because

1. they create data that other applications must have,
2. they scored high on the list of important business criteria, and

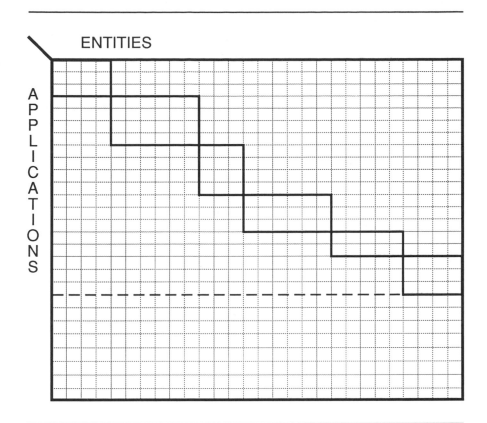

ENTITIES

APPLICATIONS

Figure 10.4. Structure of the split matrix.

3. they have a nonquantifiable importance to the business or EAP.

The lower part has the rest of the applications sequenced by data dependency and business criteria scores. Applications in this group are not unimportant, just not as critical or essential as those in the upper part.

The split matrix can be put to good use. First, it can be used to explain the implementation sequence. It is difficult for anyone to contest the data-driven sequencing principle and the matrix will visually assess the impact of suggesting changes to sequence.

Second, the split matrix usually shows that implementing about one-third of the applications will result in the creation of most (about 90 percent) of the shared data resource. The data resource will be available for access before many of the applications are built that use the data. Query, executive information systems, and data warehouse activities, for example, can begin relatively soon in the migration strategy.

Task 5   Show the sequence of existing system replacement and technology acquisition. Having ordered the applications in the architecture into an implementation sequence, the sequence in which the existing applications are defined in the Information Resource Catalog can be determined. Use the impact assessment from step 4 of the Applications Architecture Phase. The impact relationship specifies whether the existing application will be completely replaced, partially replaced, or retained possibly with enhancements. List the existing applications from the IRC in the order of their relationship to the architecture applications in the implementation sequence. This cross-reference list, referred to by some organizations as an application migration strategy, can have the following format:

Architecture Application	Impact	Existing Application
First application	Replaces	Application—A*
	Partially replaces	Application—B
	Replaces	Application—C*
Second application	Retains	Applications—D*
Third application	—	(none)
Fourth application	Partially replaces	Application—B*

The asterisk after the name of an existing application in the table above is used to indicate the last reference to that application in the sequence. Existing application B above is completely replaced after the fourth architecture application is implemented.

The sequence for acquiring and using technology platforms can be similarly determined. Use the relationship of technology platforms to the applications architecture from step 4 of the Technology Architecture Phase. List the technology platforms in the order of their initial use by an application. This list, referred to by some organizations as a technical migration strategy, can be used in step 3 of this phase to estimate the costs over time of acquiring and using the technology platforms.

STEP 2—ESTIMATE THE EFFORT, RESOURCES, AND PRODUCE A SCHEDULE

Purpose

The previous step established a sequence for the data and applications architectures. The purpose of this step is to estimate the amount of effort required for implementation, determine the resources needed, and produce a schedule for implementing architectures. The EAP team may be supplemented for this step with additional people who have experience estimating the effort to implement systems and developing schedules.

Deliverables

1. Resources needed for implementation are determined.
2. Effort estimates for the implementation of each application are made.
3. Schedule for the implementation and/or migration is set.

Tasks and Guidelines

Task 1 Estimate the time to acquire and implement software packages. · The applications architecture did not specify which applications would be purchased and which would be developed internally; the EAP team should make a preliminary determination of this based on what the application is to do, the capabilities of available software packages, and the opinions of professionals external to the EAP team.

Specific software packages available from vendors that are

likely to meet the requirements of an application may be identified, but that is not necessary. There is not enough time for a thorough evaluation of every software package alternative. Applying the 80/20 principle, the decision in this step to implement an application via purchasing a software package rather than internal development only needs to be reasonably accurate for planning purposes.

Currently, most software packages are independent, self-contained systems that are not intended to be integrated into an enterprisewide, shared data environment. Therefore, the EAP team may eliminate most software packages from consideration. The alternative of purchasing a software package for an application may be eliminated because

1. the data and application code of a package cannot easily be shared, modified, expanded, or integrated with other enterprise systems;
2. technology platforms may be incompatible; or
3. a package does not satisfy the basic requirements defined in the architecture.

It may be more costly in the long run to puchase and modify a software package than to develop applications internally. The EAP team must evaluate the tradeoffs, benefits, and costs of software packages and balance both short-term and long-term factors.

I.S. organizations in industries that have traditionally been dependent on software packages—such as banking—may realize that purchasing applications software will not lead to an integrated, shared data environment that will support the long-term goals of the enterprise. A fundamental cultural change to shift from purchasing a software to internal development may be required. If such a change would not be acceptable, then there is little incentive to employ EAP to achieve the mission stated in Chapter 1.

For each application that is expected to be implemented by purchasing a software package, estimate the time and resources needed to evaluate, select and acquire the package, install it, modify the application, and to put the application into production. A software package can implement more than one architectural application. Evaluate the impact to the overall implementation sequence of a software package that implements multiple architectural applications.

Task 2 Make estimates about available resources and estimate the effort to implement the applications. The EAP team should make assumptions regarding the availability of resources, including people (analysts, programmers, users, data analysts), software tools, and technology platforms (mainframes, workstations, networks). The availability of people is generally the most critical resource to consider. There may be practical constraints on resources, such as workspace or computer capacity, and there may be political limitations on head count or expansion.

Assume or select a development methodology or system development lifecycle and a toolset to be used for the implementation. Identify other productivity factors that would affect the estimates of effort. Estimate the amount of effort and length of time to develop applications. Factors to consider include the type of application, complexity, quantity and kind of development resources, number of inputs, outputs, files and databases, learning curve, batch or online, centralized or distributed, and so on.

There are at least three approaches that can be used to produce the time and effort estimates. The first is to rely on the experience and expertise of EAP team members to make estimates. A second approach is for the team to seek out the advice of system scheduling experts and use their estimates. A third approach is to use a computer product for making the estimates regarding applications development. Two products available for this purpose are ESTIMACS[2] and Checkpoint.[3] These products are very helpful for determining preliminary estimates for development efforts, preliminary schedules, and resource and cost estimates. An estimation product should be a component of the EAP toolset. Review the estimates from the toolset; if they are not in accordance with the collective experience of the EAP planning team and other I.S. experts from the organization, then resolve discrepancies and adjust the estimates.

There are two very important benefits to EAP from using estimation and scheduling products. First, estimating the development effort, assigning resources, and producing a development schedule are tedious, time-consuming activities. Not only do these products save valuable time toward the later stage of EAP, but they can evaluate what-if alternatives, incorporate last-minute adjustments, and estimate costs over the life of an application. A second reason to use these products is credibility. A plan to implement the architectures must be credible to be accepted, and estimates are a critical part of the plan. Whose estimates have higher credibility—members of the EAP team with their own political agendas, or a product whose unbiased proprietary formulas are used by major corporations all over the world?

Task 3 Produce an implementation schedule.   The effort estimates and resource assumptions from task 2 need to be combined to produce an implementation schedule that has the relative start and completion dates, elapsed time, and total effort, such as the one shown in Figure 10.5. The products mentioned above can provide assistance for making the schedule and generating Gantt charts to display the schedule such as the one shown in Figure 10.6. Resources need to be assigned and balanced. Application development phases can overlap and share resources. The schedule for implementing the architectures of EAP may cover five to ten years.

In producing the schedule, it is also important for the I.S. function to fulfill its near-term commitments and obligations to the business. When the implementation begins, most developers will continue to work on projects that are already under way, or to maintain existing systems. These prior development and maintenance obligations must be met. The amount of resources dedicated to the implementation and maintenance of architectural systems will increase over time.

This concept is illustrated in Figure 10-7. During the first year of implementation, most I.S. resources are dedicated to existing maintenance and development commitments. As existing systems are replaced in subsequent years, resources will free up and be assigned to architectural systems. This gradual resource allocation must be considered when determining the implementation schedule.

APPLICATION FULL NAME	ESTIMATED DAYS	START MONTH	END MONTH	DUR MONTHS
TRANSITION PHASE				
EMPLOYEE INFO MAINTENANCE	160	2	6	4
CONTRACT PRICING TABLES				
CLASSIFICATION				
CLIENT/PROSPECT MAINTENANCE	400	2	7	5
ORDER PROCESSING	800	5	13	8
ASSIGNMENT LIST & EVALUATION	200	9	13	4
TERRITORY ALIGNMENT	100	11	14	3
	═══			
TOTAL FOR PROJECT GROUP A	**1660**	**2**	**14**	**12**
SALES FORECASTING	200	14	18	4
CALL ACTIVITY	320	15	20	5
SALES REPORTING—NEW	460	18	24	6
CONSULTANT ACTIVITY	300	21	26	5
MONITORING				
SUSPECTS	120	23	26	3
	═══			
TOTAL FOR PROJECT GROUP B	**1400**	**14**	**26**	**12**
PRODUCTION TRACKING	320	26	33	7
PRODUCTION ESTIMATING	160	29	34	5
PAPER INVENTORY	230	31	35	4
ACCOUNTS PAYABLE INTERFACE	150	33	37	4
MISCELLANEOUS BILLING	170	33	37	4
COMPLAINT PROCESSING	120	34	38	4
	═══			
TOTAL FOR PROJECT GROUP C	**1020**	**26**	**38**	**12**
GRAND TOTAL	**4800**	**0**	**60**	**60**

Figure 10.5. Applications estimates and implementation plan (partial listing).

APPLICATION NAME	Scheduled Start	Scheduled Finish	Year 1												Year 2												Year 3						
			J	F	M	A	M	J	J	A	S	O	N	D	J	F	M	A	M	J	J	A	S	O	N	D	J	F	M	A	M	J	J	A	S	O
Transition to Implementation	January 2	April 2																																		
Employee Info Maintenance	April 1	July 26																																		
Contract Pricing Tables	April 1	July 26																																		
Classification System	April 1	July 26																																		
Client/Prospect Maintenance	April 3	September 3																																		
Order Processing	July 1	February 28																																		
Assignment List & Evaluation	October 1	January 27																																		
Territory Alignment	December 1	February 28																																		
Sales Forecasting	March 1	June 26																																		
Call Activity	April 1	August 25																																		
Sales Reporting	July 1	December 29																																		
Consultant Activity Monitoring	September 1	January 25																																		
Suspects Information System	November 1	January 29																																		
Production Tracking	February 1	September 3																																		
Production Estimating	May 1	September 24																																		
Paper Inventory	July 1	October 27																																		
Accounts Payable Interface	September 1	December 28																																		
Miscellaneous Billing	September 1	December 28																																		
Complaint Processing	October 1	January 27																																		

Figure 10.6. Implementation plan schedule (partial listing).

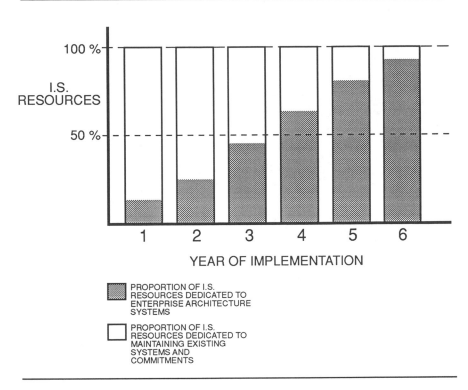

Figure 10.7. I.S. resources dedicated to architecture implementation.

Task 4   Obtain a preliminary acceptance of the implementation/migration strategy from key executives.   Meet privately with the key executives responsible for accepting the final plan. Explain the resource assumptions and the implementation schedule. Listen to their comments and discuss potential problems and tradeoffs. If necessary, revise the resource estimates and produce another schedule that is acceptable. One organization, for example, had estimated 7.3 years to implement the architectures. However, that was an unacceptable time frame to management, since the planning horizon of the company was five years, and no plan over five years would be accepted per company policy. In the revision of their schedule, the EAP team assumed a higher number of resources, assumed that a broad commitment to quality and productivity would result in the use of products such as CASE, adopted a rapid applications system development lifecycle, and was able to produce a plan that could implement the architectures in five years. This plan was ultimately accepted by management.

STEP 3—ESTIMATE THE COSTS AND BENEFITS OF THE PLAN

Purpose

The economic benefits, profit, or rate of return are paramount to organizations making a decision to accept a plan. Some organizations base their decision to implement the architectures solely on financial considerations. For organizations that give costs and benefits the highest priority in accepting an EAP plan, a cost and benefits analysis will have to be part of that plan. There are several books and articles on cost-benefit analysis that delve into this important subject in more detail than can be devoted here.[4] Suggestions for managing this step for EAP are provided below.

Some EAP projects do not require cost-benefit analysis. One organization, for example, had made the assumption that if the architectures could be implemented without adding to the headcount of I.S., then the plans would be accepted. Another decided that as long as the overall I.S. budget did not increase above present levels, the plans would be accepted.

Deliverables

1. Cost-benefit analysis
2. Summary of benefits and opportunities

Tasks and Guidelines

Task 1 Perform a cost-benefit analysis. The analysis should cover both *development and operational* costs. The major categories of costs are

- people,
- hardware and technology,
- software, and
- communications and networks.

The benefits should quantify, in dollars, the savings or income generated by the applications. Categories of benefits include

* head count reduction (efficiency/productivity),
* lower unit production costs, storage costs, or shipping costs (efficiency/productivity),
* estimated income from increased sales or market share (competitive edge),
* better product quality control (effectiveness), and
* better, more timely decisions (effectiveness).

The thoroughness of the analysis should be determined by the EAP team, the corporate decision-making process and culture, and the availability of credible cost data. Adhere to corporate standards for cost-benefit analysis. Because credibility is so important, consult the financial controllers of the organization and involve them in the cost-benefit analysis. If this cost-benefit analysis is of high importance to the organization and the acceptance of the EAP plan depends on the analysis, then this is *not* the task to short-cut due to lack of time.

It is also important in this task to be conservative, thorough, and careful. Numbers should be traceable, so document the source of all cost or savings figures. Variances, ranges, or plus-minus numbers should be provided as an indication of accuracy and confidence. Cost and benefit figures should be confirmed in writing by an authorized person. Never be unable to substantiate the source of cost or benefits figures completely. Cost and savings should *only* be estimated by *first-hand* "experts." Estimates that are the opinions of the EAP team should be clearly labelled. Errors or inconsistencies in this task could discredit the architectures and plans.

Summarize the costs and benefits in tables and graphs that show annual net cost-benefit and cumulative cost-benefit. Highlight the break-even point and rates of return. Figure 10.8 is an example of how these graphics might look.

Task 2 Obtain preliminary management approval of the cost-benefit analysis. Summarize the cost-benefit figures and supporting tables into a format that will enable top manage-

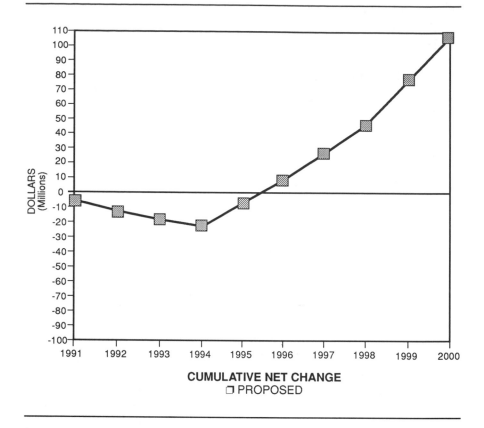

Figure 10.8. Administrative database costs.

ment to make a decision, request changes to the plans, or to resolve issues. Meet with management and the financial controllers of the organization to obtain their preliminary acceptance and approval of the cost-benefit analysis. Be prepared to answer all what, why, who, where, when, and how questions regarding each figure in the analysis. Be prepared, confident, and self-assured when speaking to executives about costs and benefits. To be otherwise would create suspicions about the validity of the figures and may undermine or destroy credibility.

Based on the comments provided by management, revise the cost-benefit figures, the effort estimates, implementation plan, or schedules until all aspects of the plan are acceptable or satisfactory to management. *Do not* wait until the final presentation to attempt to gain approval for the plan. At the end of EAP, there may be no time to make revisions, and the architectures and plans will be accepted or rejected based on the initial analysis. Keep a record of the revisions and tradeoffs made during this review, and the impact of these revisions on supporting the business functions.

Task 3 List the intangible opportunities and benefits. Develop a list of intangible opportunities and benefits that describe the contribution of the architectures and plan to the business. Categorize the benefits as short term, medium range, and long range.

STEP 4—DETERMINE SUCCESS FACTORS AND MAKE RECOMMENDATIONS

Purpose

Implementing a quality shared data environment in which people have access to required data will involve *change*. In order to effect change, decisions must be made. This step will determine the success factors needed to implement the architectures and plans and will formulate recommendations to management to effect favorable decisions. The approval of the architectures and plans means that all recommendations have been accepted and favorable business decisions rendered on all counts.

Deliverables

1. Preliminary report of success factors, implementation strategies, and recommendations for decisions is made.
2. Training requirements are determined.
3. Transition phase schedule is planned.

Tasks and Guidelines

Task 1 Prepare the recommendations. List the critical success factors for implementing the plan. In this context, success factors are conditions—either not presently in place or in jeopardy of an unfavorable change—that will contribute to or enable the implementation of the plan to proceed toward a successful conclusion. For EAP projects, the list of critical success factors may include the following:

- *Establishment of new I.S. organizations or functions*
  Functions such as data resource management, data administration, quality assurance, and system architecture may need to be established within I.S. to be involved in or to be responsible for the implementation of the architectures.

- *Immediate initiation of the Transition Phase*
  After the architectures and plans are presented, the more time that passes before the plans are accepted, the less chance they have of being accepted. Therefore, it is important to begin the Transition Phase—the activities that occur after EAP—immediately upon completion of EAP.

- *Approval of plan*
  If the plan is not approved, the architectures may not be implemented as defined. Therefore, the implementation depends on approving the plan in its entirety. The architectures and plans must not be treated like a governmental budget subject to line item veto. Either the entire plan is accepted for the full planning horizon, or the entire plan is rejected. The plan should not be viewed as a one-year decision to be reassessed next year. There must be a long-term commitment to quality, a multiyear decision.

- *Adoption of new system development methods*
  Methods aimed at increasing productivity and achieving the implementation schedule must be adopted as new standards. System development methodologies such as information engineering, object-oriented analysis and programming, or prototyping may have been assumed to formulate a reasonable, feasible implementation plan.

- *Evaluation/selection/acquisition/installation of new technologies*
  The technology architecture may have defined the need for hardware platforms, distributed networks, software pack-

ages, AD/Cycle, and other technologies required to implement the architectures. Some of these technologies may be required at the beginning of the implementation. Delays for appraising technology acquisition could retard the entire plan.

- *Standards and procedures*
  Standards and procedures for information systems may need to be updated in order to implement the architectures and plans. Approving EAP means accepting that the standards and procedures will be changed.

- *Policy statements issued and approved*
  Policies for data ownership and technology acquisition may need to be written and approved. As with standards and procedures, approving EAP means accepting that some policies will be changed.

- *Leadership of the implementation*
  Organizations and people need to be assigned the responsibility and authority for implementing the architectures and plans, especially for the first few years. Each department within I.S. must have its roles and responsibilities defined regarding the implementation.

- *Budget approval*
  The budget to implement the architectures and plans must be approved. Without funding, the implementation cannot proceed. Approving the plan means accepting the cost figures and is tantamount to approving the budget.

- *Training*
  Implementation usually requires new, expanding, and shifting skills for methods, techniques, applications development, and technology. Adequate training should be procured early in the implementation process. Accepting the plan acknowledges that the training requirements will be approved.

- *Reorganization of I.S.*
  The I.S. organization may need to adapt to the implementation and shift responsibilities as needed to ensure the successful implementation of the architectures and plans.

Describe in detail each critical success factor for the implementation of the architectures and plans. The EAP team should agree on the following for each critical success factor:

- Description of the critical success factor
- Objective or purpose and reason it is critically important
- Recommendations and the desired management decision
- Strategies for implementing the recommendations, and the ramifications in terms of cost and time

Prepare a report on the recommendations based on the discussions in the team meetings. One person should write the report on the critical success factors and recommendations. Each member of the EAP team should review and edit the draft of this report, which typically becomes a chapter of the final report for EAP.

In the team discussions, focus on how to express the critical success factors and recommendations. Use positive language, and avoid the use of negatives such as "If you don't approve [this] then [something bad] will happen." Be clear, succinct, and objective explaining the success factors and recommendations.

Task 2   Confirm the recommendations with management.
Present the recommendations to management and negotiate an agreement. Be convincing and confident when discussing recommendations with management; offer valid arguments. Refer back to the suggestions for obtaining management approval in Chapter 3. If a recommendation is rejected, then either change the architectures and plans so that the condition is no longer critical, or reformulate the recommendation to win approval. *All* of the final plans and recommendations must be feasible and acceptable to management for EAP to be considered successful. Maintain a record of the decisions and changes made to the architecture.

Task 3   Define the training requirements. Define the training requirements for departments and personnel within I.S., and for the users of applications and technology. New technologies, applications, standards, and policies will require training. Stating the kinds of training that will be needed will clarify the organizational impact of accepting the architectures and plans.

Task 4   Develop a transition phase schedule.   The success factors discussed above are often implemented during the Transition to Implementation Phase. This transition phase generally begins immediately after the formal end of EAP and continues until the implementation of the architectures is under way. Prepare a schedule for the activities that need to begin after EAP is completed. This transition phase may be as short as two months or as long as a year, depending on the number of decisions that need to be made, how prepared the organization is to implement the architectures, and how much change to the enterprise is involved. Chapter 12 presents some of the steps that are typically part of the transition phase.

DISCUSSION QUESTIONS

1. Will a formal cost-benefit analysis be necessary for your EAP?
2. One of the most difficult challenges of the EAP team is to convince the management of the enterprise to accept the sequence and schedules of the implementation. What steps will you take to ensure that your implementation plan is accepted by management?
3. Are there specific critical success factors for implementing your architectures and plans that were not mentioned in step 4?
4. Will your toolset handle the matrix multiplication and the row-column manipulation to facilitate the sequencing of applications?
5. What kinds of people should supplement the EAP for the steps in this phase?

REFERENCES

[1]Cohen, Leo J. *Creating and Planning the Corporate Data Base System Project*, Mountain House Publishing, Waitsfield, VT, 1981.

[2]ESTIMACS. Computer Associates, Mt. Laurel, NJ.

[3]Checkpoint. Software Productivity Research, Inc., 77 South Bedford Street, Burlington, MA 01803-5154.

[4]See the books and articles listed in the bibliography by Marilyn Parker.

11

Planning Conclusion

INTRODUCTION

The intent of this chapter is *not* to teach how to write an effective report or make an effective presentation. There are books, articles, and seminars that address these topics. Rather, its purpose is to provide guidelines and suggestions for *managing* this final phase of Enterprise Architecture Planning. References on effective report writing and presentations have been included in section 8 of the Bibliography.

This chapter describes two of the most important steps of EAP. After months of effort to define the business model, the Information Resource Catalog, the architectures, and a migration strategy, the acceptance of this work may depend on the final report and presentations. Therefore, it is *very* important to allow adequate time for these planning conclusion steps. Give the scheduling of the final report and presentations serious consideration during the Planning Initiation Phase. It is the choice of the EAP project manager whether the planning conclusion steps are a separate phase in the workplan, or are the last step of the Implementation Plan Phase.

Three mistakes are commonly made by EAP project managers regarding the planning conclusion steps. One mistake at the beginning of EAP is to feel that the planning conclusion is so "far down the road" that "we will cross that bridge when we get there." Unfortunately, that attitude tends to diminish the objective of EAP, and the lack of goal-oriented project planning increases the likelihood that the final "bridge" will not even be reached, let alone crossed.

Another common mistake of EAP project managers is to underestimate the effort of these final steps. Usually, two or three weeks are needed to prepare good reports and presentations for EAP.

A third mistake made as EAP progresses is to "borrow time" originally allocated to planning conclusion, when extra effort caused additional time to be consumed by prior steps. More entities than expected may be defined in the data architecture, more interviews conducted for the enterprise survey, or complicated areas of the business may need more levels of functions in the business model. Do *not* assume that the duration of planning conclusion will be less if (a) more resources are assigned to these last two steps, (b) the work is distributed among team members, (c) team members work harder toward the end of EAP, (d) the presentations and reports are shortened, or (e) the reports are written concurrently with prior steps. Despite the best intentions, the accumulated time taken from planning conclusion will weaken the final products and jeopardize success. A diligent application of the 80/20 principle throughout EAP should avoid time and resource shortages for these last steps.

Do not schedule the planning conclusion to be completed late in December when year-end pressure is extreme, focusing is difficult, and few people are available for creating a well-written, high-quality final report and presentation. How many people will attend a final presentation held the day before or after a holiday?

The most detailed business model and highest-quality architectures can be wasted if the final report is not understood, the presentations are not well attended, or if the management of the enterprise is not convinced to accept the recommendations and plans. This unfortunate outcome can be avoided by properly managing the EAP project and especially these final steps.

Steps to Planning Conclusion

There are two steps to planning conclusion.

1. Prepare the final report.
2. Make presentations to management.

STEP 1—PREPARE THE FINAL REPORT

Purpose

The purpose of this step is to prepare and deliver the final report for Enterprise Architecture Planning.

Deliverable

1. Final report of EAP

Tasks and Guidelines

Task 1 Develop an outline for the final report. The outline for the final report should be consistent with the corporate culture. The contents of the report are also dependent on the materials that have been distributed during prior phases of EAP and other company standards. Figures 11.1 and 11.2 are two sample tables of contents for final reports prepared for two projects that were conducted differently. The first report was for an EAP project that had not distributed the architectures; hence much of the report explained and included the architectures, as well as the costs, benefits, and critical success factors. The second EAP report was for a project that had distributed the architectures in prior reports, and, consequently, the architectures were not part of the final report. The focus of this second report was the migration strategy, and nearly one-third of the report was devoted to management strategies for the development of a shared data environment.

Task 2 Write the report. Assign responsibilities to team members to write and compile the sections of the report. The title

**STRATEGIC DATA
DEVELOPMENT PLAN**

Table of Contents   **Page**

1. EXECUTIVE SUMMARY
   1.1 Introduction and Objectives 3
   1.2 Data Development Plan 6
   1.3 Critical Success Factors and Recommendations 14
   1.4 Costs and Benefits 17
   1.5 Project Team 18

2. PROJECT APPROACH
   2.1 Project Background and Objectives 21
   2.2 Methodology and Encyclopedia 23
   2.3 Interviews 29

3. SYSTEMS ARCHITECTURE
   3.1 Business Model 37
   3.2 Data Architecture 52
   3.3 Application System Portfolio 114
   3.4 Current and Future Operating Environment 182

4. IMPLEMENTATION STRATEGY AND SCHEDULE
   4.1 Sequence of Applications 191
   4.2 System Projects and Schedule 194
   4.3 Conversion of Current Production Systems 207

5. CRITICAL SUCCESS FACTORS AND RECOMMENDATIONS 211

6. COST AND BENEFITS
   6.1 Current System Operational Costs 219
   6.2 Architectural Cost and Savings 221
   6.3 Benefits 239

APPENDIXES
   1. Organizational Chart
   2. Current I.S. Systems
   3. Business Functions and Information Sources
   4. ESTIMACS Questions and Responses

Figure 11.1. Final report outline example 1.

ENTERPRISE COMPUTING ENVIRONMENT

Table of Contents   **Page**

INTRODUCTION

MANAGEMENT SUMMARY 4
   The Need for an Enterprise Approach 4
   The Benefits of an Enterprise Approach 5
   Expenditures on Information Technology 8
   Critical Success Factors 9
   Implications of Not Adopting an Enterprise Approach 9
   Recommendations 10
   Conclusion 10

ASSUMPTIONS 11

APPROACH USED 12
   Background 12
   Introduction to EAP 12
   EAP Phases 13

THE PLANNING PROCESS 22
   The Long Range 22
   The Mid-Range 22
   The Short Range 22
   Annual Review 23

THE LONG RANGE 25
   Maintenance and Support 25
   Applications Target 25
   Data Target 29
   Technology Target 32

THE MID-RANGE (YEARS 2 AND 3) 42
   Applications Target 42
   Data Target 49
   Technology Target 49

THE SHORT RANGE (YEAR 1) 50
   Current Projects 50
   Applications Target 57
   Maintenance and Support 58
   Data Target 63
   Technology Target 63

Figure 11.2. Final report outline example 2.

MANAGEMENT STRATEGIES FOR INFORMATION TECHNOLOGY 64
  Major Strategies 64
  Planning Strategy for Information Technology 65
  Organization Strategy for Information Technology 73
  Leadership Strategy for Information Technology 80
  Control Strategy for Information Technology 85

MANAGEMENT STRATEGIES—SHORT RANGE 91
  Plan 91
  Organize 92
  Lead 93
  Control 94
OTHER REPORTS 95

Figure 11.2. *Continued*

for the report should be politically acceptable to executives and consistent with the corporate culture. Portions of the report may have been prepared in prior EAP steps, but most of the contents will probably be from the implementation plan (Chapter 10).

Write the executive overview last, and include figures from the body of the report that support the findings and recommendations. Avoid technical jargon. This is a business report for executives and managers, and it will be distributed widely throughout the organization. It is also a political document, so choose all words and expressions thoughtfully. In these kinds of reports, it is best to avoid

- strong, emotional words,
- unsubstantiated statements,
- non sequiturs (conclusions that don't support the facts),
- unlabeled opinions,
- naming people, and
- controversy.

Do not take a stand on an unresolved or unsupported issue that would cause disagreement or bring the validity of the entire report into question. However, the team is responsible for presenting recommendations regarding critical success factors for implementing the architectures and plans. Depending on the corporate culture, it may be best not to raise politically sensitive issues in the report, but seek an acceptable resolution through other channels. When writing about unresolved issues, appear objective by presenting all points of view fairly and in unbiased, unemotional terms. To avoid questions aimed at credibility, clearly identify the sources for all facts and figures. Voluminous support material can be placed in appendices or separate documents.

Task 3   Prepare a draft of the final report.   Team members should edit all parts of the document. The quality of the writing is important. Check spelling, grammar, and vocabulary; eliminate pronouns. Fast turnaround is paramount when delivery dates for the EAP products are at hand. The overseers of EAP should review a draft of the entire report. Also solicit comments on the draft from experienced, politically astute individuals within the enterprise.

Bring in an outside expert who is known and respected by the CEO and/or other top management to review and attest to the credibility of the architectures, plans, and the methodology used for Enterprise Architecture Planning. For example, if it is known that the CEO graduated from the University of Michigan Business School with an MBA, employ a professor from that business school to review the EAP material and report. Professors frequently take on short-term consulting assignments and can perform this kind of work. Even a casual comment during a presentation to the CEO that a Michigan professor reviewed the EAP results and found them to be credible and in accordance with modern practices for I.S. planning can have significant impact.

The report should be professional in appearance. Graphic artists and desktop publishing personnel should make the report look attractive, impressive, and have a sense of quality. Use company-standard bindings and section dividers. Consider the lead time for printing and binding in the EAP workplan so that the document can be delivered on its due date. A final report that appears poorly prepared will not be credible or given the attention it warrants.

Task 4   Distribute the report throughout the enterprise. Make a list of all executives and management in the enterprise who should receive a copy of the final report for EAP. Have extra reports printed to meet any unexpected requests. Generally, the distribution of the final report should coincide with the delivery of the final presentation.

STEP 2—MAKE FINAL PRESENTATIONS TO MANAGEMENT

Purpose

The purpose of this step is to prepare and deliver final presentations to the management of the enterprise that explain the results of EAP and ultimately to obtain the final approval and support to proceed with the implementation of the recommendations and plans.

Deliverables

1. Presentation materials are prepared.
2. Presentations are delivered.

Tasks and Guidelines

Task 1   Prepare the presentation materials.   Write a presentation outline and estimate the amount of time each section should take. To further refine the outline, obtain advice from an experienced presentation preparer. It is important to make the conclusion or main point in the first 100 seconds of the presentation. The audience will contain high-level executives, and it is unlikely they will listen very long to hear the main point. Many executives will decide in the first two minutes whether to listen to the results of EAP or to turn their attention elsewhere, possibly leaving the room, unless the speaker establishes something important and worth hearing.

One technique for capturing attention is to develop a surefire *grabber* that will capture attention and persuade someone to accept the results of EAP immediately. In EAP presentations, the grabber is usually an analogy that compares the business of providing data to providing the products or services of the enterprise. It should take only 100 seconds to make the irrefutable point that the present situation is not satisfactory, that previous systems development practices have been inappropriate, and that the implementation of the architectures and plans are needed to conduct the "data business" properly.

Another useful tactic for keeping executive attention is to use props to show the thoroughness of the enterprise survey, explain the concept of a data entity, or to illustrate aspects of future systems. For example, place a table or cart at the side of the presentation room in a clearly visible position, with binders containing the forms and samples of information sources gathered during the Enterprise Survey Phase. During the presentation, when mentioning the findings or effort that went into EAP, stand next to these materials. It is important for the audience to understand that the architectures and plans are not the product of a CASE tool or the opinion of some guru, but the result of a collaborative effort based on a thorough knowledge of the business.

Props are useful for explaining the concept of an entity in the data architecture. Hold up an object that every attendee will readily recognize, such as a product, and provide a definition for the object, point to its characteristics, and identify its relationships to other kinds of objects. Demonstrations can be useful to illustrate major benefits or capabilities of the architectures. Paint a scenario in which critical business goals are being achieved.

Schedule the presentation at a convenient time and location for the key attendees, executives or managers that have some role in the acceptance and approval of the architectures and plans. Confer with each individual to schedule the presentation, and confirm their attendance via memo. Include a list of attendees with the memo. If the presentation is scheduled more than 10 days in advance, send a message to each person as a reminder one or two days before the presentation.

Task 2 Deliver the presentation. When more than one person will make the presentation, "choreograph" the parts. Write notes for the main points of each slide and put them into a two-sided notebook with the slides or overhead transparencies. Presentation graphics software may have facilities for printing notes with the slides. Label the parts of the presentation and practice each person's part. Be sure that every important point is made and that the presentation does not drag. Select an alternate to be a "stand-in" if a participant cannot make a rehearsal, and check the timing.

Be clear, concise, and correct about everything stated in the presentation. It is important to tell management what *they* want to hear, not what you want to say. After months of work, there is a natural desire to discuss the intensive effort of the EAP process and the quality of the architectures. However, the audience is not interested in the amount of effort, the methodology, or congratulating the team for a job well done. Instead, the attendees want to hear the results of EAP and to understand what it means for them. They are most interested in the impact on their business if the EAP architectures and plans are accepted. It is important to develop the presentation from this "What's in it for me?" point of view.

Another presentation factor of great importance is the credibility of the speaker. The final presentation should be delivered by a person or people with an established reputation. For example, if the presentation is to be given to each department of the organization, then a major portion of it can be conducted by the EAP team representatives from the respective departments.

Speak with confidence and authority, or your results will be suspect. Answer all questions directly, concisely, and with self-assuredness. Some questions should be postponed until the end of the presentation, but be sure to answer them then. Stick to the agenda and schedule. A presentation can be made to top management in a single session, and, depending on the political and cultural situation, presentations may be made to the management of each department throughout the enterprise. Neglecting a key executive or department could severely impact the acceptance of the architectures and plans.

Task 3   At the end of EAP, have a team party.   The last, albeit unofficial, task of EAP is to have a party for the team. A great amount of time and effort has gone into developing the architectures and plans. It has been a team effort, and the members will have developed a spirit of teamsmanship and cooperation, so it is fitting to celebrate the successful completion of EAP with a party.

DISCUSSION QUESTIONS

1. Do you have resources available to help prepare a professional-looking final report?
2. Who should or can edit the draft of the report for strong, emotional words, unsubstantiated statements, non sequiturs, unlabeled opinions, personal references, and controversy?
3. Who will prepare the distribution list for the final report?
4. Is there an outside, credible expert to audit the EAP recommendations and plans for the CEO or primary decision maker?
5. Who will deliver the final presentations? Will it be one person or a team of people?
6. What would be a good, sure-fire "grabber" for the presentation?
7. What props could be used in the presentation to explain the architectures?
8. Will the report be published in-house or sent to an outside printer? How much time will be allocated for printing?
9. Will attendees receive copies of the presentation materials?
10. How many team members will be assigned writing responsibilities for drafting the final report? Who will be responsible for editing the final report and making sure the style is consistent and in one voice?

12

Transition to Implementation

INTRODUCTION

The final report and presentation mark the official end to Enterprise Architecture Planning. It is absurd to believe that the day after the final report and presentation are delivered, that all I.S. resources would be directed at implementing the architectures. Rather, a transition period that spans from the end of EAP to the beginning of architecture-based systems development should begin immediately upon completion of EAP. This transition period can range from several months to a year, depending on the readiness of the I.S. organizations to begin implementing the architectures.

The Zachman Framework, introduced in Chapter 1, explains the dimensions and levels of information system architectures. EAP is the process for creating levels one and two of the Zachman Framework: the enterprisewide definitions for data, applications (process), and technology (network). Each application and database will be implemented via some kind of process (usually called a system development life cycle) that creates the lower Zachman Framework levels corresponding to design, development, and the implemented components. Thus, from the Zachman perspective, there is a change in the Transition to Implementation Phase from the definition level to the design level, from the enterprisewide level to the individual system level.

The purpose of this chapter is to describe briefly *some* of the steps and tasks that need to occur during a successful transition from the definition stages of EAP to the design stages of implementation. During the transition period, most of the recommendations formulated as part of the migration strategy are accepted and implemented.

The steps listed below are usually part of the Transition to Implementation Phase. The order of their presentation does not imply priority or sequence. Indeed, most of these steps would overlap and be performed at the same time. Some of the steps may not be needed for a particular transition, or additional steps could be required that are not mentioned in this chapter.

Steps for Transition to Implementation

1. Plan the transition.
2. Adopt a system development approach.
3. Arrange for computer resources.
4. Refine the architectures.
5. Institute organizational changes.
6. Recruit implementation personnel.
7. Provide training.
8. Establish programming standards.
9. Establish procedural standards.
10. Develop a detailed schedule for the first set of applications.
11. Confirm the end of transition.

STEP 1—PLAN THE TRANSITION

Task 1   Specify the objectives for the transition.   These are the typical objectives of the transition:

- *Add detail to the architectures.*
  Since EAP has been guided by the 80/20 principle and has been constrained by time limitations, there may be aspects of the architectures and plans that have had detail omitted. After the architectures and plans are accepted, the transition to implementation is the time when further refinement and detail can be added.

- *Gather additional requirements for applications.*
  The descriptions of the applications in the applications architecture are at a summarized, ballpark level. During the transition, time should be allocated to gather additional requirements, especially for the first set of applications to be developed.

- *Acquire and install the hardware and software described in the technology architecture.*
  Determine the requirements to select and test specific hardware and software for implementing the architectures.

- *Produce detailed project workplans.*
  Every application defined in the application architecture will go through a systems development lifecycle. During EAP, the implementation plans were developed at an enterprise level for all applications. During transition, detailed project workplans should be formulated for each individual application to be developed.

- *Implement the EAP recommendations regarding the I.S. organization.*
  This includes decisions about policies and standards, new positions or roles, budgeting, performance evaluation, and so on. In general, the transition to implementation is the time to gear up for "full-steam ahead" implementation of the architectures and plans.

Task 2   Create a transition phase workplan.   Put all transition phase steps, such as those included in this chapter, into a workplan. Much of this workplan should have been created as part of formulating the recommendations in step 4 of Chapter 10. Estimate the amount of effort and the elapsed time to complete each step. The implementation of the first group of applications may be able to begin prior to completing all of the transition steps.

Task 3   Assign responsibilities for the transition.   Have members of the EAP team in positions responsible for the implementation of the architectures. EAP team members are usually qualified for positions of responsibility since they have contributed their time on the EAP project and understand both the architectures and the plans. Additionally, these team members have a vested interest in the success of the overall implementation. The participation of a group responsible for the integrity of data, often known as Data Administration or Data Resource Management, is essential, since the aim is to create a shared data environment.

Task 4   Keep the enthusiasm and momentum high.   The awareness and enthusiasm for EAP peaks at the conclusion when reports and presentations are delivered. It is important to maintain the momentum. Have a high-level executive kick off the transition. Encourage the use of new techniques and tools within I.S. Hold off-site meetings when planning for transition. Use consultants to subsidize personnel shortages, deficiencies in experience, and to ensure that progress is made.

Task 5   Designate a leader for the transition.   The transition needs a person with strong leadership and direction skills who can organize the implementation and institute the recommendations of EAP.

STEP 2—ADOPT A SYSTEM DEVELOPMENT APPROACH

Task 1   Update the system lifecycle.   Determine whether existing systems lifecycle methods and standards of I.S. are appropriate for creating a shared data environment. Consider including methods such as information engineering,[1] joint applications design,[2] rapid application development,[3] prototyping,[4] and object-oriented programming and analysis.[5]

Decisions regarding lifecycle methodology, techniques, and products are both technical and political. Here are a few suggestions for overcoming some of the normal resistance to change:

- Have pilot projects, start small, demonstrate success with the new approach.
- Obtain the support of an important executive.

- Obtain a broad-based approval of the architectures and plans.
- Have the business organization or users assume some implementation responsibilities.
- Use consultants during the transition to implementation.

When adopting a system-development approach, incorporate tasks to use and maintain the architectures. For example, in the prototyping lifecycle shown in Figure 12.1, step 2.3 verifies that the application requirements are consistent with the enterprise-wide architectures and will update the architectures to reflect additional enterprise knowledge learned during the implementation.

Task 2   Use modern tools and techniques to support systems development.   Integrated Computer-Aided Software Engineering (CASE) and other system-development products should be used to support the system-development approach.

STEP 3—ARRANGE FOR COMPUTER RESOURCES

Task 1   Acquire the computer resources.   Evaluate, select, acquire, and install the technology platforms and tools needed to implement the architectures and plans. The following list has some of the technologies that might be selected:

- Data warehouse
- Repository
- Personal computers, workstations
- CASE, software reengineering
- Communications equipment and protocols
- Mainframe upgrades
- LANs, file servers
- Knowledge bases, artificial intelligence

Acquire hardware and software *before* they become critical needs. Follow company standards and procedures for hardware and software acquisition and procurement.

APPLICATIONS PROTOTYPING METHODOLOGY

1. Review Application Development Plan

    1.1 Review Application/Function Definition
    1.2 Review Data Definitions
    1.3 Prepare Application Development Schedule
    1.4 Confirm Management Commitment

2. Define the Application Requirements

    2.1 Design High-Level Functional Specifications
    2.2 Verify Function Specifications with Users, and Gather Additional Requirements
    2.3 Update Enterprise Architectures
    2.4 Differentiate Prototype Requirements from Production System Requirements
    2.5 Publish Prototype Requirements Definition

3. Build Initial Prototype

    3.1 Design and Create the Database
    3.2 Design Menus, Screens, Batch Reports, and User Procedures
    3.3 Design, Code, and Test the Programs
    3.4 Populate the Prototype Database

4. Prototype Iteration and Approval

    4.1 Demonstrate the Prototype and Revise
    4.2 End User Prototype Review and Approval
    4.3 Define and Document all Functions and Performance Requirements and Enhancements Necessary for a Production System

5. Prototype Evolution

    5.1 Implement and Test All Requirements to Production Standards
    5.2 Restructure and Reload the Test Database
    5.3 Tune the System for Performance
    5.4 Test the Application and Obtain Approval for Production

6. Application Installation

    6.1 Move Programs into Production
    6.2 Restructure/Reload the Production Database
    6.3 Publish Documentation
    6.4 Train the Users
    6.5 Schedule the Disengagement of Old System

Figure 12.1. Sample applications prototyping methodology.

Task 2   Create a stable data resource.   Use the DBMS and repository to create a stable environment for managing the data. Have adequate data storage capacity for both test and production, especially when using a prototyping lifecycle. Products to aid database design are useful, but beware of products that promise "better designs" or enormous productivity gains. Such claims are usually unfounded. People are the most important component of any plan to improve productivity. Provide training for new methods, procedures, and technologies.

STEP 4—REFINE THE ARCHITECTURES

Task 1   Revise the architectures.   The final report and architecture documents from EAP will continue to be reviewed by people in the I.S. and business organizations. Acknowledge the feedback and comments about the final report and architectures. The final report should have been widely distributed in the last phase of EAP. During the transition, the comments and suggestions should be used to make the architectures better.

The relationship between the objects in the EAP dictionary should be reviewed and verified during the transition. In particular, review the relationships between business functions and entities, applications and business functions, and applications and entities.

Task 2   Add more detail and update the architectures.   Concentrate on the requirements of the first group of applications. As a consequence of the 80/20 principle, some of the architectures may lack detail or be somewhat incomplete. Detail that was left out due to EAP project time constraints or the 80/20 principle should be added during the transition.

STEP 5—INSTITUTE ORGANIZATIONAL CHANGES

Task 1   New departments.   Establish departments for Systems Architecture, Data Resource Management (DRM), Data Administration (DA), Quality Assurance, Data Security, Network Administration or other organizational units recommended by the

EAP team. Every new organization unit should have a charter document that contains the following:

1. mission statement,
2. responsibilities, interactions with other departments,
3. structure and position descriptions, and
4. unit plans regarding staffing, funding, resources, and projects.

Task 2   Reorganize the I.S. area.   The implementation of the enterprise architecture may require a redistribution of responsibilities within the I.S. area.

Task 3   Issue policy statements.   Policies may need to be stated regarding

- data ownership
- technology acquisition

Policy statements often require the approval of top management and require much time for review. This step should therefore begin early in the transition to implementation.[6]

STEP 6—RECRUIT PERSONNEL

Task 1   Write or revise job descriptions, including new positions.   Architectures, new methods and tools, standards revisions, and I.S. reorganizations usually mean that position descriptions need to be revised. The Human Resource department is often involved in preparing and approving position descriptions.

Task 2   Fill positions.   There may be a need for programmers, data analysts, systems designers, hardware and communications specialists, and so forth, specified in the EAP migration strategy and implementation plans. Though they may have limited technical background, consider recruiting project managers and system analysts from the business units.

Task 3   Employ consultants.   Consultants can assist with recruiting, training, and providing staff until specific positions can be hired and trained. Consultants have expertise with new-system-development approaches, software, and networks. Consultants can also prepare organizational charters, standards and procedures, and can recruit for the permanent positions.

STEP 7—PROVIDE TRAINING

Task 1   Determine training requirements.   Provide training for all new technologies, particularly relational data design, repository, CASE, networks, and new-system-development approaches. The training department within I.S. or Human Resources can be responsible for surveying the available courses.

Task 2   Circulate lists of courses available from internal and external sources.   Encourage the right people to attend these courses.

Task 3   Develop a written training plan or schedule for all personnel within I.S. and the business units involved. The training plan should specify the courses that each individual will take, and when and where he will take them.

Task 4   Update the reference library.   Have a well-stocked library with books, articles, and training materials on all aspects of systems, communications, and architectures.

STEP 8—ESTABLISH PROGRAMMING STANDARDS

The following is a list of some of the programming standards that may need to be established or changed. Many of these will change as the result of moving to a shared data and shared applications environment.

- Screen layouts
- Error handling
- Graphical User Interfaces
- Naming conventions
- Data security
- Table driven
- Options/rules
- Coding conventions
- Documentation
- File upload and download
- Module structure
- Use of color
- Batch controls
- Menu navigation
- Client/server responsibilities
- Architecture layers
- Code sharing
- User views

STEP 9—ESTABLISH PROCEDURAL STANDARDS

The following is a list of some of the procedural standards—those that aid in managing the shared data environment—that may need to be established or changed.

- Equipment operation
- Data transmission
- Log-on procedures
- Central/local backup
- Data replication
- Problem resolution
- Archiving data

- Security
- Forms control
- Ad hoc query
- Data entry
- File transfer
- Local personal computer use
- WAN/LAN administration

STEP 10—DEVELOP A DETAILED SCHEDULE FOR THE FIRST SET OF APPLICATIONS

Planning during EAP was at an application level, without considering each phase and step of a system lifecycle. Before the implementation of an application begins, a detailed system-development plan must be created. Follow the new lifecycle standards to create this plan. Describe the tasks, time frame and duration, deliverables, responsibilities, and participants. Be consistent with the EAP plans and recommendations.

Anticipate an initial learning curve, especially for new tools and technologies. Efficiency can be achieved by overlapping some development tasks of applications, but do not sacrifice time devoted to testing new tools, technologies, and system development methodologies. Plan for contingencies and unexpected events that may occur during system-development projects.

STEP 11—CONFIRM THE END OF THE TRANSITION

Unlike the beginning of the transition, which generally has a specific date, the end of transition usually has no such fixed date. The purpose of transition is to prepare for the implementation of the architectures, and, at some point, it will be recognized that this has been completed and the implementation of the architectures is under way. This point will often coincide with the end of a month or quarter when a formal status report is prepared and this conclusion is drawn.

That status report or a memo marks the formal conclusion of transition and acknowledges that the architectures are being implemented. At this time, unless further approval for proceeding is in doubt, continue with the implementation and migration plan.

REFERENCES

[1]Finkelstein, Clive. *An Introduction to Information Engineering: From Strategic Planning to Information Systems*, Addison-Wesley, Reading, MA, 1989;

Martin, James. *Information Engineering: Planning & Analysis*, Vol. 2, Prentice-Hall, Englewood Cliffs, NJ, 1990; and

Martin, James. *Information Engineering: Design & Construction*, Vol. 3, Prentice-Hall, Englewood Cliffs, NJ, 1990.

[2]Wood, Jane, and Denise Silver. *Joint Application Design*, John Wiley & Sons, New York, 1989.

[3]Martin, James. *Rapid Application Development*, Macmillan Publishing Company, New York, 1991.

[4]Boar, Bernard H. *Application Prototyping: A Requirement Definition Strategy for the 80's*, John Wiley & Sons, New York, 1984.

[5]Coad, Peter, and Edward Yourdon. *Object-Oriented Analysis*, Prentice-Hall (Yourdon Press), Englewood Cliffs, NJ, 1990;

Martin, James, and James Odell, *Object-Oriented Analysis and Design*, Prentice-Hall, Englewood Cliffs, NJ, 1992.

Shlaer, Sally, and Stephen J. Mellor. *Object-Oriented Systems Analysis: Modeling the World in Data*, Prentice-Hall (Yourdon Press), Englewood Cliffs, NJ, 1988; and

Won Kin, and Frederick H. Lochovsky. *Object-Oriented Concepts, Databases, and Applications*, Addison-Wesley, Reading, MA, 1989.

[6]Pinghera, John, and Henry Phills. "The Information Policy of AT&T," *Data Base Newsletter* 16.5, September/October 1988.

Products for the EAP Toolset

The following is a partial list of commercial products that can be used for one or more phases of EAP. Descriptions of products and vendors can be found in the references listed at the end of this Appendix.

PLANNING AND DATA DESIGN SOFTWARE

CA-DB:ARCHITECT (Computer Associates)

DESIGNMANAGER (MSP)

ER-Designer/Modeler (Chen & Associates)

ERwin/ERX (Logic Works)

Expert CIO and SYSTEMS/IRM (P-CUBE Corp.)

IDEF/LEVERAGE (D. Appleton Company)

Information Planner (KnowledgeWare)

IRMA (A.D. Little)

ISMOD (IBM)

PC PRISM (Intersolv)

PLAN/1 (Andersen Consulting)

Planning Workbench of IEW and ADW (KnowledgeWare)

PREDICT CASE (Software AG)

PRIDE—EEM and CAP (M. Bryce & Associates)

PRO PLANNER (Holland Systems)

Systems Engineer (LBMS)

TIP PLAN and DEFINE (Mendon Group Limited)

EXTENSIBLE DATA DICTIONARIES

Brownstone Solution (Brownstone)

CasePac (Computer Associates)

DATACOM/DDOL, IDMS/IDD (Computer Associates)

DATAMANAGER (MSP)

DB Excel (Reltec)

PACBASE and PACDesign (CGI Systems)

PSL/PSA (LBMS)

CASE PRODUCTS

4Front (Intersolv and Deloitte-Touche)

EXCELERATOR (Intersolv)

FOUNDATION (Andersen Consulting)

IE:EXPERT (Information Engineering Systems Corp.)

IEW and ADW (KnowledgeWare)

IEF: Information Engineering Facility (Texas Instruments)

MetaVision (Applied Axiomatics)

ORACLE CASE Architecture (Oracle Corp.)

POSE (Computer Systems Advisors)

POWERHOUSE (Cognos)

ProKit Workbench (McDonnel Douglas IS Group)

Re-Engineering Product Set (Bachman Information Systems)

SILVERRUN (Computer Systems Advisors)

TEAMWORK (Cadre Technologies)

System Architect (Popkin Software)
The Visible Analyst Workbench (Visible Systems)

OTHER PC PRODUCTS

DBMS: R:Base, Paradox, Dbase IV

Spreadsheets: Lotus, Excel, SuperCalc

Project Management: Timeline, Project Workbench

Presentation Graphics: Harvard, Freelance, Diagraph, Powerpoint

Word Processing: Word for Windows, WordPerfect, Ami Pro

Estimation: ESTIMACS, CheckPoint, ASSET-R

Simulation/Animation: SIMSCRIPT, NETSIM, AGE, DESIG N/CPN

Interactive IE Guides: IE-Expert (James Martin &Co.), Foresight (CEC), Navigator (Ernst & Young), MATE (Advanced Development Methods), CASE/FRAMEWORK (CASE Methods Development Corp.)

REFERENCES

CASE Product Guide 1992, Sentry Publishing Company, 1900 West Park Drive, Westborough, MA 01581, 508-366-2031, $99.

1991 CASE Trends Product and Industry Guide, CASE Trends, PO Box 294-MO, Shrewsbury, MA 01545-9956, 508-842-4500, $129.

Appendix **B**

Consulting Companies

The following is a partial list of companies that offer facilitative consulting support for EAP. Of course, methodologies will differ somewhat. These companies are relatively small and are usually headed by a preeminent consultant/writer/speaker. For this list and the ones that follow, only the location for the corporate or home office is provided, though the firm may have offices in additional cities.

AtkinsonTremblay (Toronto, Montreal)

Axiom Information Consulting (San Francisco, CA)

Computer and Engineering Consultants (Southfield, MI)

D. Appleton Company (Manhattan Beach, CA)

Data Administration, Inc. (Princeton, NJ)

Data Architects (Atlanta, GA)

Data Sciences Group (Tampa, FL)

DBD Systems (Rockville Centre, NY)

Holland Systems (Ann Arbor, MI)

IBIS Corporation (Ann Arbor, MI)

Information Engineering Systems Corporation (Alexandria, VA)

Information Planning Technologies (Princeton, NJ)

James Martin & Co. (Reston, VA)

Nolan Norton, Inc. (Lexington, MA)

Pacific Information Management (Santa Monica, CA)

Performance Development Corp. (Princeton, NJ)

GENERAL I.S. CONSULTING COMPANIES

These large consulting companies provide design, programming, management, and operations support services to I.S. organizations. There may be a small group or a few people within these companies that could provide facilitative or operative consulting services for traditional systems planning or for EAP.

American Management Systems (Arlington, VA)

Computer Horizons/Relational Strategies (New York, NY)

Computer Task Group (Buffalo, NY)

DMR (Wellesley Hills, MA)

LGS (Montreal, Ontario)

Systemhouse (Arlington, VA and Ottawa, Ontario)

GENERAL MANAGEMENT CONSULTING COMPANIES

The following general management consulting firms usually provide operative planning services. However, the traditional or critical success factor (short-term) approach is used most often.

Arthur D. Little (Cambridge, MA)

Booz-Allen (New York, NY)

Boston Consulting Group (Chicago, IL)

A. T. Kearny (Chicago, IL)

McKinsey (New York, NY)

BIG SIX CONSULTING FIRMS

These large consultancies with offices in most major cities generally provide the operative kind of planning, using the traditional and CSF approaches. There are small groups within these firms that are beginning to apply and gain experience with EAP and Information Engineering, with the exception of Ernst & Young, who has made a major commitment to information engineering and the Knowledgeware products.

Anderson Consulting

Coopers & Lybrand

Deloitte, Touche

Ernst & Young

Peat Marwick

Price Waterhouse

Duration Estimate for Steps of Each Phase

The table below contains rough estimates of the average relative duration of the phases and steps of EAP. Initiation phase steps are not included.

PHASE and STEP	% of Phase	% of EAP
I—Preliminary Business Model		**7%**
Step 1: Document the Organization Structure	10%	
Step 2: Identify and Define Functions	75%	
Step 3: Distribute the Functional Business Model	15%	
II—Enterprise Survey		**23%**
Step 1: Schedule Interviews	10%	
Step 2: Prepare for the Interviews	15%	
Step 3: Perform the Interviews	50%	
Step 4: Enter Data into the Toolset	15%	
Step 5: Distribute the Full Functional Business Model	10%	

PHASE and STEP	% of Phase	% of EAP
III—Current Systems and Technology Architecture		**15%**
Step 1: Determine the Scope, Objectives, and IRC WorkPlan	10%	
Step 2: Prepare for Data Collection	15%	
Step 3: Collect the IRC Data	25%	
Step 4: Enter the Data	5%	
Step 5: Validate IRC and Produce a Draft of the IRC Report	15%	
Step 6: Draw Schematics	10%	
Step 7: Distribute the IRC	10%	
Step 8: Administer and Maintain the IRC	10%	
IV—Data Architecture		**15%**
Step 1: List Candidate Data Entities for Definition	5%	
Step 2: Define the Data Entities, Attributes, and Relationships	70%	
Step 3: Relate Data Entities to the Business Functions	15%	
Step 4: Distribute the Data Architecture	10%	
V—Applications Architecture		**15%**
Step 1: List Candidate Applications	10%	
Step 2: Define the Applications	50%	
Step 3: Relate Applications to Functions	15%	
Step 4: Analyze Impact to Current Applications	15%	
Step 5: Distribute the Applications Architecture	10%	
VI—Technology Architecture		**10%**
Step 1: Identify Technology Principles and Platforms	15%	
Step 2: Define the Platforms and Distribution	50%	
Step 3: Relate the Technology Platforms to Applications and Business Functions	20%	
Step 4: Distribute the Technology Architecture	15%	

PHASE and STEP	% of Phase	% of EAP
VII—Implementation Plan		**15%**
Step 1: Sequence the Applications	20%	
Step 2: Effort, Resources, Schedule	15%	
Step 3: Costs and Benefits	10%	
Step 4: Recommendations	10%	
Step 5: Transition Phase Plan	5%	
Step 6: Final Report	20%	
Step 7: Final Presentation	20%	
		100%

Sample Function Definitions

The following sample function definitions are based on actual business model reports from enterprises going through the EAP process. The purpose of these samples is to show alternative formats for presenting business functions and information sources, and to suggest the kinds of data that can be compiled about business functions and information sources during the enterprise survey.

BUSINESS FUNCTION DEFINITION REPORT

FUNCTION NAME: Accounts Payable

SHORT NAME: Accounts Payable   FUNCTION NUMBER: 1

SUBFUNCTION OF: Financial Management   SORT KEY: GD

DESCRIPTION: Tracks invoicing and payment to vendors for products and services rendered.

FREQUENCY: 15 times per day

DURATION:

TEAM MEMBER PROVIDING INFORMATION: Chris Coffee, Damon Latham

FUNCTIONS COMPRISING (DEFINING) THIS FUNCTION

1. Verify Invoices and Filing
2 Batching of Invoices
3. Produce Check
4. Matching of Invoice and Check
5. Administer Mileage
6. Monitor Rental Agreement Expire Dates

ORGANIZATION UNITS PERFORMING THIS FUNCTION

1. Mgr. Accounting
2. Payroll/Accounts Payable

INFORMATION SOURCES USED BY THIS FUNCTION

1. Check Register
2. Payment Report of Invoices from Vendors
3. Invoices from Vendors Processed Manually
4. Voucher Register
5. Credit Invoice Summary of Vendors
6. Invoice Transactions
7. Budget Center Listing
8. Mileage Report
9. Invoice
10. Accounts Payable Stores Control Report
11. Batch Balance and Edit Report
12. Debit and Credit Invoices from Vendors
13. Check Requisition
14. Source Code Identification

INFORMATION SOURCE DEFINITION REPORT

SOURCE NAME: Budget Center Listing

SOURCE NUMBER: 5047   FORM NUMBER:__

MEDIUM: Form   TYPE: (manual, automated): M

DESCRIPTION: Listing of budget centers by responsibility.

NUMBER OF COPIES: 1

SAMPLE OBTAINED: Y

TEAM MEMBERS PROVIDING THIS INFORMATION: Jamie Boch, Natalie Emmons

USED IN FUNCTION: Accounts Payable (1)

FROM FUNCTION: 115   COPIES: 1

TO FUNCTION: COPIES: 1

VOLUME: 1

ACCURACY: OK

CURRENCY: Always out of date

DETAIL: Insufficient detail

FORMAT: OK

INFORMATION & TECHNOLOGY OPPORTUNITIES:

INFORMATION USAGE: Source usage. Referenced.

BUSINESS FUNCTIONS & INFORMATION USAGE

FUNCTION NAME: Answer Client Questions

FUNCTION NUMBER: 19

PERFORMED: 10 times per day

DURATION: 15 minutes

FUNCTION PURPOSE:	Handle client calls regarding labels, indexing, trade names, and product line newsletter.
DESCRIPTION:	Receive calls from clients—answer questions re: labels, indexing, trade names, product line newsletters. Most are answered while on the phone, or call distribution about mailing labels, indexing. Weekly sales activity record #77 for each contact.
IMPROVEMENTS:	5 minutes to 1/2 hour on average for each call. Computing would cut this time down substantially.

INFORMATION USED

NUMBER	INFORMATION SOURCE
77	Weekly Sales Activity Record
78	Trade Name Memo
79	Mail Label Order Form
80	Reprint Order Form
81	Product Line Newsletter Form
82	Buyline Memo
83	Who's New Form and Covering Memo
84	Client Card

INFORMATION PROVIDED BY: Walter Weber

BUSINESS FUNCTIONS & INFORMATION USAGE

FUNCTION NAME: Review/Assign Catalog Design Request

FUNCTION NUMBER: 58

PERFORMED: 25 times per month

DURATION: 4 hours

FUNCTION PURPOSE: To design or redesign a client's catalog in support of sales.

DESCRIPTION: Receive Design Request #146, Case Folder #147, and Control Slip #158 from consultant. Review material and assign the design to a catalog designer or art director and enter on Assignment Log #148. Give source material to designer.

DECISIONS: Distribution of design projects to the most appropriate designer based on the the designer's ability, bent, availability, style and desired style of catalog.

IMPROVEMENTS: Source data provided by consultant via computer graphics.

INFORMATION USED

NUMBER	INFORMATION SOURCE
146	Consultant Request
147	Case Folder
148	Art Design Assignment Log
149	Action Slip/Control Slip

INFORMATION PROVIDED BY: Sandi Marie

DETAILED FUNCTION DEFINITION

FUNCTION NAME: RECEIVE MATERIAL

FUNCTION NUMBER: 55

PARENT: RECEIVING (243)

DESCRIPTION: Upload material from trucks; Verify quantities to purchase orders; Process paper work into computer; Verify freight bill & charge nonstock to proper accounts; Users receive material purchased on system contracts & 3 part releases; arrange delivery of D.C. & capital.

STATUS: Active   FREQUENCY: 6618 times per month

DURATION: 6 Minutes

DECISIONS: Whether material is correct as ordered.

INFORMATION USED: Truckers manifest (pro bills); Copies of Purchase Order (sample); Terminal for entering receipts into Inv. Management System; Trucker Pro Bills; System Contract-3 Part Release (sample).

IMPROVEMENT OPPORTUNITIES: Electronic Receiving; Bar coding items by vendor.

USER COMMENTS: Inputs to be made on a more timely basis: receiving (actual), delivery points (storage), "Receiving slips should be reinstituted. . ."; "Stock should be kept on plant site and not downtown"; "usage items closer to end use"; "better warehouse I.D."; "Employee sales items more easily identified as to warehouse location."

POSSIBLE CHANGES:

INTERVIEWED: MARK LATHAM   DATE: 02/09/91

ORGANIZATION UNITS:

WAREHOUSE SUPERVISOR (129)
RECEIVING & HEAVY STORAGE FOREMAN (230)
MATERIAL RECEIVERS (231)
WHSE HEAVY STORAGE (232)

DETAILED FUNCTION DEFINITION

FUNCTION NAME: SOLVE RECEIVING PROBLEMS

FUNCTION NUMBER: 56

PARENT: RECEIVING (243)

DESCRIPTION: Resolve problems with vendors relating to: Incorrect material shipped; Short/over shipment; Damaged material; Loss on delivery to plants; In proper packaging. releases; arrange delivery of D.C. & capital.

STATUS: Active　　　　　　　FREQUENCY: 10 times per day

DURATION: 10 minutes

DECISIONS: Whether there is a problem; course of action to rectify problem; who should be informed and involved; Raise claim if cost of item warrants it.

INFORMATION USED: Copy of Purchase Order (sample); Vendor packing slip; Over/short inspection report; Claims report on carriers; Vendor Spread Sheet; FAX Machine; Telephone; Terminal.

IMPROVEMENT OPPORTUNITIES: Establish a vendor rating system to determine which vendors are acceptable, those needing improvement and those which should be eliminated.

POSSIBLE CHANGES:

INTERVIEWED: MIKE EMMONS　　　　　　　DATE: 02/10/91

ORGANIZATION UNITS:

WAREHOUSE SUPERVISOR (129)
RECEIVING & HEAVY STORAGE FOREMAN (230)
MATERIAL RECEIVERS (231)
WHSE HEAVY STORAGE (232)

DETAILED FUNCTION DEFINITION

FUNCTION NAME: DATA ENTRY

FUNCTION NUMBER: 267

PARENT: MANAGE COMPUTER INFORMATION (258)

DESCRIPTION: Transcription of written information to machine readable form.

STATUS: Active   FREQUENCY: 4 times per day

DURATION: 8 hours

DECISIONS: Setting priorities based upon production run schedule.

INFORMATION USED: Input for keying (forms); Production run schedule;
                       Generates input data for production run(s).

IMPROVEMENT OPPORTUNITIES: Steadier arrival of input data would
                             prevent large backlogs; Request from
                             Smelter to return to batch data entry for
                             XXX system.

POSSIBLE CHANGES:

INTERVIEWED: STEVE JONES   DATE: 02/09/91

ORGANIZATION UNITS:

    TRAINING (16)
    DATA ENTRY (119)
    WHSE DATA ENTRY OPERATOR (233)

Appendix **E**

Sample Business Model Document

TABLE OF CONTENTS

Introduction . . . .

Business Model . . . .

Function Improvement Opportunities . . . .

Support of Functions by Computer Applications . . . .

Next Steps . . . .

ATTACHMENTS [NOT CONTAINED IN THIS APPENDIX]

Function Structure . . . .

Organization Structure . . . .

Function Improvement Opportunities . . . .

EAP Team . . . .

Function Definition Form . . . .

BUSINESS MODEL DOCUMENT

1.   INTRODUCTION

1.1   Methodology

The EAP project assembled a team of business analysts from the departments throughout the division [not identified in this appendix]. The team first was trained in the methodology for EAP with an emphasis on the Business Model Phase.

One of the first tasks of the EAP team members was to confirm and expand the organization chart to assure the accuracy within their departments [chart not shown in this appendix]. This identified the appropriate people to be interviewed for each identified business function.

As a team, a preliminary top-level tree structure of the enterprise functions was defined, with the first level defining *value-added* functions and *support* functions [chart not shown in this appendix].

For the enterprise survey, each team member was to expand the definitions of functions for his department(s). The results of this activity were published in the preliminary business model document.

Through January, February, and early March, the business analysts conducted interviews to confirm the preliminary definitions, gathered samples of relevant information used, and solicited suggestions for possible function improvements. The results from these interviews were entered into the EAP database. Business model reports were consolidated and then distributed to the business analysts for editing, additions, and corrections.

1.2   What Is a Business Model?

A business model *defines* the business of an organization. It answers the question "*What* do we do?" This takes the form of describing and defining the *functions* of the business. A function is defined as "a set of actions performed to produce a result in support of business objectives."

A function

- has a name.
- may have a description.
- may be decomposed into sub functions.
- is performed by at least one organizational unit.
- uses information.
- may have improvement opportunities.

A function is defined entirely by its subfunctions. Thus, a complete tree-structured definition can be most easily displayed using an indented list, where each level of detail in the definition is indented from the left.

The tree structure of a function definition does *not* show

- WHO performs the function (organization unit).
- HOW functions are performed or the order in which they are performed.
- WHERE a function is performed.
- WHEN a function is performed.
- IMPORTANCE or priority of a function.
- TECHNOLOGY or resources used.
- FLOWS of inputs, outputs, or personal interactions.

It is important that the business model does not describe or define functions in terms of WHO performs them. This assures that the business model will be stable despite organizational or responsibility changes over time. Though new functions may be added or deleted from the model, the basic structural integrity of the model should remain the same.

2.   BUSINESS MODEL

2.1   Model Contents

The business model consists of [number] functions and sub-functions descriptions as defined by the business analyst team. [See Chapter 4 for tree structure examples.]

Of the [number] functions, [number] are lowest-level or

"leafs" in the tree structure. A complete Function Definition report is available in hard copy or diskette form by calling Jim at x2347.

Of the [number] detailed definitions, [number] identified possible function improvement opportunities. Section 3 of this report describes these more thoroughly.

An important part of each function description is the "Information Used." The descriptions provided here form the basis of the Data Architecture Phase of the EAP project which is described in section 5 of this report.

2.2   Model Completeness

In the indented list [not included], an "*" following a function name indicates that it is a detailed function (leaf) for which no detailed definition was provided to the team. In addition, the definitions for Personnel Management and Financial Management were largely put together by the EAP team with feedback and advice from the relevant business analysts. These are lacking in samples of information and identified function improvement opportunities.

Wherever possible, these gaps will be filled in prior to completing the subsequent stages of the project. However, it is the view of the EAP team and consultant that the model as defined satisfies the 80/20 principle for completeness.

Of the [number] detailed function definitions, [n%] contain descriptions of information used by the function.

The [number] function improvement opportunities identified address a very high percentage of the [number] functions defined (n%). This is greater than expected prior to the project, and is an indication of the thorough interviewing and analysis of business functions by the EAP team.

Another measure of completeness was indicated by "linking" all current computer applications identified in the Information Resource Catalog to the business function(s) they support. This task verified that no computer system exists that does not have a corresponding function to support in the business model, that is, important functions have not been omitted.

2.3   Functions "Performed By" Organization Units

Although the definition of each function is independent of the organization unit performing that function, links have been established in the EAP database between business functions and the organization units performing those functions. This is important for identifying impact of functions and the generality of associated information.

The [number] low-level functions are linked to the [number] units in the organization model. Over [number] such links exist. This indicates a relatively high functional overlap—that is, one business function being performed by an average of [n] organization units. Therefore, many functions defined in the business model have impacts across departments and across business locations.

For example, the following functions are performed by most organizations units:

- Timekeeping
- Department budgeting
- Department cost analysis
- Issuing supplies
- Personal computer systems management
- Presenting training courses
- Initiating maintenance work orders
- Hiring qualified people
- Addressing employee concerns
- Maintaining employee records
- Function improvement

Some functions that are performed by all production plants include:

- Physical and chemical property determination
- Accounting
- Scheduling plant production
- Complying with safety regulations and standards
- Monitoring function performance

3. FUNCTION IMPROVEMENT OPPORTUNITIES

While a few of the [number] function improvement opportunities contain suggestions for organization change or physical operation improvement as opposed to information improvement, almost all opportunities have some relevant information component. Attachment X [not included] is a listing of the function improvement opportunities by function within the definition tree structure.

The technology spectrum of suggestions includes robotics in the warehouses, electronic data interchange with vendors and carriers, fully electronic timekeeping, expanded process control in the plants, expanded dial-up browsing of public databases, bar coding of products, and improved communication of results via a network.

In addition to the improvement opportunities indicated for individual functions, a number of separate presentations have been documented with improvement potential that spans entire functional areas.

Maintenance has proposed an "example" system for the integration of equipment and parts information and equipment history with work order processing, planning, and so on.

Purchasing and Warehousing has provided a booklet of suggested computer systems improvements and proposed a two-year plan for their accomplishment.

Timekeeping has provided documentation for an absentee history system and an integrated human resource information system (HRIS).

Engineering has proposed expert systems.

Research and Technology has extensive documentation for Electronic Data Interchange (EDI) standards for general business applications and industry applications, and has demonstrated the requirements for a customer information system.

Human Resources has shared their planned developments and proposed information improvements with the team, and presented more detailed opportunities that cannot be addressed independently.

Marketing has expressed the interests and concerns of a global marketing initiative, as well as future industry directions.

The EAP team has also recognized, through analysis of results from the Information Resource Catalog (IRC) and the relationship of existing computer applications to functions in the business model, that some areas of the business are in critical need of information integration.

All of these identified opportunities will be considered during the subsequent architecture definition phases of the EAP project.

4. SUPPORT OF FUNCTIONS BY COMPUTER APPLICATIONS

The EAP team compared the functions defined in the business model with the current applications in the IRC and asked the question:

"What functions are supported by current applications?"

The answers relating the functions to applications were entered into the EAP database and the results analyzed.

The functions that are currently supported by the largest number of applications are listed below (see Figure E.1). These are significant because they indicate

1. that the function is complicated and requires many types of information.

FUNCTIONS SUPPORTED BY MULTIPLE COMPUTER APPLICATIONS

Function	# of Applications
Gather Operating Costs to Chart of Accounts	15
Schedule Maintenance Work Orders	12
Determine Plant Throughputs/Inventories	11
Capital Project Administration	10
Department Cost Analysis	9
Distribute Functional Costs	9
Divisional Costs Analysis	9
Pay Employees	9

Figure E.1. Functions supported by multiple computer applications.

2. that the current support for the function is not integrated and therefore is subject to conflicting data.

An example of one such function is schedule maintenance work orders, which is supported directly by twelve (12) computer applications. Information from each of these twelve applications is required to perform the function accurately. The conclusion from the analysis clearly shows the need for integration and simplification and for expediting information to the users.

5.   NEXT STEPS

Information from the business model is the basis for the subsequent phases of the EAP project. Indeed, the completion of the business model marks the end of the "inventory stage" of the project, or in other words, "what we have today." The next steps for defining architectures and the implementation plan are "what it should be" and "how do we get there."

Data Architecture Phase is under way. This phase addresses the question "What information is required to do business and how is this information interrelated?" This phase will identify and define the major information components that were described in the "information used" portion of the function definitions in the business model. We call these components "data entities." Once defined, the interrelationships to other data entities are also defined and diagrammed in an Entity-Relationship (E-R) Diagram.

Application Architecture Phase. This phase addresses the question "What computer systems (applications) are required to provide the information needed to the business functions?" Based on the data architecture and business model, the application superstructure to support the defined data entities is created. Consideration is also given to existing computer applications defined in the Information Resource Catalog.

Technology Architecture Phase. The question here is "What type of computer resources are required to support the applications and data?" This stage will define the hardware (mainframe computer, minicomputers, personal computers), software (operating systems, packages, languages), and communications networks best suited to the identified applications and data architecture. This will provide a picture of which applications require the mainframe and which may have data and processing distributed to mini- or microcomputers in a downsized environment.

Migration Planning Phase. This stage formulates the strategy for moving from our current environment to the state identified by the architectures.

These stages will involve the active participation of company management to

- review the accuracy of the EAP team for accuracy in reflecting identified opportunities.
- identify possible cost savings and probable costs.
- communicate to executive management the possible directions for improvement and receive feedback on priorities.
- assure that the migration plan is practicable and meets the needs of their department.

Department heads and management will have the opportunity to review and comment at each milestone and will have direct input into the migration plan for both content and prioritization.

Sample Data
Architecture

DATA ARCHITECTURE REPORT

Enterprise Architecture Planning

TABLE OF CONTENTS

1. Introduction . . . .
2. Implications of Standard Definitions . . . .
3. Entity Relationship Diagrams . . . .
4. Data to Function Relationship Matrix . . . .
5. Data Entity Report . . . .

1. INTRODUCTION

The enterprise data architecture is the product of the data architecture phase of Enterprise Architecture Planning (EAP). It defines the major kinds of data, called entities, used by the business environment. *A data entity represents a person, place, idea, thing, or event that is important to the business and about which data must be stored.*

The enterprise data architecture is not a design or specification for a single database. Rather, it is more like a dictionary, providing standard definitions of the fundamental things involved in the business. The enterprise data architecture is like a blueprint for the entire data resource needed to support the business. Just as a blueprint is required for constructing a building, an enterprise data architecture is needed before developing a shared data resource. However, like any preliminary blueprint, the enterprise data architecture is subject to change as detailed design specifications for the implementation of databases and applications increase our understanding of fundamental business concepts.

As the first of the three architectures produced by EAP, the enterprise data architecture serves several purposes.

1. It provides the standard vocabulary for identifying, defining, and naming the major kinds of data to support the business.
2. It is used to determine the requirements for application systems that are defined to manage particular sets of data entities.
3. The relationship of the data architecture to the applications portfolio is the primary basis for sequencing the implementation of applications. Data-driven planning (i.e., developing applications that create data before applications that need to use the data) makes sense and is also the least costly direction for the migration to a shared data environment.

The business model, previously compiled by the EAP team, consists of the basic definitions of business functions and information sources as expressed by management and other people throughout the business. The definitions of the entities in the data architecture were formulated by the EAP team based on the collective knowledge about the entire business as documented in the business model.

A good data architecture is a foundation for future databases and will serve the business for many years. The properties of a high-quality data architecture are the following:

1. The definitions are understandable, that is, they make sense and are applicable to the business. Entity definitions that are too specific may not be applicable to all functions of the business. On the other hand, definitions that are too general will be awkward and cumbersome to use and maintain, and generalities are subject to misinterpretation.

2. The entities are complete and consistent. Virtually every kind of data in the business should be accommodated by this set of entities, and the definitions are consistent with each other, that is, there is no duplication or overlap. There may seem to be data missing upon first gleaning, as some commonly used business names or terms do not appear. However, the team may have considered that data to be a special case of another more general entity that has been defined.

3. The architecture is relatively stable over time, that is, the fundamental definitions are robust and flexible with respect to business changes. To achieve this stability, the entity definitions are based solely on the functions in the business model, and the entity definitions are independent of

   a. who uses data;
   b. where data is used or stored;
   c. when data is used and the sequence in which it is used;
   d. how much data is used; and
   e. the applications and technology for managing data.

2.   IMPLICATIONS OF STANDARD DEFINITIONS

In order to have a shareable data environment, every kind of data *must* have a consistent enterprisewide identification scheme. One component of a data entity is called an *identifier*, which is used uniquely to identify every occurrence of a particular kind of data. For example, every Employee has a unique number as an identifier.

Some of the entities in the enterprise data architecture have identifiers that are commonly used today such as Account (Account Number). However, there are other kinds of data that do not have a consistent enterprisewide identifier today such as Requisition (Requisition Number). Three reasons that an entity may not have a standard identifier today are:

1. The data is maintained by or is spread over multiple systems that have been developed independently for different purposes, or by separate departments resulting in several identifiers used across the organization.
2. Current identifiers may be too limiting, and may have structural or interpretable codes built into them such as "Cost Center Code," Product Code," or "Vehicle Serial Number.
3. The data represented by an entity may not exist in electronic form.

In some instances, business practices may need to change to accommodate new standard identifiers. It may be necessary to update procedures, redesign reports, reengineer applications, or restructure databases. Specific recommendations for the least costly and most adaptable changes will be proposed as part of the migration planning phase of EAP.

At this point, these are some of the significant potential changes in business practices:

- Employee numbers are currently assigned with an embedded meaning—one number range for hourly, another for salaried. Contractors are not assigned numbers although they may function as employees in every respect except for compensation and some kinds of benefits.
- The multiplicity of accounting identifiers currently being used is an ongoing cause of confusion and errors, for example, Project Number, SP-Number (Engineering), Account Number, and Work Order Number.
- Currently, locations around the enterprise are either loosely identified or are identified by various complex codes with dual purposes, such as Area/Zone Code, Workplace Number.

This complicates such business functions as Maintenance, Cost Distribution, and Supplies Delivery.

- The vast number of documents required in the enterprise (drawings, manuals, procedures, files) are classified, indexed, and stored in a variety of media and formats. Today, the ability to retrieve or locate documents by anyone but the "owner" is very limited.

- Products of our business are not uniquely identified and, therefore, are difficult to track in shipment. Bar coding of products with a unique identifier is one method being suggested to simplify product tracking.

The remaining sections of this document contain the following reports:

ENTITY SUMMARY:	A list of the entities and their definitions in a dictionary format.
FULL-ENTITY REPORT:	All components defined for an entity including description, identifier, attributes, and related entities.
ENTITY RELATIONSHIP DIAGRAMS:	Pictorial illustrations of the relationships between entities from particular functional perspectives of the business.
DATA-TO-FUNCTION MATRIX:	Shows the usage of data by the business functions in tabular format.

3.   ENTITY RELATIONSHIP DIAGRAMS

The entity relationship diagrams show pictorially the interrelationships of entities. A single diagram that would include all of the entities and relationships would be nearly impossible to read or use. Therefore, the entities and relationships are divided into groups for diagramming purposes. The diagrams contained in this section represent a view of the data architecture from the perspective of functional areas.

An entity relationship diagram consists of boxes and lines connecting the boxes. An entity name, such as Employee, is inside the box. The name of the relationship, such as "fills," appears next to the line connecting the Employee entity (box) to another entity box for Position.

A relationship describes some of the rules or conditions about the entities of the business. Crow's-feet at the end of the relationship line indicates that many of that entity participate in the relationship, while two lines indicate that only one occurrence of the entity is involved. For example, the relationship indicating "a Business Process is governed by a Plan" has crow's-feet at both ends. This indicates a Plan can govern many Business Processes and a Business Process can be governed by many Plans. However, the relationship "a Business Process is measured by a Process History" has two lines on the Process end and a crow's-foot at the other. This indicates a Business Process can be measured by several Process Histories, but one Process History can only measure one Business Process.

An entity may be related to other instances of the same entity. This is shown in the diagrams by a line connecting an entity to itself. Such a line with two cross lines usually indicates a hierarchical structure. For example, a Business Process may be decomposed into several component Business Processes.

4.   DATA-TO-FUNCTION RELATIONSHIP MATRIX

This report shows the usage of data by business function in a tabular format. The hierarchical business functions form the rows of the table and the entities are the columns. The entities are grouped into categories and a name is given to the category.

The entries in the table indicate how data is used. Three kinds of entity usage may be given:

C   Created means that the function may create new instances (identifier values) of an entity. For example, the function "Plan a Building" will create data about a new Facility—new in the sense that data about this Facility did not exist in the Enterprise's information resource previously.

U *Updated* means that the function may access and change (i.e., add to, alter, or delete) data about the entity. For example, the function "Generate Periodic Product Quality Statistics" will alter or add to data about a Product Type.

R *Referenced* means that the function needs to access data about the entity but will not significantly update or change that data.

The function-to-entity matrix has several important uses

1. The matrix clearly shows that there is substantial sharing of data among business functions. Though this was known intuitively before this project began, the matrix goes beyond proving that hypothesis and identifies the data that needs to be shared and managed as a resource.

2. The matrix will be used to define the scope of future application systems. Traditionally, applications have been developed to support particular organization units and their procedures. Traditional applications tend to be very large and involve many kinds of data. When data is managed as a resource, applications are designed to support particular business functions and to manage particular data entities. In the future, there will be many small applications rather than a few large ones. The scope of some future applications can be determined by scanning down the columns of this matrix to understand the usage of data in the business.

3. This matrix, in conjunction with another that relates applications to business functions, will be used to sequence the development of the data resource and to formulate a migration strategy.

5.   DATA ENTITY REPORT

The full description and information about every entity is presented in this report. Each entity begins a new page and the name of the entity appears at the top of the page. With the name is a number that was assigned by the EAP team for internal tracking purposes only and has no inherent meaning.

The first item under the name is *alias*, which are other terms by which an entity may be known. For example, Contract may also be known as Agreement.

The *description* gives the definition of each entity. The complete set of entity definitions of the data architecture forms the basic vocabulary of the enterprise. Though some definitions may seem to be broad and general, the team has determined that generality to be necessary to accommodate both the vast variety of perspectives enterprisewide and the numerous business changes that occur in our dynamic marketplace.

The *identifier* is an attribute of the entity that serves to uniquely identify a single occurrence of the entity. It is usually an assigned number.

A few entities may be special cases of another entity, for example a Capital Appropriation Request is a special case of a Requisition, yet it is distinctive enough to be specifically identified. These entities are flagged in the line *is a kind of* followed by the internal identification number of the more general entity.

Attributes serve to further define and clarify the meaning of each data entity. Attributes, not to be confused with data elements or fields, may be complex and contain many data elements when eventually implemented in files and databases. For example, one attribute of Product Type is Physical Specifications, which would contain a variety of physical characteristics and properties depending on the particular Product Type. However, it is an attribute of Product Type because it is fundamental to understanding the meaning of the term "product type." Entities will eventually become hundreds or thousands of files and data elements. Only those attributes deemed important for understanding the meaning of an entity are included in the data architecture.

Relationships show the interrelationship and dependency of the definitions of entities. For example, under Employee we have the relationship indicating that an Employee has an Occupation (Job or Title) with the notation 'M:1' (read as "many to one"). That means that one Employee may have only one Occupation, but many Employees can have the same Occupation.

Appendix **G**

Sample Application Architecture Report

TABLE OF CONTENTS

1.0 DEFINITION OF AN APPLICATIONS ARCHITECTURE .....

2.0 PURPOSE OF THE APPLICATIONS ARCHITECTURE ......

3.0 APPROACH ....

4.0 DELIVERABLES ....

    4.1 List of Applications ....

    4.2 Applications Architecture Description ....

    4.3 Applications Supporting Major Business Functions ......

    4.4 Application Benefits Summary ....

    4.5 Detailed Business Functions not Supported by the Applications Architecture ....

    4.6 Current Applications not Impacted by the Applications Architecture ....

    4.7 Applications to Data Entity Matrix and Usage ....

    4.8 Application Stakeholders ....

1. DEFINITION OF AN APPLICATIONS ARCHITECTURE

This report is the major deliverable of the Application Architecture Phase of the Enterprise Architecture Planning project. It defines the applications required to support the business functions and manage the information within our business environment.

The application architecture is not a specification for a particular application. Rather, it is a high-level description of the capabilities and benefits of *all* applications to support the business. It also identifies the business functions supported by the applications, the data created, updated, or referenced by the applications, and current applications that are impacted. The application architecture serves as an architectural blueprint of the entire application resource needed to support the business and its shared data environment. However, just like any preliminary blueprint, the application architecture is subject to refinements as more detailed design specifications are developed during the implementation of the applications defined herein.

A *good* applications architecture exhibits the following properties:

1. The applications are *understandable*. They are applicable to the business and the definitions make sense.
2. It is *complete* and *consistent*. All of the data created, updated, and referenced by the business, as defined in the data architecture, can be managed by the complete set of applications. Support is provided to all business functions that need it.
    All applications are consistent with each other and do not overlap. Applications that create or update the same data entity are managing different instances of that data in a consistent manner. For example, the EMPLOYEE entity is created by the Employee Information System through the Recruiting business function. When the employee's salary is determined and further adjusted, the Compensation System will update the Compensation Data associated with EMPLOYEE. As the employee is paid by the Payroll System, this application will update the employee's Compensation History. The Employee Time Management System will reference

the EMPLOYEE entity as it records the actual hours an employee worked, including overtime and project work. The EMPLOYEE entity also has a Medical History which will be updated by the Health and Safety System when the employee receives a replacement medical or work restriction. Courses attended by an employee are recorded by the Training Management System in the educational and training data of EMPLOYEE.

3. The application architecture is *stable*. This stability has been achieved by basing the definitions in the application architecture on the business model and data architecture. Thus, the applications definitions are *independent* of
   * *who* uses the application;
   * *where* the application is used or stored;
   * *when* the application is used;
   * *how* the application works; and
   * the *technology* with which the application is implemented.

2.   PURPOSE OF THE APPLICATIONS ARCHITECTURE

As the second of three architectures defined in Enterprise Architecture Planning, the primary purpose of the applications architecture is to define the applications that will provide data to business functions to achieve our corporate direction. Each application is intended to

* improve the business effectiveness or productivity,
* provide a strategic advantage over our competitor, and
* manage particular kinds of data or perform a business function.

3   APPROACH

The applications architecture was created by the EAP project team during March through May. The team was trained and guided by Dr. Steven Spewak of Information Planning Technologies. The Business Model, Information Resource Catalog, and data architecture (deliverables of previous phases of the EAP methodology) along with the opportunities identified during the Enterprise Survey Phase were used to define the applications for managing our shared data resource.

The team developed a preliminary list of applications, and through a series of discussions, refined the preliminary definitions in accordance with the properties of a good applications architecture. Appropriate names were chosen and the following identified for each application: capabilities, benefits, business functions supported, current applications impacted, and data entities created/updated/referenced.

All of this information was entered into the EAP project database. The team then reviewed all 387 opportunities collected during the enterprise survey. The team determined that 320 of these opportunities could be fulfilled by the applications architecture. The remaining opportunities were not feasible or did not involve information technology. Additional reports were produced to verify the relationship of applications to business functions, current systems, and data entities.

4.   DELIVERABLES

4.1   List of Applications

This report is an alphabetical list of the applications that comprise the application architecture. Each application is described by its name and purpose. The Application Number follows the application name and is used for internal tracking purposes only.

4.2   Applications Architecture Description

This report contains the complete description and information about each application in the applications architecture. Each application begins a new page with the name and purpose of the application appearing at the top of the page followed by

Description / Capabilities: Further describes the application by identifying its capabilities—what it does but not *how* it works. Capabilities are not listed in the order of importance or priority.

Benefits: Identifies the benefits expected to be realized when the application is implemented.

Detailed Business Functions Supported: Identifies the business function (name and number) supported *significantly* by the application. The business function is at the most detailed level, the lowest in the hierarchical decomposition, for that particular portion of the business.

Current IRC Applications Affected: Identifies the current system (as documented in the Information Resource Catalog) that will be impacted significantly by implementing the application. The impact has been recorded as follows

C—completely replace the current system,

P—partially replace the current system, or

R—retain the current system.

Data Entity Relationships: Identifies the data entities managed by the application. The data usage column specifies whether the application creates (C), updates (U), or references (R) a data entity. This information is very important for determining the order in which applications should be developed. That is, an application that creates a data entity should be implemented before an application that updates that entity.

SAMPLE APPLICATION

BUSINESS ANALYSIS SYSTEM (28)

Purpose: Decision making and impact assessment for analyzing business
opportunities.

Description/Capabilities:

1. Accesses external and internal financial, market, technical, and business information for analysis to assist in making the correct business decision.
2. It will also identify required business resources, functions, and government regulations.
3. The application will be able to perform "what if" analysis.

Benefits:

1. Ability to perform "what if" analysis rapidly using various scenarios.
2. Provides electronic access to key business information.

Detailed Business Functions Supported

ANALYZE & IMPROVE EXISTING FUNCTION (224)
ANALYZE & IMPROVE EXISTING PRODUCTS & PROCESSES (221)
CORPORATE PRODUCT RATIONALIZATION (11)
DEFINE & DEVELOP NEW PRODUCT PROCESSES (222)
DEFINE & DEVELOP NEW PRODUCT PROCESSES (226)
DETERMINE RESOURCE REQUIREMENTS (115)
ESTABLISH BUSINESS GOALS (13)

Current IRC Applications Affected:	*Impact*
HEAD COUNT BY DEPARTMENT (282)	R
MANPOWER PLANNING (238)	P
MATERIALS POPULATION (245)	R
ZERO-BASED RESOURCE BUDGET (252)	C

Data Entity Relationships:	*Data Usage*
BUSINESS PROCESS (19)	R
DOCUMENT (32)	R
EQUIPMENT TYPE (28)	R
FACILITY (38)	R
GOODS AND SERVICES TYPE (27)	R
INCIDENT (34)	R
LOCATION (14)	R
ORGANIZATION UNIT (2)	R
PERFORMANCE MEASURES AND STANDARDS (13)	R
PLAN (18)	C
POSITION (3)	R
PRODUCT TYPE (9)	R
SKILL (4)	R
SUPPLIER (25)	R

4.3 Applications Supporting Major Business Functions

These diagrams identify the applications that support the business functions in each of the major business functional areas. Each application name is enclosed in a rectangular box. The data entities shared by all of these applications appear in the disc-like figures in the diagram. Since an application can support several business functions, an application may appear on several diagrams.

4.4 Detailed Business Functions Not Supported by the Applications Architecture

This report identifies detailed or lowest-level business functions that are not supported by the application architecture. The business functions on this list are either performed manually and require no direct application support (i.e., Resolve Employee Performance Issues) or are beyond the scope of the business model (i.e., Influence Changes to Government Regulations).

Business Functions Not Supported by the Applications Architecture

ADVERTISE PRODUCTS & SERVICES (20)
ANNOUNCE NEW PRODUCTS & SERVICE (19)
COMMITTEE ADMINISTRATION (94)
CONDUCT EXTERNAL PRESENTATIONS (32)
CONDUCT TOURS (30)
CONTRIBUTE TO CHARITIES & SOCIETIES (28)
DEFINE HUMAN RESOURCES POLICIES (92)
DEFINE MISSION & VALUE STATEMENTS (12)
DEFINE WORKMANSHIP STANDARDS (240)
DETERMINE PRODUCT LIFE CYCLE (21)
EMPLOYMENT EQUITY (124)
ESTABLISH COMMUNICATION PROGRAMS (90)
FACILITATE SELF-MANAGED WORK TEAMS (126)
INFLUENCE CHANGES TO GOVERNMENT REGULATIONS (34)

INTERVIEW EMPLOYMENT CANDIDATES (121)
SALES PRESENTATION (205)
MANAGE RECOGNITION PROGRAMS (77)
OBTAIN AUTHORIZATION TO HIRE (119)
PHYSICAL DISPOSAL (281)
PREPARE APPROPRIATE DOCUMENTATION (280)
PRODUCT REVIEW & FEEDBACK TO OTHER DIVISIONS (191)
PROMOTE EDUCATIONAL PARTNERSHIPS (27)
PROVIDE USER SUPPORT (138)
RESOLVE EMPLOYEE PERFORMANCE ISSUES (79)
SUCCESSION PLANNING (125)
TECHNOLOGY RESEARCH & DEVELOPMENT (3)
TRAIN CUSTOMER STAFF (206)

4.6 Current Applications Not Impacted by the Applications Architecture

This report identifies the current systems documented by the Information Resource Catalog that are not affected by the application architecture. The systems listed below are either very specialized (i.e. Automatic Program Generation) or are physically located outside of the "enterprise" and are used for data retrievals that are independent of the application architecture (i.e. Product Design System).

AUTOMATIC PROGRAM GENERATION (94)
CIRCUIT BOARD DESIGN SYSTEM (WORKSTATION) (148)
CIRCUIT BOARD DESIGN SYSTEM (MAINFRAME) (147)
LXXX PROGRAMMING DEVELOPMENT/TEST SOFTWARE (93)
WIRE TERMINATION MACHINE (212)
PRODUCT DESIGN SYSTEM (156)

4.7 Applications-to-Data Entity Matrix and Usage

This report illustrates the usage of data by the application architecture in a tabular format. The applications of the application architecture form the rows of the table and the data entities form the columns. The entries in the table indicate how data is used. An application may either create (C), update (U), or reference (R) a data entity. A blank entry means the data is not used by the application. This table has several important uses:

1. It shows where sharing of data occurs within the application architecture.
2. It will be used to sequence the implementation of the applications since applications that create data should be implemented before applications that update or reference that data. The matrix can be used to determine interim data interfaces that may be required and capabilities that may need to be transferred from one application to another.

4.8   Application Stakeholders

This report identifies the applications that support business functions associated with a particular organization unit. The organization unit names appear in alphabetical order. Beneath the organization unit name is the application name followed by its application number. Since the same business function can be performed by several organization units, an application can support more than one organization unit. This report indicates the extent of application sharing throughout our business.

Applications supporting all ORG units

BENEFITS ADMINISTRATION SYSTEM (16)
BUSINESS ANALYSIS SYSTEM (1)
COMPENSATION SYSTEM (17)
COMPUTER/COMMUNICATION SYSTEM MANAGEMENT (23)
DOCUMENT MANAGEMENT (24)
EMPLOYEE INFORMATION SYSTEM (18)
EMPLOYEE TIME MANAGEMENT SYSTEM (46)
FINANCIAL ANALYSIS SYSTEM (6)
FINANCIAL PLANNING SYSTEM (7)
FINANCIAL REPORTING SYSTEM (8)
HEALTH AND SAFETY SYSTEM (19)
INCIDENT MANAGEMENT SYSTEM (31)

MACHINE PROGRAMMING SYSTEM (32)

ORGANIZATION ADMINISTRATION SYSTEM (21)

PROCESS MANAGEMENT SYSTEM (33)

PROCUREMENT MANAGEMENT SYSTEM (13)

PRODUCT ASSEMBLY PLANNING SYSTEM (34)

PRODUCT ORDERING SYSTEM (45)

PRODUCTION CONTROL SYSTEM (38)

PRODUCTION DOCUMENTATION SYSTEM (39)

PROJECT MANAGEMENT SYSTEM. (20)

QUALITY ASSURANCE SYSTEM (35)

RATE DETERMINATION SYSTEM (41)

RECEIVING SYSTEM (14)

TRAINING MANAGEMENT SYSTEM (22)

WORKLOAD BALANCING SYSTEM (43)

Applications supporting the Controller's Department

ACCOUNTS PAYABLE (3)

ACCOUNTS RECEIVABLE (4)

ASSET MANAGEMENT (9)

AUDIT MANAGEMENT SYSTEM (47)

BENEFITS ADMINISTRATION SYSTEM (16)

COMPENSATION SYSTEM (17)

COMPUTER/COMMUNICATION SYSTEM MANAGEMENT (23)

EMPLOYEE INFORMATION SYSTEM (18)

FINANCIAL ANALYSIS SYSTEM (6)

FINANCIAL PLANNING SYSTEM (7)

FINANCIAL REPORTING SYSTEM (8)

GENERAL LEDGER (10)

INVENTORY MANAGEMENT SYSTEM (12)

PAYROLL SYSTEM(11)

PROCUREMENT MANAGEMENT SYSTEM (13)

PRODUCT ORDERING SYSTEM (45)

PRODUCTION CONTROL SYSTEM (38)

PROJECT MANAGEMENT SYSTEM (20)

Bibliography

1. GENERAL EAP AND SDP (INCLUDING BUSINESS MODELING)

Ackley, David, and David C. Tryon. "The Process-Object-State Method: Toward a Normative Framework for Model Integration," *Data Resource Management*, Auerbach Publishers, Vol. 1, No.3, Summer 1990.

Anderson, Robert E., and Raymond K. Cornbill. "When Strategic Information Planning and Management Misses the Mark," *Information Strategy: An Executive's Journal*, Vol. 1, No. 2, Winter 1985.

Appleton, Daniel S. "Applying Lessons from the Industrial Revolution to the Information Revolution," *Chief Information Officer Journal*, Vol. 2, No. 3, Winter 1990.

Aranow, Eric. "Modeling Exercises Shape Up Enterprises," *Software Magazine*, Vol. 11, No. 1, January 1991.

Arthur Young Information Technology Group. *The Arthur Young Practical Guide to Information Engineering*, John Wiley & Sons, New York, 1987.

Atkinson, Robert A. "The Real Meaning of Strategic Planning," *Journal of Information Systems Management*, Vol. 8, No. 4, Fall 1991.

Atkinson, Robert A., and Judith Montgomery. "Reshaping IS Strategic Planning," *Journal of Information Systems Management*, Auerbach Publishers, Vol. 7, No. 4, Fall 1990.

Brancheau, James, and James Wetherbe. "Information Architectures: Methods and Practice," MISRC Working Paper 86-06, University of Minnesota, Minneapolis 55455 (1986).

Brancheau, James C., Larry Schuster, and Salvatore T. March. "Building and Implementing an Information Architecture," *Data Base*, Vol. 20, No. 2, Summer 1989.

Burke, Jerry N. "Inmon's ISA and the Zachman Grid," *Data Resource Management*, Vol. 1, No. 3, Summer 1990.

Chantico Technical Management Series. *Strategic and Operational Planning for Information Systems*, QED Publishing Group, Wellesley, MA, 1985.

Cheung, Steven C. K. "Avoiding the Pitfalls of Information Systems Planning," *Data Resource Management*, Auerbach, Summer 1990.

Cohen, Leo J. *Creating and Planning the Corporate Data Base System Project*, QED Publishing Group, Wellesley, MA, 1984.

Corbin, Darrell S. "Bottom-Up IRM Planning: How It Worked at Rockwell," *Information Strategy: The Executive's Journal*, Vol. 3, No. 1, Fall 1986.

Crescenzi, Adam D. "The Dark Side of Strategic IS Implementation," *Information Strategy*, Auerbach, Fall 1988.

Curtice, Robert M. *Strategic Value Analysis: A Modern Approach to Systems and Data Planning*, Prentice-Hall, Englewood Cliffs, NJ, 1987.

Curtice, Robert M. "A Formula That Equates IS and Prosperity," *Information Strategy*, Auerbach, Vol. 4, No. 4, Summer 1988.

Curtice, Robert M., and Dave Stringer. "Visualizing Information Planning," *Computerworld* (in-depth), January 14, 1991.

Devlin, B. A., and P. T. Murphy. "An Architecture for a Business and Information System," *IBM Systems Journal*, Vol. 27, No. 1, 1988.

Dickson, Gary, and James Wetherbe. *The Management of Information Systems*, McGraw-Hill, New York, 1985.

Finkelstein, Clive. *An Introduction to Information Engineering: From Strategic Planning to Information Systems*, Addison-Wesley, Reading, MA, 1989.

French, Alfred J. *The Business Knowledge Investment: Building Architected Information*, Prentice-Hall (Yourdon Press), Englewood Cliffs, NJ, 1990.

Gallo, Thomas E. *Strategic Information Management Planning*, Prentice-Hall, Englewood Cliffs, NJ, 1988.

Gaskill, Daniel W. "Maximizing the Value of Information," *Database Programming & Design*, Vol. 2, No. 9, September 1989.

Goodhue, Dale L., Judith A. Quillard, and John F. Rockart. "Managing the Data Resource: A Contingency Perspective," *MIS Quarterly*, September 1988.

———. Laurie J. Kirsch, Judith A. Quillard, and Michael D. Wybo, "Strategic Data Planning: Lessons from the Field," *MIS Quarterly*, Vol. 16, No. 1, March 1992.

Head, Robert V. *Strategic Planning for Information Systems*, QED Publishing Group, Wellesley, MA, 1982.

Head, Robert V. *Planning Techniques for Systems Management*, QED Publishing Group, Wellesley, MA, 1984.

Henderson, John C., and Jay G. Cooprider. "Dimensions of I/S Planning and Design Aids: A Functional Model of CASE Technology," *Information Systems Research*, Vol. 1, No. 3, September 1990.

Hessinger, Paul R. "Key to Success with DB2," *A Computer Task Group Special Report*, Buffalo, NY, 1987.

Holcman, Samuel B. "A Review of Three Information Strategy Planning Tools," *Data Base Newsletter*, Vol. 16, No. 4, July–August 1988.

Horton, F. W. *Information Resources Management*, Prentice-Hall Inc., Englewood Cliffs, NJ, 1985.

IBM, *Business Systems Planning*, GE20-0527-4 (1984). Available from IBM.

IBM, *A Management System for the Information Business* (3 volumes), GE20-0748-0, BE20-0749-0, GE20-0750-0 (1983). Available from IBM.

Information Systems Management. "Strategic Planning" column written by Robert E. Wallace (1986–1990) and Robert A. Atkinson (1990).

Inmon, W. H., and Caplan, Jeffrey. *Information Systems Architecture*: Development in the 90's, QED Publishing Group, Wellesley, MA, 1992.

Inmon, W. H., and Michael L. Loper. "Integrating Information Systems Using a Unified Data Architecture," *Data Resource Management*, Vol. 1, No. 2, Spring 1990.

James, Phillip N. "A Framework for Strategic and Long-Range Information Resource Planning," *Information Strategy*, Fall 1985.

Johnson, James R. "Enterprise Analysis," *Datamation*, December 15, 1984.

Karimi, Jahangir. "Strategic Planning for Information Systems: Requirements and Information Engineering Methods," *Journal of Management Information Systems*, Vol. 4, No. 4, Spring 1988.

Kerr, James. "The Power of Information Systems Planning," *Database Programming & Design*, Vol. 3, No. 12, December 1990.

————. "A Blueprint for Information Systems," *Database Programming & Design*, Vol. 2, No. 9, September 1989.

————. *The IRM Imperative: Strategies for Managing Information Resources*, John Wiley & Sons, New York, 1990.

King, William. "Strategic Planning for MIS," *MIS Quarterly*, Vol. 2, No. 1, March 1978.

Lederer, Albert L., and Kenneth J. Calhoun. "Why Some Systems Don't Support Strategy," *Information Strategy*, Summer 1989.

Lederer, Albert L., and Aubrey L. Mendelow. "Information Systems Planning: Incentives for Effective Action," *Data Base*, Vol. 20, No. 3, Fall 1989.

Lederer, Albert L., and Andrew Putnam. "Bridging the Gap: Connecting Systems Objectives to Business Strategy with BSP," *Journal of Systems Management*, Auerbach, Summer 1987.

————. "Connecting Systems Objectives to Business Strategy with BSP," *Information Strategy*, Auerbach, Winter 1986.

Lederer, Albert L., and Vijay Sethi. "The Implementation of Strategic Information Systems Planning Methodologies," *MIS Quarterly*, September 1988.

————. "Pitfalls in Planning," *Datamation*, June 1, 1989.

Leware, Gilbert W. "Achieving Business Goals Through Information Systems Technology," *Data Resource Management*, Vol. 2, No. 3, Summer 1991.

Martin, James. *Strategic Data Planning Methodologies* (1st ed.), Prentice-Hall, Englewood Cliffs, NJ, 1982.

————. *Strategic Information Planning Methodologies* (2d ed.), Prentice-Hall, Englewood Cliffs, NJ, 1989.

————. *Information Engineering: Planning & Analysis* (book 2), Prentice-Hall, Englewood Cliffs, NJ, 1990.

————. *Information Engineering: Design & Construction* (book 3), Prentice-Hall, Englewood Cliffs, NJ, 1990.

McLean, E. R., and J. V. Soden. *Strategic Planning for MIS*, John Wiley and Sons, Inc., New York, 1977.

Meador, Jo Guasasco. "Building a Business Information Model," *Journal of Information Systems Management*, Vol. 7, No. 4, Fall 1990.

————. "Guidelines for Developing a Data Base Plan," *Data Resource Management*, Vol. 2, No. 1, Winter 1991.

Modell, Martin E. "Building Business Models: The Entity Relationship Approach," *Data Resource Management*, Vol. 1, No. 3, Summer 1990.

Moriarty, Terry. "Framing Your System," *Database Programming & Design*, Vol. 4, No. 6, June 1991.

Moskowitz, Robert. "Strategic Systems Planning Shifts to Data-Oriented Approach," *Computerworld (In-depth)*, March 12, 1986.

Mulryan, Dennis W. "Architecture: Translating Business Vision Into Business Design" and "Home Base Inc.: Uniting Architecture Design and Business Strategy," *Stage By Stage*, Nolan-Norton & Co., Vol. 8, No. 1, 1988.

Nolan, Richard L. "Top-Down-Driven Architecture Design," *Stage By Stage*, Nolan-Norton & Co., Vol. 8, No. 1, 1988.

Nolan, Richard L. *Managing the Data Resource Function* (2d ed.), West Publishing Co., St. Paul, MN, 1982.

Parker, Claire M. "Developing an Information Systems Architecture: Changing How Data Resource Managers Think About Systems Planning," *Data Resource Management*, Vol. 1, No. 4, Fall 1990.

Parker, M. M. "Enterprise Information Analysis: Cost-Benefit Analysis and the Data-Managed System," *IBM Systems Journal*, Vol. 21, No. 1, 1982.

Parker, Marilyn M., H. E. Trainor, and Robert J. Benson. *Information Economics: Linking Information Technology to Business Performance*, Prentice-Hall, Englewood Cliffs, NJ, 1988.

———. *Information Strategy and Economics*, Prentice-Hall, Englewood Cliffs, NJ, 1988.

Parker, Marilyn M., and Robert J. Benson. "A Strategic Planning Methodology: Enterprisewide Information Management," *Data Resource Management*, Auerbach, Summer 1990.

———. "Enterprise Wide Information Management State-of-the-Art Strategic Planning," *Journal of Information Systems Management*, Vol. 6, No. 3, Summer 1989.

Sanders, G. Lawrence. "Strategic Database Planning," *Database Programming & Design*, Vol. 3, No. 11, November 1990.

Siegal, Paul. *Strategic Planning of Management Information Systems*, Petrocelli Books, New York, 1975.

Sinclair, Stuart. "The Three Domains of Information Systems Planning," *Journal of Information Systems Management*, Spring 1986.

Spewak, Steven H. "The DRM Mission: Quality Data," *Data Resource Management*, Vol. 2, No. 1, Winter 1991.

Sullivan, C. H. "An Evolutionary New Logic Redefines Strategic Systems Planning," *Information Strategy: An Executive's Journal*, Vol. 3, No. 2, Winter 1987.

Synott, William R. "The Building Blocks of IRM Architecture," *Information Strategy: An Executive's Journal*, Vol. 1, No. 3, Spring 1985.

Targowski, Andrew. *The Architecture and Planning of Enterprise-Wide Information Management Systems*, Idea Group Publishing, Harrisburg, PA, 1990.

Tom, Paul L. *Managing Information as a Corporate Resource*, Scott Foresman & Co., Glenview, Illinois, 1987.

Valderrabano, J. L., and V. Venkatakrishnan. "Business Impact of Strategic Data Planning," *Journal of Information Systems Management*, Vol. 7, No. 1, Winter 1990.

Venkatraman, N. "Research on MIS Planning: Some Guidelines from Strategic Planning Research," *Journal of Management Information Systems*, Vol. 2, No. 3, Winter 1986.

Vesely, Eric Garrigue. *Strategic Data Management: The Key to Corporate Competitiveness*, Prentice-Hall (Yourdon Press), Englewood Cliffs, NJ, 1990.

Ward, John, Pat Griffiths, and Paul Whitmore. *Strategic Planning for Information Systems*, John Wiley & Sons, Chicester, England, 1990.

Zachman, John. "Business Systems Planning and Business Information Control Study: A Comparison," *IBM Systems Journal*, Vol. 21, No. 1, 1982.

———. "A Framework for Information Systems Architecture," *IBM Systems Journal*, Vol. 26, No. 3, 1987.

2. STRATEGIC SYSTEMS AND BUSINESS PLANNING (INCLUDING CULTURE)

Bedell, Eugene F. *The Computer Solution: Strategies for Success in the Information Age*, Dow Jones-Irwin, Homewood, Illinois, 1985.

Bouldin, Barbara M. *Agents of Change: Managing the Introduction of Automated Tools*, Prentice-Hall (Yourdon Press), Englewood Cliffs, NJ, 1989.

Brooks, Frederick P., Jr. *The Mythical Man-Month*, Addison-Wesley Publishing Co., Reading, MA, 1975. Reprinted with corrections in 1982.

Buday, Robert (editor). "Strategic Systems," Special Supplement Section of *Information Week*, May 26, 1986.

Cox, John, and Parks Dimsdale. "Selling New Ideas Properly Aids Their Acceptance Within an Organization," *Industrial Engineering*, December 1986.

Denison, Daniel R. *Corporate Culture and Organizational Effectiveness*, John Wiley & Sons, New York, 1990.

Edelman, Franz. "The Management of Information Resources: A Challenge to American Business," *MIS Quarterly*, Vol. 5, No. 1, March 1981.

Fried, Louis, and Richard Johnson. "Gaining the Technology Advantage: Planning for the Competitive Use of IT," *Information Systems Management*, Vol. 8, No. 4, Fall 1991.

Green, Carolyn W. "IRM and the Implementation of Change," *Data Base Newsletter*, Vol. 18, No. 3, May/June 1990.

Henderson, John C. "A Methodology for Identifying Strategic Opportunities for DSS," CISR Working Paper No. 131, MIT Sloan School, Cambridge, MA, 1985.

Hurst, Blaine. "Facilitating Change: The Key to Success with Information Technology," *Chief Information Officer Journal*, Vol. 3, No. 4, Spring 1991.

Ives, Blake, and Gerald Learmonth. "The Information System as a Competitive Weapon," *Communications of the ACM*, Vol. 27, No. 12, December 1984.

King, William R., and David I. Cleland (editors). *Strategic Planning and Management Handbook*, Van Nostrand Reinhold, New York, 1987.

Leware, Gilbert W. "Strategic Business Planning: Aligning Business Goals with Technology," *Information Systems Management*, Vol. 8, No. 4, Fall 1991.

Linder, Jane. "Harnessing Corporate Culture," *ComputerWorld (In-Depth)* September 23, 1985.

Marchand, Donald, and Forest Horton, Jr. *Infotrends*, John Wiley & Sons, New York, 1986.

McFarlan, F. Warren. "Information Technology Changes the Way You Compete," *Harvard Business Review*, Vol. 62, No. 3, May–June 1984.

McNurlin, Barbara Canning (editor). "Creating a Vision and Selling It," *I/S Analyzer*, Vol. 26, No. 9, September 1988.

———. "Influencing Corporate Policy," *I/S Analyzer*, Vol. 26, No. 6, June 1988.

Millar, Victor E. "Information for Competitive Advantage," *Information Strategy*, Fall 1985.

Parsons, Gregory L. "Information Technology: A New Competitive Weapon," *Sloan Management Review*, Fall 1983.

Porter, Michael. *Competitive Advantage*, Free Press, New York, 1985.

Porter, Michael, and Victor E. Millar. "How Information Gives You Competitive Advantage," *Harvard Business Review*, July–August 1985.

Rackoff, Nick, Wiseman, Charles, and Walter A. Ullrich. "Information Systems for Competitive Advantage: Implementation of a Planning Process," *MIS Quarterly*, December 1985.

Ranftl, Robert M. "Seven Keys to High Productivity," *Research Man-*

agement, Vol. 29, No. 5, September 1986. (Reprinted in *IEEE Engineering Management Review*, Dec. 1988.)

Rockart, John, and C. Bullen. "A Primer on Critical Success Factors," Center for Information Systems Research CISR Working Paper No. 69, MIT Cambridge, MA, 1981.

Rockart, John, and David DeLong. *Executive Support Systems: The Emergence of Top Management Computer Use*, Dow Jones-Irwin, Homewood, IL, 1988.

Rockart, John, and Michael Treacy. "The CEO Goes On-line," *Harvard Business Review*, Vol. 60, No. 1, January–February 1982.

Sankar, Y. "Organizational Culture and New Technologies," *Journal of Systems Management*, ASM, April 1988.

Steiner, George A. *Strategic Planning: What Every Manager Must Know*, The Free Press (MacMillian), New York, 1979.

Synnott, William. *The Information Weapon: Winning Customers and Markets with Technology*, John Wiley & Sons, New York, 1987.

Tichy, Noel M. *Managing Strategic Change: Technical, Political, and Cultural Dynamics*, John Wiley & Sons, New York, 1983.

Wiseman, Charles. *Strategy and Computers: Information Systems as Competitive Weapons*, Dow Jones-Irwin, Homewood, IL, 1985.

3. DATA ARCHITECTURE (CONCEPTUAL DATA MODELING)

Appleton, Daniel. "Law of the Data Jungle," *Datamation*, October 1983.

"Business Rules: The Missing Link," *Datamation*, October 1983.

———. "The Technology of Data Integration," *Datamation*, November 1985.

———. "Rule Based Data Resource Management," *Datamation*, May 1986.

Bachman, Charles, and Chris Gane. "The Bachman Approach to the Lou's Slips Marina Problem," *Data Base Newsletter*, Vol. 17, No. 2, March/April 1989.

Batini, C., M. Lenjerni, and S. Navathe. "Comparative Analysis of Methodologies for Database Schema Integration," *Computing Surveys*, ACM Vol. 18, No. 4, December 1988.

Booch, Grady. *Object-Oriented Design with Applications*, Benjamin/ Cummings Publishing Co., Redwood City, CA, 1991.

Bracket, Michael H. *Practical Data Design*, Prentice-Hall, Englewood Cliffs, NJ, 1990.

Bruce, Thomas A. *Designing Quality Databases with IDEF1x*, Dorset House Publishing, NY, 1992.

Chen, Peter P. "The Entity-Relationship Model—Toward a Unified View of Data," ACM Transactions on Database Systems, Vol. 1, No. 1, March 1976.

Coad, Peter, and Edward Yourdon. *Object-Oriented Analysis*, Prentice-Hall (Yourdon Press), Englewood Cliffs, NJ, 1990.

Curtice, Robert, and Paul Jones. *Logical Data Base Design*, QED Publishing Group, Wellesley, MA, 1988.

Database Programming and Design, "Database Design" column written by Barbara Von Halle (February 1990–), see August 1991, July 1991, December 1990, November 1990, May 1990, April 1990, March 1990, and February 1990.

Durell, William R. "Using Affinity Analysis for Strategic Data Planning," *Data Resource Management*, Vol. 2, No. 1, Winter 1991.

Flavin, Matt. *Fundamental Concepts of Information Modeling*, Yourdon Press Monograph (now Prentice-Hall), New York, 1981.

Flemming, Candice C., and Barbara von Halle. *Handbook of Relational Database Design*, Addison Wesley, Reading, MA, 1989.

GUIDE International Corporation. *Data Resource Management Planning Methodology*, Publication No. GPP-84, IL, 1982.

Hall, John, Keith Robinson, and Christopher M. P. Bird. "An Overview of Entity Life History Analysis and Event Process Outline Specification," "ELH Analysis and EPO Specification: Building Simple Histories," and "ELH Analysis and EPO Specifications: Adding Operations and State-Variables and Specifying the Outline," *Data Base Management*, Auerbach Publishers, 22-01-40, 22-01-41, and 22-01-42, Summer 1990.

Hull, Richard, and Roger King. "Semantic Database Modeling: Survey, Applications, and Research Issues," *ACM Computing Surveys*, Vol. 19, No. 3, September 1987.

ICAM Definition (IDEF) Method for Function Modeling. IDEFUG-M-1X-8511, IDEF Users Group Secretariat, Ann Arbor, MI, 1985.

Inmon, William H. *Data Architecture: The Information Paradigm*, QED Publishing Group, Wellesley, MA, 1989.

McKee, Richard and Jeff Rogers. "Data Modeling Techniques: A Matter of Perspective," *Data Resource Management*, Vol. 3, No. 3, Summer 1992.

Meador, Jo Guasasco. "Defining the Business Information Requirements for a Data Architecture Framework," *Data Resource Management*, Vol. 1, No. 4, Fall 1990.

———. "Building the Systems Model for a Data Architecture Framework," *Data Resource Management*, Vol. 1, No. 4, Fall 1990.

National Bureau of Standards, Guide on Logical Database Design, NBS

Special Publication 500-122, U.S. Department of Commerce, February 1985.

Martin, James, and James Odell. *Object-Oriented Analysis and Design,* Prentice-Hall, Englewood Cliffs, NJ, 1992.

Nijssen, G. M., and T. A. Halpin. *Conceptual Schema and Relational Database Design: A Fact Oriented Approach,* Prentice-Hall, NJ, 1989.

Peckham, Joan, and Fred Maryanski. "Semantic Data Models," *ACM Computing Surveys,* Vol. 20, No. 3, September 1988.

Potter, Walter D., and Robert P. Trueblood. "Traditional, Semantic, and Hyper-Semantic Approaches to Data Modeling," *Computer (IEEE),* June 1988.

Ross, Ronald. *Entity Modeling: Techniques and Applications,* Database Research Group, MA, 1987.

Rumbaugh, James, Michael Blaha, William Premerlani, Frederick Eddy, and William Lorenson. *Object-Oriented Modeling and Design,* Prentice-Hall, Englewood Cliffs, NJ, 1991.

Shlaer, Sally, and Stephen J. Mellor. *Object-Oriented Systems Analysis: Modeling the World in Data,* Prentice-Hall (Yourdon Press), Englewood Cliffs, NJ, 1988.

Spewak, Steven H. "The Three Dimensional Data Model," *Data Base Newsletter,* Vol. 10, No. 2, March 1982.

Teorey, Toby J., and James P. Fry. *Design of Database Structures,* Prentice-Hall, Englewood Cliffs, NJ, 1982.

Thompson, J. Patrick. *Data with Semantics: Data models and Data Management,* Van Nostrand Reinhold, New York, 1989.

Veryard, R. *Pragmatic Data Analysis,* Blackwell Scientific Publishing, Computer Science Press, Rockville, MD, 1984.

Whitener, Theresa. "Building Database Stability," *Database Programming & Design,* Vol. 1, No. 6, June 1988.

4. CURRENT SYSTEMS AND TECHNOLOGY

Burk, Cornelius F., and Forest W. Horton, Jr. *INFOMAP: A Complete Guide to Discovering Corporate Information Resources,* Prentice-Hall, Englewood Cliffs, NJ, 1988.

5. APPLICATIONS ARCHITECTURE

Best, Laurence J. *Application Architecture: Modern, Large-Scale Information Processing,* John Wiley & Sons, New York, 1990.

Boar, Bernard H. *Application Prototyping: A Requirement Definition Strategy for the 80's,* John Wiley & Sons, New York, 1984.

Martin, James. *Rapid Application Development*, Macmillan Publishing Company, New York, 1991.

McFarlan, F. Warren. "Portfolio Approach to Information Systems," *Harvard Business Review*, Vol. 59, No. 5, September–October 1981.

Mushet, Mike. "Application Systems Planning," *Journal of Information Systems Management*, Winter 1985.

Venner, Gary S. "Managing Applications as a Software Portfolio," *Journal of Information Systems Management*, Vol. 5, No. 3, Summer 1988.

Wood, Jane, and Denise Silver. *Joint Application Design*, John Wiley & Sons, New York, 1989.

6. TECHNOLOGY ARCHITECTURE

Carlson, Christopher K., Ella P. Gardner, and Stephen R. Ruth. "Technology-Driven Long-Range Planning," *Journal of Information Systems Management*, Vol. 6, No. 3, Summer 1989.

Ceri, S., and G. Pelagitti. *Distributed Databases: Principles and Systems*, McGraw-Hill, Inc., New York, 1984.

Computer Associates. *CA90s: Computing Architecture for the 90's*, available from Computer Associates International, 1990.

Coulouris, George, and Jean Dollimore. *Distributed Systems: Concepts and Design*, Addison-Wesley, Boston, MA, 1989.

Gunton, Tony. *Infrastructure: Building a Framework for Corporate Information Handling*, Prentice-Hall, Englewood Cliffs, NJ, 1989.

Hutchison, David. *Local Area Network Architectures*, Addison-Wesley, Boston, MA, 1988.

Martin, James, and Kathleen K. Chapman. *Local Area Networks: Architectures and Implementation*, Prentice-Hall, Englewood Cliffs, NJ, 1989.

Martin, James, and Joe Leban. *DECnet Phase V, an OSI Implementation*, Digital Press, Bedford, MA, 1992.

Martin, James. *Client-Server Application Development*, Volume 1: *Systems and Software*, Volume 2: *Methodology*, Savant Institute, Carnforth, Lancs., UK, 1992.

Teorey, Toby J., Jarrir Chaar, Kunle Olukotun, and Amjad Umar. "Allocation Methods of Distributed Database," *Database Programming & Design*, Vol. 2, No. 4, April 1989.

Walford, Robert B. *Network System Architecture*, Addison-Wesley, Boston, MA, 1990.

———. *Information Systems and Business Dynamics*, Addison-Wesley, Boston, MA, 1990.

7. QUALITY

Gitlow, Howard S., and Shelly J. Gitlow. *The Deming Guide to Quality and Competitive Position*, Prentice-Hall, Englewood Cliffs, NJ, 1987.

Juran, J. M. *Juran on Planning for Quality*, The Free Press (MacMillan), New York, 1988.

Scherkenbach, William W. *The Deming Route to Quality and Productivity: Road Maps and Roadblocks*, Mercury Press, Rockville, MD, 1988.

Walton, Mary. *The Deming Management Method*, The Putnam Publishing Group (Perigee Books), New York, 1986.

8. MAKING PRESENTATIONS

Adamy, David. *Preparing and Delivering Effective Technical Presentations*, Artech House, Norwood, MA, 1987.

Beeri, David F., ed. *Writing and Speaking in the Technology Professions: A Practical Guide*, IEEE Press, Piscataway, NJ, 1991. (Order #P0278-2).

Communications Briefings (editors). *The Executive's Guide to Successful Presentations, Communication Briefings*, Pitman, NJ, 1989.

Frank, Milo O. *How to Get Your Point Across in 30 Secones—or Less*, Simon and Schuster, Inc., New York, 1986.

Inglis, Scott, and Joanna Kozubska. "Planned Presentations," *Management Decision*, Vol. 24, No. 5, 1987. (Reprinted in Engineering Management Review, Vol 16, No. 4, December 1988. From the IEEE Engineering Management Society.)

Woelfle, Robert M. (editor). *A Guide for Better Technical Presentations*, IEEE Press, New York, 1975.

9. CONFERENCES AND SEMINARS

All About IRM, annually in July; contact Barnett Data Systems, 19 Orchard Way, Rockville, MD 20854, (301) 762-1288.

CASE WORLD, sponsored by Digital Consulting Inc., 204 Andover Street, Andover, MA 01810, (508) 470-3880.

Enterprise-Wide Information Management, annually in September, sponsored by IBM and GWU, 1 Brookings Dr., St. Louis, MO 63130, (314) 889-5380.

A Framework for Information Systems Architecture: A Zachman Framework Conference, held in Washington, DC; contact Barnett Data Systems (see above).

GUIDE, meets three times each year, committees on architecture and
repository.

Strategic Data and Systems Planning, held each spring in Washington,
DC from 1984 through 1990, contact Barnett Data Systems for the
proceedings (see above).

Strategic Data and Systems Planning, annually in the fall beginning in
1991; contact Technology Transfer Institute, 741 Tenth Street,
Santa Monica, CA 90402, (213) 451-2104.

Public semicars on this subject are offered by

Barnett Data Systems (301) 762-1288

Computer & Engineering Consultants (313) 569-0900

Digital Consulting, Inc. (508) 470-3880

Performance Development Corporation (609) 921-3770

Technology Transfer Institute (213) 451-2104

10.   ASSOCIATIONS

Association for Computing Machinery (ACM) (SIGBDP, SIGMOD,
SIGSE)

Association for Systems Management (ASM)

Data Administration Management Association (DAMA)

Data Processing Management Association (DPMA)

IEEE Computer Society and Engineering Management Society

Information Resources Management Association (IRMA)

International DB2 Users Group (IDUG)

Society for Information Management (SIM)

11.   JOURNALS AND PERIODICALS

Case Report, Auerbach Publishers, One Penn Plaza, New York, NY
10119.

CIO, IDG Communications, 5 Speen Street, P.O. Box 9208,
Framingham, MA 01701.

Chief Information Officer Journal, Falkner & Gray, 106 Fulton Street,
NYC 10038.

ComputerWorld, CW Publishing, 375 Cochituate Road, Box 9171,
Framingham, MA 01701.

Database Programming & Design, Miller Freeman Publications, 500
Howard St., San Francisco, CA 94105.

Data Base, publication of SIGBDP of the ACM, 11 W. 42nd St., NYC
10036.

Data Base Management, Auerbach Publishers, One Penn Plaza, NYC
10119.

Data Resource Management, Auerbach Publishers, One Penn Plaza, NYC 10119.

Data Base Newsletter, Database Research Group, 129 Tremont St., Ste 500, Boston, MA 02108.

Datamation, Cahner's Publishing, 275 Washington St., Newton, MA 02158.

IBM Systems Journal, IBM, Armonk, NY 10504.

Information Resources Management Journal, IDEA Group Publishing, Olde Liberty Square, Jonestown Road, Suite 230, Harrisburg, PA 19111.

Information Strategy: The Executives Journal, Auerbach Publishers (see above).

Information Week, CMP Publications, 600 Community Dr., Manhasset, NY 11030.

Journal of Information Systems Management, Auerbach Publishers (see above).

Journal of Management Information Systems, M.E. Sharpe, 80 Business Park Drive, Armonk, NY 10504.

MIS Quarterly, Society for Information Management, 111 East Wacker Dr., Chicago, IL 60601.

Software Engineering: Tools Techniques Practice, Auerbach Publishers (see above).

Software Magazine, Sentry Publishing, P.O. Box 542, Winchester, MA 01890.

Technology Analysis & Strategic Management, Carfax Publishing Co., P.O. Box 25, Abington, Oxfordshire, OX14 3UE, United Kingdom.

12.   DATA BASE NEWSLETTER ARTICLES

The *Data Base Newsletter* is published bimonthly by the Data Base Research Group located at 31 State Street, Suite 800, Boston, Massachusetts 02109 (617-227-2583). It began publication in 1977, and Ronald G. Ross has been its editor since September of that year. Over the years, the DBN has printed many articles related to Enterprise Architecture Planning. This bibliography contains a list in reverse-chronological order of DBN articles on the topics of enterprise architectures, conceptual data modeling, business modeling, and strategic data planning.

"An Interview with Ian Palmer (James Martin & Co.)," by Ron Ross, 19:5, September/October 1991.

"Zachman Framework Extensions: An Update," by Ron Ross, 19:4, July/August 1991.

"Rules for the Zachman Framework Architecture," by Ron Ross, 19:4, July/August 1991.

"Information Engineering and Strategic Planning," short articles by Stu Coleman (Pacific Information Management), Clive Finkelstein (Information Engineering Systems Corp), Wayne Lapaire (LGS Group), Ian Palmer (James Martin Associates), Timothy Rinaman (Information Engineering Systems Corp), David Ritter (Computer & Engineering Consultants), Jack Warren (NOVA Petrochemicals), and Glen Weekley (Computer Task Group), 19:2, March/April 1991.

"Information Engineering and Strategic Planning," a letter by Bob Curtice (Arthur D. Little), 18:6, November/December 1990.

"Strategic Information Engineering: How Bekins Initiated the Process," by Thomas T. Schwaninger (Bekins), 17:6, November/December 1989.

"An Interview with John A. Zachman, IBM Corporation," 17:5, September/October 1989.

"Methodology Frameworks: Putting Things in an Enterprise Perspective," by Stu Coleman (Pacific Information Management), 17:5, September/October 1989.

"Strategic Information Planning at First Interstate Bank of Arizona," by Michael Sosnowski, 17:4, July/August 1989.

"The Conceptual Schema" by Daniel S. Appleton (DACOM), 17:4, July/August 1989.

"A Review of Three Information Strategy Planning Tools," by Sam Holcman (Computer & Engineering Consultants), 16:4, July/August 1988.

"Tips and Tricks in the Construction of a Data Usage Matrix," by Steven Cheung (Arthur Young) and Earl Hadden (Pacific Information Management), 16:3, May/June 1988.

"Information Engineering: Problems Impeding Acceptance," by Thomas F. Haughey, 16:3, May/June 1988.

"Requirements for Information Strategy Planning Tools," by Sam Holcman (Computer & Engineering Consultants), 16:2, March/April 1988.

"Strategic Data Planning at AT&T," by John M. Pinghera (AT&T), 15:6, November/December 1987.

"Tips, Tricks, and Traps in Building an Enterprise Information Model," by Steven C. K. Cheung (Cominco), and David R. Ells (Information Systems Services), 15:5, Sept/Oct 1987.

"Strategic Data Planning at Cameron, USA," by Richard Avery (Cameron), 15:4, July/Aug 1987.

"Domains and Data Validation," by Dan Tasker, 15:3, May/June 1987.

"Measuring the Success of Strategic Data Planning," by Thomas R. Finneran, 14:6, November/December, 1986.

"Strategic Data and Systems Planning at First Interstate Services Company," by Susan K. Marshall and Thomas T. Schwaninger, 14:5, September/October 1986.

"Implementing a Strategic Data Plan," by Richard Mader (Federated Department Stores), Part III: 14:2, March/April 1986; Part II: 14:1, January/February 1986; Part I: 13:6 November/December 1985.

"Strategic Data Planning at Amoco," by William W. Baker (Database Design) and Raymond C. Bell (Amoco), 13:4, July/August 1985.

"A Guide to Strategic Information Planning," by William W. Baker (Database Design), 13:4, July/August 1985.

"Integrating Information Systems into Strategic Planning," by John C. Henderson (MIT) and John G. Sifonis (Arthur Young), 13:2, March/April 1985.

"Business Systems Planning, A Newsletter Interview with Art Viles, IBM Corporation," 12:6, November/December 1984.

"An Architecture for Information Resource Management," by Eric Joyall (London Life Insurance), 12:5, September/October 1984.

"Strategic Information Planning at the First National Bank of Chicago," by Walter S. Augustine and Michael J. Kearney, 12:3, May/June 1984.

"Strategic Data Planning, A Newsletter Interview with Robert H. Holland, Holland Systems Corp.," 12:3, May/June 1984.

"Strategic Data Planning at a Major Utility," by Martin Turner, 11:4, July/August 1983.

"The BEST Method for Strategic Data Planning," by Ronald G. Ross, Part 3: 11:4, July/August 1983; Part 2: 11:3, May/June 1983; Part 1: 11:2, March/April 1983.

"The Three Dimensional Data Model," by Steven H. Spewak (Information Planning Technologies), 10:2, March 1982.

"Organizational Modeling: What Is It, Why Do It?," by Ronald G. Ross, 9:5, September 1981.

"Strategic Planning for Data Base," by Leo J. Cohen (PDC), 9:2, March 1981.

"The Seven Steps of a Data Base System Project," by Leo J. Cohen (PDC), 6:5, September 1978.

Index

80/20 principle, 35, 189, 236

A
Abstraction, 185
Affinity analysis, 192
Application
    architecture, 14 199, 224
    sequencing principle, 240
    -to-data matrix, 243, 250
    -to-entity matrix, 248
    -to-functions cross, 211
    -to-organization unit, 211
Architectures, 1
Assimilation, 185
Attribute, 169, 175

B
Benefits of
    an Information Resource
        Catalog (IRC), 141
    Enterprise Architecture
        Planning, 6
Best methodology, 27
Business modeling, 14, 85

Business systems architecture, 231

C
CASE, 41, 58, 143
Charles Wiseman, 203
Checkpoint, 255
Competitive Advantage, 97
Computer-Aided Software
    Engineering (CASE), 285
Computers and Strategy, 203
Conceptual enterprise network, 231
Consultants
    facilitative, 70
    Operative, 70
    selection criteria, 70
Conway, 4
Cost-benefit analysis, 260, 261
Criteria for good applications
    architecture, 210
Critical success factors, 52, 92, 264
CRUD matrix, 189, 201

Current systems and technology, 14

D
Data
architecture, 14, 169, 224
dependency, 10, 249, 250
dependency principle, 246
driven, 9
entities, 169
quality, 4
Deming, 4
14 points for Quality, 4

E
E-R
diagramming conventions, 187
methodology, 50
EAP, 1
project workbook, 76
team, 66
toolset products, 63
"wedding cake", 113
workplan, 72, 76
Enterprise, 38
Entity, 174
definition, 177
usage matrix, 242
-to-business function, 189
-to-current application, 189
ESTIMACS, 255
Executive information system (EIS), 241

F
Favorable characteristics for an enterprise, 40
Final report for Enterprise Architecture Planning, 271
Flexible systems, 41

Function, 95
Definition Form, 111
-to-entity, 203
Functional
business model, 9
decomposition, 100
Fundamental Rule of Functional Decomposition, 95

G
Generalization, 185
Good enterprise data architecture, 188

H
Hardware requirements, 56

I
IBM's BSP, 53
Impact analysis, 218
Implementation
plan steps, 239
Plans, 15
Indented structure list, 93
Information
engineering, 192, 284
Resource Catalog, 72
Information source(s), 117, 122
source from, 126
IRC workplan, 145

J
Jan Linder, 44
John Zackman, 11
Joint Application Design, 116, 284
Juran, 4

L
Leo Cohen, 242
Long-range plan, 2

M
Matrices, 189, 211
Matrix, 203
Migration
  Plans, 15
  strategy, 259

O
Object-oriented programming
  and analysis, 284
Objectives of the transition, 282
Outside expert, 275

P
Planning initiation, 14
Potential obstacles, 20
Process driven, 9
Programming standards, 289
Prototyping, 284
  lifecycle, 287

R
RAD (Rapid Application
  Development), 41, 284
Relationship, 176
Richard Nolan, 44

S
Separation,. 185
Seven steps of planning
  initiation, 38
Shared Data environment, 216
Source data, 242
Split matrix, 250
Steps
  for building an IRC, 143
  for Technology Architecture,
    224
  for transition to
    implementation, 282

to applications architecture,
  199
to data architecture phase,
  170
to planning conclusion, 271
Strategic business planning, 86
Subtype entity, 181
Success factors, 4
Supertype, 181
Systems lifecycle, 284

T
Technology architecture, 14, 223
Technology platforms, 227
  principles, 225
Three steps to business
  modeling, 85
Toolset requirements, 56
Training requirements, 289
Transition phase
  schedule, 267
  workplace, 283

U
Unfavorable characteristics for
  an enterprise, 42

V
Value
  chain, 246
  -added chain, 249

W
W. Edwards Deming, 4

Z
Zachman framework, 11, 169,
  199, 223, 281